The Songs of Jesus

REDEEMER

The Songs of

JESUS

A Year of
Daily Devotions
in the Psalms

TIMOTHY
KELLER

with KATHY KELLER

VIKING

VIKING
An imprint of Penguin Random House LLC
375 Hudson Street
New York, New York 10014
penguin.com

ISBN 978-0-525-95514-6

Printed in the United States of America
1   3   5   7   9   10   8   6   4   2

Set in Warnock Pro and Pirouette
Designed by Amy Hill

To the Midwood family
Louise
Jesse, Meg, and Abby
And in honor of our dear friend David (1949–2014),
Husband, father, grandfather, friend, mentor,
and minister of the Gospel
Who is singing songs with Jesus with all his might

INTRODUCTION

The Psalms were the divinely inspired hymnbook for the public worship of God in ancient Israel (1 Chronicles 16:8–36). Because psalms were not simply read, but sung, they penetrated the minds and imaginations of the people as only music can do. They so saturated the heart and imagination of the average person that when Jesus entered Jerusalem it was only natural that the crowd would spontaneously greet him by reciting a line from a psalm (Mark 11:9; Psalm 118:26).

The early Christians sang and prayed the psalms as well (Colossians 3:16; 1 Corinthians 14:26). When Benedict formed his monasteries he directed that the psalms all be sung, read, and prayed at least once a week. Throughout medieval times the psalms served as the most familiar part of the Bible for most Christians. The Psalter was the only part of the Bible a lay Christian was likely to own. At the time of the Reformation, the psalms played a major role in the reform of the church. Martin Luther directed that "the whole Psalter, psalm by psalm, should remain in use." John Calvin prescribed metrical psalms as the main diet of song in worshipping congregations.[1] Calvin wrote: "The design of the Holy Spirit [was] . . . to deliver the church a common form of prayer."[2]

All theologians and leaders of the church have believed that the Psalms should be used and reused in every Christian's daily private approach to God and in public worship. We are not simply to read psalms; we are to be immersed in them so that they profoundly shape how we relate to God. The psalms are the divinely ordained way to learn devotion to our God.

Why? One reason is that it is what Luther called a "mini Bible." It gives an overview of salvation history from creation through the giving of the Law at Mount Sinai, the establishment of the tabernacle and temple, the exile due to unfaithfulness, and it points us forward to the coming messianic redemption and the renewal of all things. It treats the doctrines of revelation (Psalm 19), of God (Psalm 139), and of human nature (Psalm 8) and sin (Psalm 14).

The psalms are more than just an instrument for theological instruction, however. One of the ancient church fathers, Athanasius, wrote, "Whatever your particular need or trouble, from this same book [the psalms] you can select a form of words to fit it, so that you . . . learn the way to remedy your ill."[3] Every situation in life is represented in the book of psalms. Psalms anticipate and train you for every possible spiritual, social, and emotional condition—they show you what the dangers are, what you should keep in mind, what your attitude should be, how to talk to God about it, and how to get from God the help you need. "They put their undeviating understanding of the greatness of the Lord alongside our situations, so that we may have a due sense of the correct proportion of things." Every feature and circumstance of life is "transmitted into the Lord's presence, and put into the context of what is true about him."[4] Psalms, then, are not just a matchless primer of teaching but a medicine chest for the heart and the best possible guide for practical living.

In calling psalms "medicine" I am trying to do justice to what makes them somewhat different from other parts of the Bible. They are written to be prayed, recited, and sung—to be *done,* not merely to be read. Theologian David Wenham concludes that using them repeatedly is a "performative act" that "alters one's relationship [with God] in a way mere listening does not."[5] We are, in a sense, to put them inside our own prayers, or perhaps to put our prayers inside them, and approach God in that way. In doing this the psalms involve the speaker directly in new attitudes, commitments, promises, and even emotions. When, for example, we do not merely read Psalm 139:23–24—"search me . . . test me . . . see if there is any offensive way in me"—but pray it, we invite God to test our motives and we give active assent to the way of life called for by the Bible.[6]

The psalms lead us to do what the psalmists do—to commit ourselves to God through pledges and promises, to depend on God through petition and expressions of acceptance, to seek comfort in God through lament and complaint, to find mercy from God through confession and repentance, to gain new wisdom and perspective from God through meditation, remembrance, and reflection.

The psalms also help us see God—God not as we wish or hope him to be but as he actually reveals himself. The descriptions of God in the Psalter are rich beyond human invention. He is more holy, more wise, more fearsome, more tender and loving than we would ever imagine him to be. The psalms fire our imaginations into new realms yet guide them toward the God who actually exists. This brings a reality to our prayer lives that nothing else can. "Left to ourselves, we will pray to some god who speaks what we like hearing, or to the part of God we manage to understand. But what is critical is that we speak to the God who speaks to us, and to everything that he speaks to us. . . . What is essential in prayer is not that we learn to express ourselves, but that we learn to answer God."[7]

Most of all the psalms, read in light of the entire Bible, bring us to Jesus. The psalms were Jesus's songbook. The hymn that Jesus sang at the Passover meal (Matthew 26:30; Mark 14:26) would have been the Great Hallel, Psalms 113–118. Indeed, there is every reason to assume that Jesus would have sung all the psalms, constantly, throughout his life, so that he knew them by heart. It is the book of the Bible that he quotes more than any other. But the psalms were not simply sung by Jesus; they also are about him, as we will see throughout this volume.

The psalms are, then, indeed the songs of Jesus.

THE PLAN OF THIS BOOK

This book is a daily devotional that takes the reader through every verse of the book of Psalms in 365 days. In one sense the psalms do not need to be made into a daily devotional—they *are* the divinely inspired devotional book.

Many find modern devotionals to be either too upbeat or too sentimental or too doctrinal or too mystical because they reflect the perspective and experience of just one human author. The psalms, by contrast, give us a range of divinely inspired voices of different temperaments and experiences. No other book, even of the Bible, can compete with it as a basis for daily prayer. The New Testament obviously presents Jesus Christ to us in far more explicit and direct ways, yet no part of the New Testament is actually written to be a course of prayed theology that helps you process every possible personal situation through the truth about God.

So the psalms are already God's devotional book. Nevertheless, most of us need the help of a guide for our first several journeys through the Psalter. Too many of the psalms have complex historical content and can be difficult to understand even after multiple readings. We can't pray a text if we find it utterly confusing.

Each devotional provides you with your daily reading from a psalm. It then gives a brief meditation on the meaning of the psalm and a prayer to help you actually use it in your heart and as a way to approach God. The prayers should be seen as "on-ramps," not as complete prayers. The reader should follow the trajectory of the prayers and keep going, filling each prayer out with personal particulars, as well as always praying in Jesus's name (John 14:13).

We structured this daily devotional so it can be used in three different ways. The simplest way is to read the psalm and the meditation slowly, and then use the prayer to begin praying the psalm yourself. The prayers offer an opportunity to continue praying to God about anything in your heart and anything personal you are facing that day. This could take no more than fifteen minutes.

The second way to use the devotional is to take the time to look up the additional scriptural references that are embedded in the meditation and sometimes in the prayer. The statements in the meditation are understandable without the references, but looking them up and reading them will greatly enhance your grasp of the meaning and may also enrich your time of prayer.

The third way to use the devotional is to get a blank journal to use along with it. Read the psalm portion twice slowly. Then ask three questions and write out your answers:

> *Adore*—What did you learn about God for which you could praise or thank him?
> *Admit*—What did you learn about yourself for which you could repent?
> *Aspire*—What did you learn about life that you could aspire to, ask for, and act on?

Once you have answered these three questions, you have your own meditation on the psalm. Now read the meditation in the book and incorporate its insights into your journal notes. Finally, turn your meditation—already categorized as adoration, confession, and aspiration—into personal prayer, using the provided "on-ramp" prayer as well. This will take you into the deep level of wisdom and insight the psalms can provide.

You are ready to start your year of devotions. May God give you "the Spirit of wisdom and revelation, so that you may know him better" (Ephesians 1:17).

January 1

READ Psalm 1. 1 Blessed is the one who does not walk in step with the wicked or stand in the way that sinners take or sit in the company of mockers, **2** but whose delight is in the law of the LORD, and who meditates on his law day and night. **3** That person is like a tree planted by streams of water, which yields its fruit in season and whose leaf does not wither—whatever they do prospers. **4** Not so the wicked! They are like chaff that the wind blows away. **5** Therefore the wicked will not stand in the judgment, nor sinners in the assembly of the righteous. **6** For the LORD watches over the way of the righteous, but the way of the wicked leads to destruction.

THE NOURISHING WORD. Psalm 1 is the gateway to the rest of the psalms. The "law" is all Scripture, to "meditate" is to think out its implications for all life, and to "delight" in it means not merely to comply but to love what God commands. Christians have their attitude toward God changed from one of duty to free, loving self-giving because of what Jesus did for us on the cross. So to know how to meditate on and delight in the Bible is the secret to a relationship with God and to life itself. Views contrary to God's Word are no anchor in time of need. God's Word gives us the resilience of a tree with a source of living water that will never dry up.

Prayer: Lord of the Word, don't let me be seduced by the world—either naively going with the crowd or becoming a hardened cynic. Help me meditate on your Word to the point of delight. Give me stability and contentment regardless of the circumstances. How I need that! Amen.

January 2

READ Psalm 2:1–4. **1** Why do the nations conspire and the peoples plot in vain? **2** The kings of the earth rise up and the rulers band together against the LORD and against his anointed, saying, **3** "Let us break their chains and throw off their shackles." **4** The One enthroned in heaven laughs; the LORD scoffs at them.

NO INTIMIDATION. Each day the media highlights new things to fear. The "powers that be" in society tell us that obedience to God shackles us, limiting our freedom. In reality, liberation comes only through serving the one who created us. Those people and forces that appear to rule the world are all under his Lordship, and one day they will know it. God still reigns, and we can take refuge in him from all our fears. So to be intimidated by the world (Psalm 2) is as spiritually fatal as being overly attracted to it (Psalm 1).

Prayer: Lord of the world, people resent your claims on human lives. I fear to speak of you for fear of ridicule or anger. But you are not intimidated by the world "powers," nor should I be. Help me to know the joy of obedience and the fearlessness that goes with it. Amen.

READ Psalm 2:5–12. **5** He rebukes them in his anger and terrifies them in his wrath, saying, **6** "I have installed my king on Zion, my holy mountain." **7** I will proclaim the LORD's decree: He said to me, "You are my son; today I have become your father. **8** Ask me, and I will make the nations your inheritance, the ends of the earth your possession. **9** You will break them with a rod of iron; you will dash them to pieces like pottery." **10** Therefore, you kings, be wise; be warned, you rulers of the earth. **11** Serve the LORD with fear and celebrate his rule with trembling. **12** Kiss his son, or he will be angry and your way will lead to your destruction, for his wrath can flare up in a moment. Blessed are all who take refuge in him.

REFUGE IN GOD. God's response to human pride and power is to install his "son" on Zion. This points beyond Israel's king to Jesus, God's true Son. One day he will put everything right; but he will do this by going first to Zion—to Jerusalem—to die for our sins. To "kiss his son" is to rest in and live for him. If we do this, we have assurance that no matter what happens to us, ultimately everything will be all right. If we don't live for him, we end up fighting God himself. So "there is no refuge from him— only *in* him."[8]

Prayer: Lord, your answer to the chaos and strife of the world is your Son, Jesus Christ. He will eventually break brokenness, kill death, destroy destruction, and swallow every sorrow. Teach me how to take refuge in you—in your forgiveness through Jesus, in your wise will, and in my assured, glorious future. Amen.

January 4

READ Psalm 3. **1** LORD, how many are my foes! How many rise up against me! **2** Many are saying of me, "God will not deliver him." **3** But you, LORD, are a shield around me, my glory, the One who lifts my head high. **4** I call out to the LORD, and he answers me from his holy mountain. **5** I lie down and sleep; I wake again, because the LORD sustains me. **6** I will not fear though tens of thousands assail me on every side. **7** Arise, LORD! Deliver me, my God! Strike all my enemies on the jaw; break the teeth of the wicked. **8** From the LORD comes deliverance. May your blessing be on your people.

PEACE AMID DANGER. David's son Absalom was trying to kill him. The seeds of that family dysfunction are David's own fault. He had wanted Absalom's love so much he never corrected him, even when Absalom murdered one of his brothers. Now David is fleeing to save his own life. In this prayer he realizes that neither a son's love nor popular acclaim can serve as a person's worth or security. David relocates his glory and hope to God and finds peace despite danger. God is the only one who sustains you, whether an army is pursuing you or you are at home in your own bed. God sustains every breath you take.

Prayer: Lord and Savior, I am facing so many troubles, some of my own making. But I can hold my head up because I am your child and servant. So be my shield—protect me. And be my glory—give me confidence that you are with me and will bring me through this. Help me! Amen.

January 5

READ Psalm 4. **1** Answer me when I call to you, my righteous God. Give me relief from my distress; have mercy on me and hear my prayer. **2** How long will you people turn my glory into shame? How long will you love delusions and seek false gods? **3** Know that the LORD has set apart his faithful servant for himself; the LORD hears when I call to him. **4** Tremble and do not sin; when you are on your beds, search your hearts and be silent. **5** Offer the sacrifices of the righteous and trust in the LORD. **6** Many, LORD, are asking, "Who will bring us prosperity?" Let the light of your face shine on us. **7** Fill my heart with joy when their grain and new wine abound. **8** In peace I will lie down and sleep, for you alone, LORD, make me dwell in safety.

JOY APART FROM CIRCUMSTANCES. How can we have peaceful sleep at night (verse 8) and joy—even when others are prospering and we are not (verse 7)? Consider whether you have a divided heart—making success or relationships into idols—and repent (verse 2). Consider whether you have a bitter heart—and forgive (verse 4). Finally, in prayer, seek God's face, a sense of his presence and his love on your heart (verse 6). Then we can know we are safe in God, come what may.

Prayer: Lord, other "gods" compete with you for the allegiance of my heart. I nurse resentment toward people who have wronged me, and sometimes toward you. It is these things that keep me from knowing the joy of your presence and the peace of your protection. Help me remove them and fill my heart with your joy. Amen.

January 6

POURING OUT OUR HEART. Many of the psalms begin with desperate "laments"—cries for help from deep within. This is uncensored prayer, straight from the heart. Even when we have no words to express our anguish, we can lay our requests before God. He expects us to come to him for refuge from our grief, fear, and pain and not to dull those emotions with amusements and distractions that promise, but can never deliver, blessing. We are to have confidence that he is the God who told Moses that he would faithfully commit himself in love to us, in grace, despite our sins and flaws (Exodus 6:7).

Prayer: All-knowing Lord, you see what is in my heart. All-powerful Lord, I don't have the power to accomplish what needs to be done, so I spread out my requests before you. All-wise Lord, I know you hear and will act—but I know also I must wait on your wise timing, and so I will. Amen.

READ Psalm 5:7–12. **7** But I, by your great love, can come into your house; in reverence I bow down toward your holy temple. **8** Lead me, LORD, in your righteousness because of my enemies—make your way straight before me. **9** Not a word from their mouth can be trusted; their heart is filled with malice. Their throat is an open grave; with their tongues they tell lies. **10** Declare them guilty, O God! Let their intrigues be their downfall. Banish them for their many sins, for they have rebelled against you. **11** But let all who take refuge in you be glad; let them ever sing for joy. Spread your protection over them, that those who love your name may rejoice in you. **12** Surely, LORD, you bless the righteous; you surround them with your favor as with a shield.

PRAYING FOR PROTECTION. David's psalms often speak of enemies. Ancient kings were always in danger of people trying to kill them. We may have fewer enemies intent on physical violence, but there are many forces in the world that can ruin us economically, emotionally, physically, and spiritually. We must do what David did. He asks God to spread his protection over him. He is sure God will do this because he looks toward his temple, the place where sins are atoned for. Christians do the same when they remember the One who claimed to be the final temple (John 2:20–21), the ultimate sacrifice, and the conclusive proof of God's great love for us.

Prayer: Righteous Lord, I ask for protection from all the hostile forces around me. But when I get indignant about evil in others, I remember my own sin, and that I can come near you only by your grace. How I need to hate wrongdoing and yet not become angry and begin to feel superior to others! Keep me safe, but keep me humbled. Amen.

January 8

READ Psalm 6. 1 LORD, do not rebuke me in your anger or discipline me in your wrath. 2 Have mercy on me, LORD, for I am faint; heal me, LORD, for my bones are in agony. 3 My soul is in deep anguish. How long, LORD, how long? 4 Turn, LORD, and deliver me; save me because of your unfailing love. 5 Among the dead no one proclaims your name. Who praises you from the grave? 6 I am worn out from my groaning. All night long I flood my bed with weeping and drench my couch with tears. 7 My eyes grow weak with sorrow; they fail because of all my foes. 8 Away from me, all you who do evil, for the LORD has heard my weeping. 9 The LORD has heard my cry for mercy; the LORD accepts my prayer. 10 All my enemies will be overwhelmed with shame and anguish; they will turn back and suddenly be put to shame.

WAITING IS HARD. "How long, O Lord, how long?" is the cry of someone who has walked with more pain and sickness than he thought he could ever bear. God hears the prayers of the faltering because of his "unfailing love" (the Hebrew *chesedh,* the steadfast love of a covenant God who cares for us not because we are perfect but because he is) (verse 4). Though David scarcely has the heart to pray, his tears are not in vain. He gets an "answering touch" (verses 8–9)—an assurance that God is listening even though he hasn't done anything about the circumstances—yet (verse 10). God walks with us, and helps us to "run with perseverance the race" (Hebrews 12:1).

Prayer: "Thy promise is my only plea—with this I venture nigh. Thou callest burdened souls to Thee, and such, O Lord, am I."[9] I know that your love is unfailing even if I don't feel it. But I ask that in your grace you touch me and give me a sense of your presence at my side. Amen.

READ Psalm 7:1–5. 1 LORD my God, I take refuge in you; save and deliver me from all who pursue me, **2** or they will tear me apart like a lion and rip me to pieces with no one to rescue me. **3** LORD my God, if I have done this and there is guilt on my hands— **4** if I have repaid my ally with evil or without cause have robbed my foe— **5** then let my enemy pursue and overtake me; let him trample my life to the ground and make me sleep in the dust.

SMEAR CAMPAIGN. How do we deal with gossip and slander and the loss of our reputation? David shows us straightaway. He doesn't *say*, "I will take refuge in God," but rather *shows* that he already has, that he is already safe. How can he feel that way before he knows whether the smear campaign will be thwarted? The answer: if we trust in God's wisdom and will, then we have peace regardless of the immediate outcome. It is only God's opinion of us that counts, and that will prevail.

Prayer: Lord, some criticisms are terribly unfair. My deepest comfort is knowing that you see all things and will in the end set all things right. So I will not desperately defend myself or strike out at my accusers and insinuators. You know the truth, and that suffices for me. I leave this all in your hands. Amen.

January 10

READ Psalm 7:6–11. **6** Arise, LORD, in your anger; rise up against the rage of my enemies. Awake, my God; decree justice. **7** Let the assembled peoples gather around you, while you sit enthroned over them on high. **8** Let the LORD judge the peoples. Vindicate me, LORD, according to my righteousness, according to my integrity, O Most High. **9** Bring to an end the violence of the wicked and make the righteous secure—you, the righteous God who probes minds and hearts. **10** My shield is God Most High, who saves the upright in heart. **11** God is a righteous judge, a God who displays his wrath every day.

GOD ON HIGH. David has not done the things of which he is accused (verse 8). He wants God to take his throne on high (verse 7) and right all wrongs. He rightly leaves retribution to God, who alone has the wisdom to know what people deserve as well as the power and right to give it to them. So should we. But how can we be sure that *we* will survive Judgment Day? Christians know that before the Lord is lifted up on a throne to judge, first he will be lifted up on a cross to atone for sin (John 12:32). So on the final day a joy-filled, redeemed people will assemble at his feet (verse 7).

Prayer: Righteous Lord, I have many who *falsely* accuse me. Defend me from them! But I also know my sin, and my heart *rightly* accuses me. I rest in Jesus's atoning death for me. *"Be Thou my Shield and hiding Place, that, sheltered by Thy side, I may my fierce accuser face, and tell him Thou hast died!"*[10] Amen.

January 11

READ Psalm 7:12–17. **12** If he does not relent, he will sharpen his sword; he will bend and string his bow. **13** He has prepared his deadly weapons; he makes ready his flaming arrows. **14** Whoever is pregnant with evil conceives trouble and gives birth to disillusionment. **15** Whoever digs a hole and scoops it out falls into the pit they have made. **16** The trouble they cause recoils on them; their violence comes down on their own heads. **17** I will give thanks to the LORD because of his righteousness; I will sing the praises of the name of the LORD Most High.

THE SELF-DEFEAT OF EVIL. Because we live in a broken world, much injustice will go unpunished until the final day of judgment. However, most of the time, God's justice works itself out within the fabric of history. Evil carries within it the seeds of its own destruction. Not only is it a bore—leading to dissatisfaction and emptiness (verse 14)—but it recoils on itself. You fall into the pit you have dug for others. Haters are hated, deceivers are deceived, gossips are gossiped about. Remember this until you are not intimidated, discouraged, or tempted by the wrongdoing you see around you.

Prayer: Lord, I admit that some of my resentment of those who wrong me is tinged with envy. They live as they choose, and they seem happier than I am. But that is an illusion. Evil is like cancer cells—they grow, but only toward collapse and destruction. Help me see that clearly, so I can forgive them and not be tempted by them. Amen.

January 12

READ Psalm 8. **1** LORD, our Lord, how majestic is your name in all the earth! You have set your glory in the heavens. **2** Through the praise of children and infants you have established a stronghold against your enemies, to silence the foe and the avenger. **3** When I consider your heavens, the work of your fingers, the moon and the stars, which you have set in place, **4** what is mankind that you are mindful of them, human beings that you care for them? **5** You have made them a little lower than the angels and crowned them with glory and honor. **6** You made them rulers over the works of your hands; you put everything under their feet: **7** all flocks and herds, and the animals of the wild, **8** the birds in the sky, and the fish in the sea, all that swim the paths of the seas. **9** LORD, our Lord, how majestic is your name in all the earth!

WONDERFUL CARE. The universe reveals God's glory. Aren't humans just specks of dust in this vastness? Physically, yes; yet we fill the mind of God (verse 4). The astonishment of the psalmist should be ours: Why should God care about us? Because he has made us in his image and given us the world he created to care for as his agents. Living with care for the land, sea, and air and all who live there, and doing justice for every human being stamped with his image, brings God glory. As a human race we are not doing this very well! But Jesus has come, and eventually the world will be under *his* feet (verse 6; Hebrews 2:5–9) and then everything will be made right.

Prayer: Majestic God, how is it possible that we *fill* your mind? You love and care for us so much you were willing to become a weak infant and vulnerable child, all in order to save us. Now help me, in all my daily interactions, to treat every person I meet as a being infinitely precious in your sight. Amen.

January 13

READ Psalm 9:1–12. **1** I will give thanks to you, LORD, with all my heart; I will tell of all your wonderful deeds. **2** I will be glad and rejoice in you; I will sing the praises of your name, O Most High. **3** My enemies turn back; they stumble and perish before you. **4** For you have upheld my right and my cause, sitting enthroned as the righteous judge. **5** You have rebuked the nations and destroyed the wicked; you have blotted out their name for ever and ever. **6** Endless ruin has overtaken my enemies, you have uprooted their cities; even the memory of them has perished. **7** The LORD reigns forever; he has established his throne for judgment. **8** He rules the world in righteousness and judges the peoples with equity. **9** The LORD is a refuge for the oppressed, a stronghold in times of trouble. **10** Those who know your name trust in you, for you, LORD, have never forsaken those who seek you. **11** Sing the praises of the LORD, enthroned in Zion; proclaim among the nations what he has done. **12** For he who avenges blood remembers; he does not ignore the cries of the afflicted.

THANKS. This psalm helps us toward the spiritual health of a thankful heart. We must discern God's "wonderful deeds" in our lives, a phrase that can refer to dramatic miracles like the parting of the Red Sea. However, we must also learn to see the more subtle ways God comforts us just when we were ready to give up, or brings the right friend or book or line of thinking into our lives just when we needed it. Recognize and tell of God's daily, wonderful deeds, and you will have a note of grateful joy as the background music to your life.

Prayer: O Lord, you never forsake the troubled and the afflicted. When I think of your innumerable mercies to me, small and large, I can only cry.... What thanks I owe you, and what love! Help me to see the ways you support and guide me every day, so that I will always find new reasons to thank you. Amen.

January 14

READ Psalm 9:13–20. **13** L ORD, see how my enemies persecute me! Have mercy and lift me up from the gates of death, **14** that I may declare your praises in the gates of Daughter Zion, and there rejoice in your salvation. **15** The nations have fallen into the pit they have dug; their feet are caught in the net they have hidden. **16** The L ORD is known by his acts of justice; the wicked are ensnared by the work of their hands. **17** The wicked go down to the realm of the dead, all the nations that forget God. **18** But God will never forget the needy; the hope of the afflicted will never perish. **19** Arise, L ORD, do not let mortals triumph; let the nations be judged in your presence. **20** Strike them with terror, L ORD; let the nations know they are only mortal.

NEVER FORGET. This psalm moves suddenly from thanksgiving to a cry for help amid suffering. Life is like that. But David grabs hold of a truth that keeps him from sinking. The core sin is to forget that God is God and that we are not. And this is justice— those who forget God will be forgotten, but those who remember God will be remembered forever (Isaiah 56:5). Christians know of one who remembered God yet was completely forsaken (Matthew 27:46). But because Jesus died *in our place,* we can be even surer than David that God will always be there for us.

Prayer: Lord, so many of my problems stem from not remembering you. I forget your wisdom and so I worry. I forget your grace and so I get complacent. I forget your mercy and so I get resentful of others. Help me remember who you are every moment of the day. Amen.

January 15

READ Psalm 10:1–11. **1** Why, LORD, do you stand far off? Why do you hide yourself in times of trouble? **2** In his arrogance the wicked man hunts down the weak, who are caught in the schemes he devises. **3** He boasts about the cravings of his heart; he blesses the greedy and reviles the LORD. **4** In his pride the wicked man does not seek him; in all his thoughts there is no room for God. **5** His ways are always prosperous; your laws are rejected by him; he sneers at all his enemies. **6** He says to himself, "Nothing will ever shake me." He swears, "No one will ever do me harm." **7** His mouth is full of lies and threats; trouble and evil are under his tongue. **8** He lies in wait near the villages; from ambush he murders the innocent. His eyes watch in secret for his victims; **9** like a lion in cover he lies in wait. He lies in wait to catch the helpless; he catches the helpless and drags them off in his net. **10** His victims are crushed, they collapse; they fall under his strength. **11** He says to himself, "God will never notice; he covers his face and never sees."

PAINFUL REALITY. Augustine taught there were two "cities" or ways to live in society—one based on self-giving and one on self-serving. To worship the desires of the heart (verse 3) leads to habits of self-expression and self-assertion rather than sacrificial love. It is this way of life that appears to be ascendant in the world, with a God who seems to be far away and doing nothing about it (verse 1). The psalm describes this situation in painful detail, as a way of keeping us from even subtly going along with this manner of living. Like the psalmist, we need to resist it in prayer and in our daily life.

Prayer: Lord, keep me from being either naive about human evil, self-righteous about it, or cynical before it. Don't let me ever get used to injustice or, worse, become complicit in it. That takes constant vigilance and reflection about how I am living. Keep me loving what you love and hating what you hate. Amen.

January 16

READ Psalm 10:12–18. **12** Arise, LORD! Lift up your hand, O God. Do not forget the helpless. **13** Why does the wicked man revile God? Why does he say to himself, "He won't call me to account"? **14** But you, God, see the trouble of the afflicted; you consider their grief and take it in hand. The victims commit themselves to you; you are the helper of the fatherless. **15** Break the arm of the wicked man; call the evildoer to account for his wickedness that would not otherwise be found out. **16** The LORD is King for ever and ever; the nations will perish from his land. **17** You, LORD, hear the desire of the afflicted; you encourage them, and you listen to their cry, **18** defending the fatherless and the oppressed, so that mere earthly mortals will never again strike terror.

ENCOURAGEMENT. This second half of the psalm shows us a man who never gets the "why?" questions answered (verse 13) yet who trusts God completely. While the day of justice may be still in the future, the promise of encouragement is in the present, if we look to him. How can we trust him now if we still see oppression reigning? Christians know he so loves the helpless (verse 12), grief-stricken (verse 14), and oppressed (verse 18) that he literally became one of them and "by oppression and judgment he was taken away" (Isaiah 53:3–8). So commit yourself to him.

Prayer: Lord, the world is filled with so many tragedies and injustices! I wish I knew the "why" behind so many things. But despite appearances and what I see from my extremely limited vantage point, you have never wronged anyone. Help me trust your wisdom and give my heart the encouragement and strength that only you can give. Amen.

READ Psalm 11. **1** In the LORD I take refuge. How then can you say to me: "Flee like a bird to your mountain. **2** For look, the wicked bend their bows; they set their arrows against the strings to shoot from the shadows at the upright in heart. **3** When the foundations are being destroyed, what can the righteous do?" **4** The LORD is in his holy temple; the LORD is on his heavenly throne. He observes everyone on earth; his eyes examine them. **5** The LORD examines the righteous, but the wicked, those who love violence, he hates with a passion. **6** On the wicked he will rain fiery coals and burning sulfur; a scorching wind will be their lot. **7** For the LORD is righteous, he loves justice; the upright will see his face.

DON'T DESPAIR. When life crumbles, the desire to run away and hide in despair is strong. David counters this impulse with three insights: theological—God is still on his throne and will execute justice in his wise time (verse 4); practical—crises are really tests, opportunities to evaluate what is true and solid and what is flimsy and should be discarded (verses 4–5); and spiritual—what we really need is the knowledge of God's presence and *face* (verse 7). Only love makes you interested in gazing on someone's face. Pray until God and his love become more real to you. Then you won't run scared.

Prayer: Lord, people are saying, "It's over; just give up." But I won't panic—or should I say, "Lord, help me to not panic"? I know you are on your throne—but my heart doesn't feel that—so speak to my heart. Let me love you enough not to be scared. Amen.

January 18

READ Psalm 12. **1** Help, LORD, for no one is faithful anymore; those who are loyal have vanished from the human race. **2** Everyone lies to their neighbor; they flatter with their lips but harbor deception in their hearts. **3** May the LORD silence all flattering lips and every boastful tongue— **4** those who say, "By our tongues we will prevail; our own lips will defend us—who is lord over us?" **5** "Because the poor are plundered and the needy groan, I will now arise," says the LORD. "I will protect them from those who malign them." **6** And the words of the LORD are flawless, like silver purified in a crucible, like gold refined seven times. **7** You, LORD, will keep the needy safe and will protect us forever from the wicked, **8** who freely strut about when what is vile is honored by the human race.

THE POWER OF WORDS. Perhaps it has never been truer than now that "what is vile is honored by the human race." Christians need God's protection from lies, slander, and deception, because words have enormous power not only to distort and wound but also to overthrow a whole culture (verses 3–5, 7–8; cf. James 3:1–11). The great danger is to respond in kind. Instead we must model our words on God's—true and well crafted (verse 6). Our job is to trust in God's protection and to copy the actions of our Master and Savior, Jesus, who when he was reviled did not revile. We give glory to God when we suffer without hatred and retaliation.

Prayer: Lord, I am surrounded by people whose words are either fawning and flattering or malicious and stinging. Don't let me imitate them. Make my words honest and true, economical and few, wise and well chosen, calm and kind. Give me so much love and grace that this kind of conversation comes naturally to me. Amen.

READ Psalm 13. **1** How long, LORD? Will you forget me forever? How long will you hide your face from me? **2** How long must I wrestle with my thoughts and day after day have sorrow in my heart? How long will my enemy triumph over me? **3** Look on me and answer, LORD my God. Give light to my eyes, or I will sleep in death, **4** and my enemy will say, "I have overcome him," and my foes will rejoice when I fall. **5** But I trust in your unfailing love; my heart rejoices in your salvation. **6** I will sing the LORD's praise, for he has been good to me.

HONESTY. David is in agony and can't feel the presence of God. He cries out that God has ignored his pain and his sorrow. It is almost a howl, and the fact that it is included in the Bible tells us that God wants to hear our genuine feelings, even if they are anger at him. David never stops praying, however, and that is the key. As long as we howl toward God and remember his salvation by grace (verse 5), we will end at a place of peace. If Christians do that by hearing Jesus praying verses 1–4 on the cross, losing the Father's face as he paid for our sins, we will be able to pray verses 5–6 indeed.

Prayer: ""Tempest-tossed soul, be still; my promised grace receive'; 'Tis Jesus speaks—I must, I will, I can, I do believe."[11] Lord, this reminds me that believing the promise of your presence in my suffering takes time, and grows slowly, through stages in prayer. So I will pray until my heart rejoices in you. Amen.

January 20

READ Psalm 14. **1** The fool says in his heart, "There is no God." They are corrupt, their deeds are vile; there is no one who does good. **2** The LORD looks down from heaven on all mankind to see if there are any who understand, any who seek God. **3** All have turned away, all have become corrupt; there is no one who does good, not even one. **4** Do all these evildoers know nothing? They devour my people as though eating bread; they never call on the LORD. **5** But there they are, overwhelmed with dread, for God is present in the company of the righteous. **6** You evildoers frustrate the plans of the poor, but the LORD is their refuge. **7** Oh, that salvation for Israel would come out of Zion! When the LORD restores his people, let Jacob rejoice and Israel be glad!

FOOLISHNESS. In the Bible foolishness means a destructive self-centeredness. Fools cannot bear to have anyone over them, and so they ignore God or deny he exists. Some of this rebellion exists in every heart. Every sin is a kind of practical atheism—it is acting as if God were not there. That also means that belief in God must be a gift. This psalm is famously quoted in Romans 3:11: "There is no one who seeks God." Left to ourselves, we would never want to find God, much less know him. So take heart . . . If you want God, it is because he wants you to find him.

Prayer: Lord, I often struggle with doubts about you, and this psalm makes me realize they don't all come from my intellect and mind—many come from my heart. Part of me doesn't *want* there to be a God I have to obey. Increase my faith, through your Word and Spirit, and through believing friends, "the company of the righteous." Amen.

January 21

READ Psalm 15. **1** LORD, who may dwell in your sacred tent? Who may live on your holy mountain? **2** The one whose walk is blameless, who does what is righteous, who speaks the truth from their heart; **3** whose tongue utters no slander, who does no wrong to a neighbor, and casts no slur on others; **4** who despises a vile person but honors those who fear the LORD; who keeps an oath even when it hurts, and does not change their mind; **5** who lends money to the poor without interest; who does not accept a bribe against the innocent. Whoever does these things will never be shaken.

INTEGRITY. Who gets to draw near to God? Those who speak true words (verse 2), but in love (verse 3) and generosity (verse 5). Those who are transparent, honest, and faithful to their word, not always changing their minds (verses 4 and 5). If we deceive, vilify, and flatter, if we make empty promises and overblown claims, we cannot expect God's presence in our lives. This standard not only challenges us but also reminds us we can go to God only through his grace. No one but Jesus ever lived with perfect integrity (Hebrews 4:15), but because he is our Savior, we can go in to God (Hebrews 4:16).

Prayer: Lord, the sins of my tongue are so many! Forgive me for talking too much (because of pride), for talking too little (because of fear), for not telling the truth (because of pride and fear), for words that are harsh and cutting, for hurting others' reputations through gossip. Purify my words with your Word. Amen.

January 22

READ Psalm 16:1–6. **1** Keep me safe, my God, for in you I take refuge. **2** I say to the LORD, "You are my Lord; apart from you I have no good thing." **3** I say of the holy people who are in the land, "They are the noble ones in whom is all my delight." **4** Those who run after other gods will suffer more and more. I will not pour out libations of blood to such gods or take up their names on my lips. **5** LORD, you alone are my portion and my cup; you make my lot secure. **6** The boundary lines have fallen for me in pleasant places; surely I have a delightful inheritance.

IDOLS THAT DESERT. We may not believe in literal divine god-beings of beauty, wealth, pleasure, or fertility. But we must all live for something, and if we live for and love any thing more than God himself, we are trapped. They become things we *have* to have, so we "run," exhausted, after them. But this leads to increasing suffering (verse 4), for life inevitably takes them from us. Instead we must make God our portion (our real wealth), our cup (our real pleasure), our ultimate good.

Prayer: Lord, I want the gifts of your hand more than the glory of your face. I can root my happiness in amusements, music, food, or nice weather. But let suffering enter the picture, and they show themselves as the tawdry baubles that they are. Without your constant presence and favor, no thing is a "good thing." So I receive them with thanks, but I rest my heart and hope in you. Amen.

January 23

READ Psalm 16:7–11. 7 I will praise the LORD, who counsels me; even at night my heart instructs me. 8 I keep my eyes always on the LORD. With him at my right hand, I will not be shaken. 9 Therefore my heart is glad and my tongue rejoices; my body also will rest secure, 10 because you will not abandon me to the realm of the dead, nor will you let your faithful one see decay. 11 You make known to me the path of life; you will fill me with joy in your presence, with eternal pleasures at your right hand.

THE BEST IS YET TO COME. If God is our greatest good, we get what can't be lost and will only increase—infinitely. The Lord is at our right hand. To be at someone's right hand is to be their advocate in court or support in battle or companion for a journey. In Christ this is all literally true (Acts 2:24–36). Because he died and rose for us, he is our representative in heaven (so we are completely forgiven) and companion on earth (so we are intimately loved). And someday we will not just sense him at our side but see him face to face. In our resurrected bodies that will be endless, unimaginable pleasure (verses 9–11). Now we have nothing to fear.

Prayer: Lord, as I lay down in sleep last night and rose this morning only by your grace, so keep me in a joyful, lively remembrance that whatever happens, I will someday know my final rising—the resurrection—because Jesus Christ lay down in death for me and rose for my justification. Amen.

READ Psalm 17:1–9. **1** Hear me, LORD, my plea is just; listen to my cry. Hear my prayer—it does not rise from deceitful lips. **2** Let my vindication come from you; may your eyes see what is right. **3** Though you probe my heart, though you examine me at night and test me, you will find that I have planned no evil; my mouth has not transgressed. **4** Though people tried to bribe me, I have kept myself from the ways of the violent through what your lips have commanded. **5** My steps have held to your paths; my feet have not stumbled. **6** I call on you, my God, for you will answer me; turn your ear to me and hear my prayer. **7** Show me the wonders of your great love, you who save by your right hand those who take refuge in you from their foes. **8** Keep me as the apple of your eye; hide me in the shadow of your wings **9** from the wicked who are out to destroy me, from my mortal enemies who surround me.

A CLEAR CONSCIENCE. David is not claiming to be sinless as a human; he is denying that he is corrupt as a ruler. He has not lied to his people (verse 3) or taken bribes (verse 4). He is being falsely accused but his conscience is clear. How can we always keep a clear conscience? There are two parts to it. Do the right thing. But when you don't, immediately repent, knowing that you are "the apple of [God's] eye." In Christ, astonishingly, God does indeed see us as perfect (Philippians 3:9–10). So whether you are falsely accused or fallen and recovered, you can walk with your head up.

Prayer: Lord, help me to not care so much what others think of me. But help me to not even care so much about what *I* think of myself. Remind my heart that when you look on me you find me "in Christ" and see beauty. Let me rest in that. Amen.

January 25

READ Psalm 17:10–15. **10** They close up their callous hearts, and their mouths speak with arrogance. **11** They have tracked me down, they now surround me, with eyes alert, to throw me to the ground. **12** They are like a lion hungry for prey, like a fierce lion crouching in cover. **13** Rise up, LORD, confront them, bring them down; with your sword rescue me from the wicked. **14** By your hand save me from such people, LORD, from those of this world whose reward is in this life. May what you have stored up for the wicked fill their bellies; may their children gorge themselves on it, and may there be leftovers for their little ones. **15** As for me, I will be vindicated and will see your face; when I awake, I will be satisfied with seeing your likeness.

HOPE IN THE DARKNESS. The callous people who cross any line, flout every law, laugh at compassion, and do whatever it takes to be happy *right now* are indeed those we need to fear in this life. Living a self-absorbed life will always be at the cost of everyone else. In such a dark world, David maintains hope. He remembers that cruelty always comes home to roost (verse 14). But verse 15 goes far beyond such computation, reminding us that someday we will see the Lord as he is (1 John 3:2; 2 Corinthians 3:18). To gaze into infinite beauty and to receive such infinite love will give us a satisfaction that will last forever.

Prayer: Thank you, Lord, for the confidence your resurrection gives me that in the end all wrongs will be made right. Thank you for allowing me to rest in the assurance of my future resurrection and of living with you forever. Knowing this heals all wounds. Amen.

January 26

READ Psalm 18:1–6. **1** I love you, LORD, my strength. **2** The LORD is my rock, my fortress and my deliverer; my God is my rock, in whom I take refuge, my shield and the horn of my salvation, my stronghold. **3** I called to the LORD, who is worthy of praise, and I have been saved from my enemies. **4** The cords of death entangled me; the torrents of destruction overwhelmed me. **5** The cords of the grave coiled around me; the snares of death confronted me. **6** In my distress I called to the LORD; I cried to my God for help. From his temple he heard my voice; my cry came before him, into his ears.

I LOVE YOU, LORD. The psalms repeatedly call God a refuge, because we so constantly need it. Habitually turning to God for refuge is the only real support we have in life. In Psalm 2 David took refuge by remembering that God will put all things right eventually. In Psalm 7 he took refuge by resting on God's wise arrangement of his current life circumstances. Here we see David taking refuge by thanking God exuberantly for past blessings. When he says, "I love you, Lord," he uses an unusual Hebrew word that conveys deep emotion and passion. Cultivate such love by considering how God delivered you through the drama of the cross (Romans 5:8). That will make you strong.

Prayer: Thank you, Lord Jesus, for leaving the ultimate refuge of heaven to become radically vulnerable and to die for me, so that now, despite my sin, I can find a welcome and refuge in the arms of the Father. I love you for what you have done and for who you are. Amen.

READ **Psalm 18:7–19.** **7** The earth trembled and quaked, and the foundations of the mountains shook; they trembled because he was angry. **8** Smoke rose from his nostrils; consuming fire came from his mouth, burning coals blazed out of it. **9** He parted the heavens and came down; dark clouds were under his feet. **10** He mounted the cherubim and flew; he soared on the wings of the wind. **11** He made darkness his covering, his canopy around him—the dark rain clouds of the sky. **12** Out of the brightness of his presence clouds advanced, with hailstones and bolts of lightning. **13** The LORD thundered from heaven; the voice of the Most High resounded. **14** He shot his arrows and scattered the enemy, with great bolts of lightning he routed them. **15** The valleys of the sea were exposed and the foundations of the earth laid bare at your rebuke, LORD, at the blast of breath from your nostrils. **16** He reached down from on high and took hold of me; he drew me out of deep waters. **17** He rescued me from my powerful enemy, from my foes, who were too strong for me. **18** They confronted me in the day of my disaster, but the LORD was my support. **19** He brought me out into a spacious place; he rescued me because he delighted in me.

THE HINDSIGHT OF FAITH. David says God came down from heaven in storm (verses 8–9 and 12–13) and wind (verse 15) to save him. While he did these things at other times (cf. Joshua 10:11; Exodus 14:21), God never literally did them to help David escape from Saul. With hindsight, however, David now sees that God was active beneath the surface of things, even when he seemed absent at the time, "because he delighted in me" (verse 19). Christians know that God came down from heaven for them because he "loved [us] and gave himself for [us]" (Galatians 2:20) on the cross and delights in us in Christ (Colossians 1:22).

Prayer: Lord, the very fact that another day has been added to my life is due to your undeserved mercy and active presence. As I age another day, let me grow in the knowledge that I am completely accepted and fully loved, despite my flaws and failures, in Christ. Amen.

January 28

READ Psalm 18:20–27. **20** The LORD has dealt with me according to my righteousness; according to the cleanness of my hands he has rewarded me. **21** For I have kept the ways of the LORD; I am not guilty of turning from my God. **22** All his laws are before me; I have not turned away from his decrees. **23** I have been blameless before him and have kept myself from sin. **24** The LORD has rewarded me according to my righteousness, according to the cleanness of my hands in his sight. **25** To the faithful you show yourself faithful, to the blameless you show yourself blameless, **26** to the pure you show yourself pure, but to the devious you show yourself shrewd. **27** You save the humble but bring low those whose eyes are haughty.

Friendship with God. The word "faithful" (verse 25) refers to pledged love between covenant partners. God responds in kind (verses 25–26) so he can be not just a King but also a friend. Aristotle thought it impossible that humans could be friends with a god, because friends have things in common, and can say, "You, too?" But in becoming human, God's first great act of friendship, he became like us, drawing near to us so we could draw near to him. Since he humbled himself to get near us, only the humble, not the haughty, can be his friends. In his second great act of friendship, he gave his life for us (John 15:13). In our suffering, then, we can look at Jesus and say, "You, too?"

Prayer: Lord, it seems unimaginable that the Lord of the universe would also be the friend of my heart, but so it is. Through listening to your Word, through honest and constant prayer, through serving you even as you loved me, let me grow in friendship and intimate fellowship with you. Amen.

READ Psalm 18:28–33. **28** You, LORD, keep my lamp burning; my God turns my darkness into light. **29** With your help I can advance against a troop; with my God I can scale a wall. **30** As for God, his way is perfect: The LORD's word is flawless; he shields all who take refuge in him. **31** For who is God besides the LORD? And who is the Rock except our God? **32** It is God who arms me with strength and keeps my way secure. **33** He makes my feet like the feet of a deer; he causes me to stand on the heights.

STRENGTH THROUGH THE WORD. This psalm, from the first verse and throughout, is all about how God gives us the strength to face anything. How do we get that strength? Here David says he can scale a wall, because God's way is perfect and his Word is flawless. A perfect God could have nothing less than perfect communication with his people. It is we who read hastily, skip prayer, and fail to meditate on his Word, who find it confusing. The best gift in the world, next to the Word incarnate, Jesus himself, is God's written Word, and it will ignite your heart if you give it a chance.

Prayer: I thank you, Lord, for the Word of God, the Scripture, for its variety, wisdom, truth, wholesomeness, and power. Open my eyes so I can see more and more wondrous things in it and grow in strength to face anything that life can throw at me. Amen.

January 30

READ Psalm 18:34–45. **34** He trains my hands for battle; my arms can bend a bow of bronze. **35** You make your saving help my shield, and your right hand sustains me; your help has made me great. **36** You provide a broad path for my feet, so that my ankles do not give way. **37** I pursued my enemies and overtook them; I did not turn back till they were destroyed. **38** I crushed them so that they could not rise; they fell beneath my feet. **39** You armed me with strength for battle; you humbled my adversaries before me. **40** You made my enemies turn their backs in flight, and I destroyed my foes. **41** They cried for help, but there was no one to save them—to the LORD, but he did not answer. **42** I beat them as fine as windblown dust; I trampled them like mud in the streets. **43** You have delivered me from the attacks of the people; you have made me the head of nations. People I did not know now serve me, **44** foreigners cower before me; as soon as they hear of me, they obey me. **45** They all lose heart; they come trembling from their strongholds.

TRUE GREATNESS. Amid the celebration of military prowess exercised in defense of David's life against those sent into the wilderness to kill him is a remarkable statement—(literally) "your *gentleness* has made me great" (verse 35). The word comes from the word for "humble" or "meek." It was the gentleness God exercised toward an imperfect human being that allowed David his success, and it was the gentleness God taught him through hard lessons over the years that, in the end, was his true greatness.[12] Indeed, the height of the Lord's greatness was revealed in his ability and willingness to become weak and die for us.

Prayer: Lord Jesus, you said that you are "gentle and humble in heart" (Matthew 11:29)—but I so often am not. You were not concerned about your glory and reputation but I am. You never paid people back in anger but I do. Let your gentleness toward me make me gentle to others. Amen.

January 31

READ Psalm 18:46–50. **46** The LORD lives! Praise be to my Rock! Exalted be God my Savior! **47** He is the God who avenges me, who subdues nations under me, **48** who saves me from my enemies. You exalted me above my foes; from a violent man you rescued me. **49** Therefore I will praise you, LORD, among the nations; I will sing the praises of your name. **50** He gives his king great victories; he shows unfailing love to his anointed, to David and to his descendants forever.

THE JOY OF GRACE. In verses 4 through 19 David says *he* defeated his enemies, but here he says God did it. Is it we who work or God? Both—and this paradox (Philippians 2:12) is no contradiction. David knew, in the end, that God accomplished it all through his grace, despite David's imperfect efforts. But that did not make him passive. Work done in the belief it is all up to us becomes a joyless, deadly grind. Only those who know that salvation comes by sheer grace, not our efforts, have the inner dynamic of grateful joy (Colossians 3:15–17) that empowers the greatest efforts. So the joy of the Lord *is* our strength (Nehemiah 8:10).

Prayer: Lord, help me remember that my salvation in Christ is complete—so the great work is already done, the great debt already paid, the great disease already healed. That enables me to take on all lesser tasks and challenges with confidence and joy. I put myself in your hands—work through me. Amen.

February 1

READ Psalm 19:1-6. **1** The heavens declare the glory of God; the skies proclaim the work of his hands. **2** Day after day they pour forth speech; night after night they reveal knowledge. **3** They have no speech, they use no words; no sound is heard from them. **4** Yet their voice goes out into all the earth, their words to the ends of the world. In the heavens God has pitched a tent for the sun. **5** It is like a bridegroom coming out of his chamber, like a champion rejoicing to run his course. **6** It rises at one end of the heavens and makes its circuit to the other; nothing is deprived of its warmth.

THE SOUNDLESS WORD. Why do mountains and oceans, the sun and stars move us as deeply as great art? The answer is because they *are* great art. Nature speaks to all (verse 2) without audible words (verse 3). It is nonverbal communication that there is a God, that the world is not an accidental collocation of molecules but the meaningful work of an artist's hands. We should be reverent before our environment. It also means that all people know, at some level, about God, truth, meaning, wisdom, and beauty, even if they suppress that knowledge (Romans 1:18–21). Nevertheless, good, nonverbal communication is easily misinterpreted. We need something more.

Prayer: Maker of heaven and earth, your creation speaks and sings to us of your greatness. May I neither despise nature, failing to care reverently for its integrity, nor worship nature, failing to let it point me beyond itself to your glory, which even it only "fitfully reflects."[13] Amen.

February 2

READ Psalm 19:7–14. **7** The law of the LORD is perfect, refreshing the soul. The statutes of the LORD are trustworthy, making wise the simple. **8** The precepts of the LORD are right, giving joy to the heart. The commands of the LORD are radiant, giving light to the eyes. **9** The fear of the LORD is pure, enduring forever. The decrees of the LORD are firm, and all of them are righteous. **10** They are more precious than gold, than much pure gold; they are sweeter than honey, than honey from the honeycomb. **11** By them your servant is warned; in keeping them there is great reward. **12** But who can discern their own errors? Forgive my hidden faults. **13** Keep your servant also from willful sins; may they not rule over me. Then I will be blameless, innocent of great transgression. **14** May these words of my mouth and this meditation of my heart be pleasing in your sight, LORD, my Rock and my Redeemer.

THE PERFECT WORD. Nature tells us about God's reality and power but not about his saving grace (verses 7–14). Only the Bible can enlighten the spiritually blind (verse 8) and "refresh the soul" (verse 7). Since the Hebrew word for "soul" means one's psyche or self, the Bible has the power to show and restore your true identity. For the Bible to do all this, you must accept that it is perfectly true and trustworthy in all its parts (verses 7–9). Then don't just study it but let it search you (verses 11–14). Finally, ask Jesus, the Word made flesh, to give you his Spirit in order to find him in the written Word. The result will be wisdom, joy, and sweetness.

Prayer: Lord, I am so grateful that you don't make us guess who you are but that you speak directly to us. But if the Word is going to be sweet and life-giving to me, I must let it examine, search, and warn me. Help me have the discipline and faith to let it do that in my life. Amen.

February 3

READ Psalm 20. **1** May the LORD answer you when you are in distress; may the name of the God of Jacob protect you. **2** May he send you help from the sanctuary and grant you support from Zion. **3** May he remember all your sacrifices and accept your burnt offerings. **4** May he give you the desire of your heart and make all your plans succeed. **5** May we shout for joy over your victory and lift up our banners in the name of our God. May the LORD grant all your requests. **6** Now this I know: The LORD gives victory to his anointed. He answers him from his heavenly sanctuary with the victorious power of his right hand. **7** Some trust in chariots and some in horses, but we trust in the name of the LORD our God. **8** They are brought to their knees and fall, but we rise up and stand firm. **9** LORD, give victory to the king! Answer us when we call!

BEFORE A BATTLE. How do you get ready for some great challenge? It could be a conflict or a surgery or an undertaking that is very dangerous. The people here are on the eve of a great battle, and the temptation is to look to military might as their hope (verse 7). Instead they look to the Lord and to the king he has sent them (verse 1–6). Because God answers *him,* God's king (verse 1), he answers *them* (verse 9). How easy for us to place hope in analogous things—family, money, doctors, programs. Christians look instead to *their* anointed King, Jesus. God always answers him and honors his sacrifice (verse 1–4; cf. Hebrews 10:1–22).

Prayer: Lord, I am so anxious because I look to human wisdom, talent, and resources. They can let me down, but you cannot! Even if things don't go as I wish, if they are in your hands I am safe. And I know you will hear my prayer because you always hear my Savior's prayers. Amen.

February 4

READ Psalm 21:1–7. **1** The king rejoices in your strength, LORD. How great is his joy in the victories you give! **2** You have granted him his heart's desire and have not withheld the request of his lips. **3** You came to greet him with rich blessings and placed a crown of pure gold on his head. **4** He asked you for life, and you gave it to him—length of days, for ever and ever. **5** Through the victories you gave, his glory is great; you have bestowed on him splendor and majesty. **6** Surely you have granted him unending blessings and made him glad with the joy of your presence. **7** For the king trusts in the LORD; through the unfailing love of the Most High he will not be shaken.

REJOICING IN THE KING. Psalm 21 is thanksgiving for the answered prayers of Psalm 20. The people have triumphed because their king has. But the language describing the king now bursts its own banks. He lives "for ever and ever" and receives splendor and bliss "unending." We might think this flattering hyperbole, if we didn't know that these things are true of Jesus, the ultimate king, without exaggeration.[14] In him the splendor, the intimacy with God (verse 6), and the assurance of final triumph all are ours. And Jesus's "heart's desire" is our salvation. "After he has suffered, he will see the light of life and be satisfied" (Isaiah 53:11). Our daily joy should be as exuberant as this psalm.

Prayer: Lord Jesus, you ran your course with joy—and it cost you your life—all because your heart's desire was that we should be your people. Through you I have access to the Father and the assurance of resurrection. Let these joyous certainties animate my daily life. You are my King indeed. Amen.

February 5

READ Psalm 21:8–13. **8** Your hand will lay hold on all your enemies; your right hand will seize your foes. **9** When you appear for battle, you will burn them up as in a blazing furnace. The LORD will swallow them up in his wrath, and his fire will consume them. **10** You will destroy their descendants from the earth, their posterity from mankind. **11** Though they plot evil against you and devise wicked schemes, they cannot succeed. **12** You will make them turn their backs when you aim at them with drawn bow. **13** Be exalted, in your strength, LORD; we will sing and praise your might.

RESTING IN GOD'S JUDGMENT. The first part of this psalm is what we like to hear, but the second part, where God's King punishes his enemies, is just as much a part of God's Word as the rest. If we have lived comfortable, untroubled lives, these verses may trouble us; to anyone who has experienced injustice or oppression they are a comfort. Because Jesus will be the infallible judge, we don't have to be. We can let our grudges go and our revenge die.

Prayer: Lord, I praise you for being a God of justice, who will not let any wrongdoing go unaddressed or unpunished. Instead of being angry at those who wrong me, let me be compassionate, praying that they find your mercy through repentance. Amen.

February 6

READ Psalm 22:1–8. **1** My God, my God, why have you forsaken me? Why are you so far from saving me, so far from my cries of anguish? **2** My God, I cry out by day, but you do not answer, by night, but I find no rest. **3** Yet you are enthroned as the Holy One; you are the one Israel praises. **4** In you our ancestors put their trust; they trusted and you delivered them. **5** To you they cried out and were saved; in you they trusted and were not put to shame. **6** But I am a worm and not a man, scorned by everyone, despised by the people. **7** All who see me mock me; they hurl insults, shaking their heads: **8** "He trusts in the LORD," they say, "let the LORD rescue him. Let him deliver him, since he delights in him."

A WORD-SATURATED LIFE. Jesus answered every one of Satan's assaults with passages from Deuteronomy. As he was carrying the cross he cited the prophet Hosea, and as he was dying in agony he quoted both Psalm 22:1 and Psalm 31:5. Jesus was so saturated in the Word of God that it spontaneously came to his mind, enabling him to interpret and face every challenge. There are modern imitations of what Jesus had—relaxation techniques, stress management, positive thinking, mystical forms of contemplation. But nothing can duplicate it. God's Word was what sustained God's incarnate Word when he lived and when he died. Accept no substitutes.

Prayer: Lord, let your word be not merely something I believe but something that dwells richly inside me, so it reshapes all my thinking and feelings and even the very foundations of my heart. Let your promises, summonses, and declarations be my strength. Amen.

February 7

READ Psalm 22:9–18. **9** Yet you brought me out of the womb; you made me trust in you, even at my mother's breast. **10** From birth I was cast on you; from my mother's womb you have been my God. **11** Do not be far from me, for trouble is near and there is no one to help. **12** Many bulls surround me; strong bulls of Bashan encircle me. **13** Roaring lions that tear their prey open their mouths wide against me. **14** I am poured out like water, and all my bones are out of joint. My heart has turned to wax; it has melted within me. **15** My mouth is dried up like a potsherd, and my tongue sticks to the roof of my mouth; you lay me in the dust of death. **16** Dogs surround me; a pack of villains encircles me; they pierce my hands and my feet. **17** All my bones are on display; people stare and gloat over me. **18** They divide my clothes among them and cast lots for my garment.

THE HEART OF JESUS. This psalm of David poses a puzzle. The speaker's hands and feet are pierced (verse 16), his bony frame exposed (verse 17) as he experiences fatal dehydration (verse 15). This is not describing illness or persecution but rather an *execution*. Nothing like this ever happened to David, and the usual cries for justice are absent. It's as if this were a punishment that, though not deserved, must be submitted to. Jesus understood this psalm to be about his death (Matthew 27:46). Here, then, we have something remarkable—a look into the horror and agony of his heart, described by Jesus himself. Reading the psalm is like standing on holy ground.

Prayer: Thank you, Father, for disclosure of what Jesus went through for me. *"O wondrous love! to bleed and die, to bear the cross and shame; That guilty sinners, such as I, might plead Thy gracious name."*[15] Amen.

February 8

READ **Psalm 22:19–26.** **19** But you, LORD, be not far from me. You are my strength; come quickly to help me. **20** Deliver me from the sword, my precious life from the power of the dogs. **21** Rescue me from the mouth of the lions; save me from the horns of the wild oxen. **22** I will declare your name to my people; in the assembly I will praise you. **23** You who fear the LORD, praise him! All you descendants of Jacob, honor him! Revere him, all you descendants of Israel! **24** For he has not despised or scorned the suffering of the afflicted one; he has not hidden his face from him but has listened to his cry for help. **25** From you comes the theme of my praise in the great assembly; before those who fear you I will fulfill my vows. **26** The poor will eat and be satisfied; those who seek the LORD will praise him—may your hearts live forever!

BLESSED TO BLESS. All becomes praise in verse 22. God has *not* despised the affliction of the suffering one—and in light of the cross this means that God accepts Jesus's sacrifice (verses 22–24). The delivered servant now begins a new mission—telling the good news of God's salvation to others. Christians know that this is the mission of the resurrected Christ (Matthew 28:28–30). But the principle applies to us. Abraham was saved and blessed by God, but only so he could be a blessing to the world (Genesis 12:1–3). God never calls us in to love and change us without then sending us out to reach and serve others. We are blessed to bless.

Prayer: Lord God, you love all you have made and want all to turn to you and live. So show mercy to the many across the world who do not know you, removing any ignorance, hardness of heart, and disdain for your Gospel and so bring them home to yourself.[16] Amen.

February 9

READ Psalm 22:27–31. **27** All the ends of the earth will remember and turn to the LORD, and all the families of the nations will bow down before him, **28** for dominion belongs to the LORD and he rules over the nations. **29** All the rich of the earth will feast and worship; all who go down to the dust will kneel before him—those who cannot keep themselves alive. **30** Posterity will serve him; future generations will be told about the Lord. **31** They will proclaim his righteousness, declaring to a people yet unborn: He has done it!

HE HAS DONE IT! Our mission to the world tells the good news of God's salvation to all classes (the poor in verse 26 and the rich in verse 29), to all races and nations (verse 27), and to all generations (verse 30). What is this universal message? It is that salvation is something not that we attain but that he attains and gives. "He has done it!" cries David. "It is finished," cries Jesus (John 19:30), using the Greek *tetelestai*, a term that has the connotation of payment. "I have paid your debt to the last penny; I have drained your cup to the last drop," he says. There is now no condemnation left for us (Romans 8:1).

Prayer: Father, my mind knows the doctrine—that my salvation and standing with you depend not on my works but on Christ's works. Yet my heart doesn't fully believe it, and so I go back and forth between pride and self-loathing, depending on my performance. Let my heart fully grasp that "salvation is from the Lord" (Jonah 2:9). Amen.

February 10

READ Psalm 23. **1** The LORD is my shepherd, I lack nothing. **2** He makes me lie down in green pastures, he leads me beside quiet waters, **3** he refreshes my soul. He guides me along the right paths for his name's sake. **4** Even though I walk through the darkest valley, I will fear no evil, for you are with me; your rod and your staff, they comfort me. **5** You prepare a table before me in the presence of my enemies. You anoint my head with oil; my cup overflows. **6** Surely your goodness and love will follow me all the days of my life, and I will dwell in the house of the LORD forever.

PEACE IN THE MIDST. God has a celebration meal with us not after we finally get out of the dark valley but in the middle of it, in the presence of our enemies. He wants us to rejoice in him in the midst of our troubles. Is our shepherd out of touch with reality? Hardly. Jesus is the only shepherd who knows what it is like to be a sheep (John 10:11). He understands what we are going through and will be with us every step of the way, even through death itself, where "all other guides turn back"[17] (Romans 8:39).

Prayer: Lord, if I fed on your love, grace, and truth, I would not be in any want. In this life I will never attain that, yet you are always with me, and someday you will lead me to my true country, the home I've been looking for all my life. Help me rest in that. Amen.

February 11

READ Psalm 24:1–6. **1** The earth is the LORD's, and everything in it, the world, and all who live in it; **2** for he founded it on the seas and established it on the waters. **3** Who may ascend the mountain of the LORD? Who may stand in his holy place? **4** The one who has clean hands and a pure heart, who does not trust in an idol or swear by a false god. **5** They will receive blessing from the LORD and vindication from God their Savior. **6** Such is the generation of those who seek him, who seek your face, God of Jacob.

THE PURSUIT OF GOD. All money, talent, health, power, and pleasure in the world are God's. But the greatest treasure he can give us is life in his presence. His face—not the gifts of his hands, though they are welcome—is where we find the glory that other things fail to provide. To know his presence, however, is to "ascend" a hill or mountain (verse 3), and doing so is always a struggle. You must repent, seeking a clear conscience (verse 4). You must know your idols and reject them (verse 4). And you must wrestle in prayer to seek God's face, as did Jacob (verse 6), who said, "I will not let you go unless you bless me" (Genesis 32:26).

Prayer: Lord, you alone are the fountain of the life and love I have looked for in other places, to my misery. I want to love you for yourself alone and know your fellowship and presence. That will be a long journey and a struggle. But I commit myself to it today. Amen.

February 12

READ **Psalm 24:7–10.** **7** Lift up your heads, you gates; be lifted up, you ancient doors, that the King of glory may come in. **8** Who is this King of glory? The LORD strong and mighty, the LORD mighty in battle. **9** Lift up your heads, you gates; lift them up, you ancient doors, that the King of glory may come in. **10** Who is he, this King of glory? The LORD Almighty—he is the King of glory.

TRUE GLORY. What is God's glory? It is his infinite weight, his supreme importance. To glorify God is to obey him unconditionally. To ever say, "I'll obey if . . ." is to give something else more importance or glory than God. But while glorifying God is never less than obedience, it is more. God's glory also means his inexpressible beauty and perfection. It does not glorify him, then, if we only ever obey God simply out of duty. We must give him not only our will but also our heart, as we adore and enjoy him, as we find him infinitely attractive. And there is no greater beauty than to see the Son of God laying aside his glory and dying for us (Philippians 2:5–11)

Prayer: Lord, you loved me enough to lose all your glory for me even though you owned the whole world and everything in it! Show your glory to my heart, to my family, and to my society as well, that they may all say to you, "Come in." Amen.

February 13

READ Psalm 25:1–7. **1** In you, LORD my God, I put my trust; **2** I trust in you; do not let me be put to shame, nor let my enemies triumph over me. **3** No one who hopes in you will ever be put to shame, but shame will come on those who are treacherous without cause. **4** Show me your ways, LORD, teach me your paths. **5** Guide me in your truth and teach me, for you are God my Savior, and my hope is in you all day long. **6** Remember, LORD, your great mercy and love, for they are from of old. **7** Do not remember the sins of my youth and my rebellious ways; according to your love remember me, for you, LORD, are good.

WHOSE WITS? David's enemies are opposed to his philosophy of life. His conviction was "that a man must live by the help of God, not by his wits," a view of life his enemies despised as naive.[18] David admits that without God, the life of integrity would be no match for the self-interested, treacherous power politics of the world (verse 3). Christian integrity means leading a life of purity and celibacy if you are not married and telling the truth even when it will harm your career—things the world sees as stupid. But in the end, it is the world that will be put to shame.

Prayer: Lord, I want to live according to your Word—"*your* ways," "*your* truth" (verses 4–5)—rather than by what will make me popular and powerful. Give me the desire and integrity to live like this. And because this will make me vulnerable, protect me from those who would take the opportunity to harm me. Amen.

February 14

READ Psalm 25:8–14. **8** Good and upright is the LORD; therefore he instructs sinners in his ways. **9** He guides the humble in what is right and teaches them his way. **10** All the ways of the LORD are loving and faithful toward those who keep the demands of his covenant. **11** For the sake of your name, LORD, forgive my iniquity, though it is great. **12** Who, then, are those who fear the Lord? He will instruct him in the ways they should choose. **13** They will spend their days in prosperity, and their descendants will inherit the land. **14** The LORD confides in those who fear him; he makes his covenant known to them.

GUIDANCE. How does God guide us? The better question is not how, but *whom* God guides. What kind of person must we be so that he leads us in our decision making? We must be so immersed in God's written Word and truth (verses 4–5) that we are trained to choose rightly even in cases to which the Bible doesn't speak directly. We must be not wise in our own eyes (verse 9) but aware of our sins and limitations (verse 11). We must trust that *all* the things God sends us are grounded in his loving will (verse 10; Genesis 50:20). God "confides" in those who have all these attitudes of heart (verse 14). He makes us wise so we know the paths to take.

Prayer: Lord, don't just make me obedient to your Word, but also make me wise—knowing the right thing to do in the myriad life situations to which the Bible's rules don't directly speak. Let me grow in wisdom, judgment, and prudence, and give me the humility prerequisite for them all. Amen.

February 15

READ Psalm 25:15–22. **15** My eyes are ever on the LORD, for only he will release my feet from the snare. **16** Turn to me and be gracious to me, for I am lonely and afflicted. **17** Relieve the troubles of my heart and free me from my anguish. **18** Look upon my affliction and my distress and take away all my sins. **19** See how numerous are my enemies and how fiercely they hate me! **20** Guard my life and rescue me; do not let me be put to shame, for I take refuge in you. **21** May integrity and uprightness protect me, because my hope, LORD, is in you. **22** Deliver Israel, O God, from all their troubles!

WAITING EAGERLY. Verse 21 uses the word "hope" to translate a term that means "to wait eagerly" for God. This is not resignation or passivity but an active stance toward life. David lives in integrity and uprightness (verse 21) despite how well his enemies are doing (verse 19). He also keeps his eyes on the Lord (verse 15) and seeks his presence and touch (verse 16). Those two things—unconditional obedience and prevailing prayer—are the constituents of "waiting eagerly" for God. Waiting on God, rather than jumping the gun by taking matters into your own hands, is the epitome of wisdom, as the contrasting lives and destinies of Saul (1 Samuel 13:8–14) and David (1 Samuel 26:10–11) make clear.

Prayer: Lord, I confess I do not understand your timing. If I were in charge of history and my life I would have arranged things differently. But I cannot see the whole picture, I cannot see from beginning to end, and so I wait for you in obedience and prayer. Amen.

February 16

READ Psalm 26:1–5. **1** Vindicate me, LORD, for I have led a blameless life; I have trusted in the LORD and have not faltered. **2** Test me, LORD, and try me, examine my heart and my mind; **3** for I have always been mindful of your unfailing love and have lived in reliance on your faithfulness. **4** I do not sit with the deceitful, nor do I associate with hypocrites. **5** I abhor the assembly of evildoers and refuse to sit with the wicked.

THE SECRET OF TRUE INDEPENDENCE. When David calls himself "blameless" he does not mean "sinless," because in verse 11 he begs for mercy. Rather, as king he is charged falsely with corruption, with allying with evil men, and with taking bribes (verses 4–5, 10). By calling out to God to be his judge, he appeals neither to his friends to defend him nor to his enemies to change their minds. This is the secret of true independence, as Paul found when he said he cared not at all what people thought—friends or foes—nor even how he assessed himself. "It is the Lord who judges me" (1 Corinthians 4:4). Only God's opinion counts.

Prayer: Father, I confess that the opinions of others matter far more to me than does yours. I fear looking bad. Help me to remember how accepted I am in Christ—so I will have the freedom and poise necessary to live without fear. Amen.

READ Psalm 26:6–12. **6** I wash my hands in innocence, and go about your altar, LORD, **7** proclaiming aloud your praise and telling of all your wonderful deeds. **8** LORD, I love the house where you live, the place where your glory dwells. **9** Do not take away my soul along with sinners, my life with those who are bloodthirsty, **10** in whose hands are wicked schemes, whose right hands are full of bribes. **11** I lead a blameless life; deliver me and be merciful to me. **12** My feet stand on level ground; in the great congregation I will praise the LORD.

THE PLACE YOUR GLORY DWELLS. David loves that God's glory—his infinitely holy and beautiful presence—dwells in the temple (verse 8). Even more marvelous is the Gospel, which tells us that Jesus is the true temple (John 2:20–21). God's glory dwells in him (John 1:14) and in all those who unite with him by faith (1 Peter 2:4–5). Those odd people in the next pew? That couple with the whiny baby? Those young people who don't dress right for church? They should be objects of your love and respect because God's glory dwells in them. The weight of their glory should "be laid daily on [your] back, a load so heavy only humility can carry it, and the backs of the proud will be broken."[19]

Prayer: Father, each of my neighbors is made in your image and precious in your sight; each of my brothers and sisters has Christ and his glory in them. How can I ever be cold, irritated, or disdainful toward anyone? Give me enough love to live my life every day as I should. Amen.

READ Psalm 27:1-6. **1** The LORD is my light and my salvation—whom shall I fear? The LORD is the stronghold of my life—of whom shall I be afraid? **2** When the wicked advance against me to devour me, it is my enemies and my foes who will stumble and fall. **3** Though an army besiege me, my heart will not fear; though war break out against me, even then will I be confident. **4** One thing I ask from the LORD, this only do I seek: that I may dwell in the house of the LORD all the days of my life, to gaze upon the beauty of the LORD and to seek him in his temple. **5** For in the day of trouble he will keep me safe in his dwelling; he will hide me in the shelter of his sacred tent and set me high upon a rock. **6** Then my head will be exalted above the enemies who surround me; at his sacred tent I will sacrifice with shouts of joy; I will sing and make music to the LORD.

THE BEAUTY OF GOD. Is there certain music that gives you deep joy? Is there a view or landscape that does the same? If someone says, "What is the use of that?" you answer that the music or landscape is not a means to some other end but profoundly satisfying in itself. David's supreme priority is "to gaze on the beauty of the Lord" (verse 4). "Gazing" is not a one-time glimpse but a steady, sustained focus. It is not petitionary prayer but praising, admiring, and enjoying God just for who he is. David finds God beautiful, not just useful for attaining goods. To sense God's beauty in the heart is to have such pleasure in him that you rest content.

Prayer: Lord, it is no exaggeration to say that there is only one thing that I really need in life, and I ask for it now. It is to not merely believe in you but in prayer and experience to see and sense your beauty. Let me love you for yourself alone. Amen.

February 19

READ Psalm 27:7–14. **7** Hear my voice when I call, LORD; be merciful to me and answer me. **8** My heart says of you, "Seek his face!" Your face, LORD, I will seek. **9** Do not hide your face from me, do not turn your servant away in anger; you have been my helper. Do not reject me or forsake me, God my Savior. **10** Though my father and mother forsake me, the LORD will receive me. **11** Teach me your way, LORD; lead me in a straight path because of my oppressors. **12** Do not turn me over to the desire of my foes, for false witnesses rise up against me, spouting malicious accusations. **13** I remain confident of this: I will see the goodness of the LORD in the land of the living. **14** Wait for the LORD; be strong and take heart and wait for the LORD.

FINDING HIS BEAUTY. David is having difficulties, but the beauty of God enables him to live in confident peace (verses 1 and 6). If our hearts delight in God and his face, then we can contemplate losing earthly joys without fear. Even if our mother and father forsake us, we can face it (verse 10). Why? If our greatest treasure—communion with the living God—is safe, of what can we be afraid? Yet we are afraid of so many things. So our fears can serve an important purpose—they show us where we have really located our heart's treasure. Follow the pathway of the fear back into your heart to discover the things you love more than God.

Prayer: Lord, I will obey you simply because you are worthy of it and it is my duty. But don't let my service to you remain at that level. Show me your beauty—attract my heart, capture my imagination, so that I find joyful pleasure in serving you. Amen.

February 20

READ Psalm 28:1–5. **1** To you, LORD, I call; you are my Rock; do not turn a deaf ear to me. For if you remain silent, I will be like those who go down to the pit. **2** Hear my cry for mercy as I call to you for help, as I lift up my hands toward your Most Holy Place. **3** Do not drag me away with the wicked, with those who do evil, who speak cordially with their neighbors but harbor malice in their hearts. **4** Repay them for their deeds and for their evil work; repay them for what their hands have done and bring back on them what they deserve. **5** Because they have no regard for the deeds of the LORD and what his hands have done, he will tear them down and never build them up again.

THE STING OF INJUSTICE. David fears being "drag[ged] away with the wicked" (verse 3) to the "pit," a word that can mean a dungeon for offenders (verse 1). He cries to God at the prospect of being unfairly charged and counted as a corrupt ruler. This is a major theme of the psalms, but not one that most of us in comfortable Western societies can easily understand. "Nothing stings so sharply as injustice, and nothing should; so these verses are not simply vindictive, but put into words the protest of any healthy conscience at the wrongs of the present order, and the conviction that a day of judgment is a moral necessity."[20] Christians should also cry to God day and night against injustice (Luke 18:7).

Prayer: Lord, I pray for justice in the world—for the lifting up of the poor out of their misery, for the breaking of the power of tyrannical regimes, for the end of violence, warfare, racial conflict, and strife. Thank you that you *are* a God of justice. Amen.

February 21

READ Psalm 28:6–9. **6** Praise be to the LORD, for he has heard my cry for mercy. **7** The LORD is my strength and my shield; my heart trusts in him, and he helps me. My heart leaps for joy, and with my song I praise him. **8** The LORD is the strength of his people, a fortress of salvation for his anointed one. **9** Save your people and bless your inheritance; be their shepherd and carry them forever.

PRAYER-HEARING GOD. We can't live without prayer. David has made petitions that were both bold and specific (verses 3–5). He took time to reason with God, reminding him of why he was making his requests. Then he bursts into praise in verse 6 that God has "heard my cry." How could he know that? Perhaps God sent David a special revelation that his exact request would be answered. We have no such access. But when we make our requests known to God we can do something like this: We can thank him ahead of time for giving us what we would have asked for if we knew everything he knew (Philippians 4:6–7).

Prayer: Father, I know that you listen to me—not because I deserve it but because your Son, Jesus, my great high priest, brings my needs before your throne and you hear them all for his sake. I lift my empty hands to you and ask that you fill them with your grace and help. Amen.

February 22

READ Psalm 29. **1** Ascribe to the LORD, you heavenly beings, ascribe to the LORD glory and strength. **2** Ascribe to the LORD the glory due his name; worship the LORD in the splendor of his holiness. **3** The voice of the LORD is over the waters; the God of glory thunders, the LORD thunders over the mighty waters. **4** The voice of the LORD is powerful; the voice of the LORD is majestic. **5** The voice of the LORD breaks the cedars; the LORD breaks in pieces the cedars of Lebanon. **6** He makes Lebanon leap like a calf, Sirion like a young wild ox. **7** The voice of the LORD strikes with flashes of lightning. **8** The voice of the LORD shakes the desert; the LORD shakes the Desert of Kadesh. **9** The voice of the LORD twists the oaks and strips the forests bare. And in his temple all cry, "Glory!" **10** The LORD sits enthroned over the flood; the LORD is enthroned as King forever. **11** The LORD gives strength to his people; the LORD blesses his people with peace.

LORD OF THE STORM. Hurricanes have massive power, yet God's is greater—he is enthroned over the flood (verse 10), working out his will sovereignly in nature and history and even through storms for our ultimate good (Romans 8:28). God's power is particularly evident in his voice (verses 3–9). What God's voice or Word does *he* does (verses 5 and 8). His divine power is active in his Word. Do not underestimate, then, how much the power of God can do in your life through the Bible. The voice of the Lord can break down even our strongest defenses, defuse our despair, free us from guilt, and lead us to him.

Prayer: Lord, if I want your power in my life, I must listen to your Word. Enable me to "read, mark, learn and inwardly digest"[21] the Scriptures and therein encounter you, my living Lord. Amen.

February 23

READ Psalm 30:1–5. **1** I will exalt you, LORD, for you lifted me out of the depths and did not let my enemies gloat over me. **2** LORD my God, I called to you for help and you healed me. **3** You, LORD, brought me up from the realm of the dead; you spared me from going down to the pit. **4** Sing the praises of the LORD, you his faithful people; praise his holy name. **5** For his anger lasts only a moment, but his favor lasts a lifetime; weeping may stay for a night, but rejoicing comes in the morning.

GRACE SHALL LEAD ME HOME. This is a song of grace. While God can be angry with his people, anger is never the final word (verse 5), and so joy is always on the way, always coming to those who believe in him. In Jesus this principle goes even further to "sorrow *producing* joy (2 Corinthians 4:17; John 16:20–22)."[22] Jesus's grief and suffering produced joy for both him and us, and now, when we trust in him during dark times, our sorrow can also produce the joy of increased faith and spiritual reality.

Prayer: Lord, your Word says that our troubles are "achieving for us an eternal glory that far outweighs them all" (2 Corinthians 4:17). I can't fathom all that that means, but I have seen the beginnings of it in my life. So do the work in me that can happen only when I trust in you as I weep. Amen.

February 24

READ Psalm 30:6–12. **6** When I felt secure, I said, "I will never be shaken." **7** LORD, when you favored me, you made my royal mountain stand firm; but when you hid your face, I was dismayed. **8** To you, LORD, I called; to the Lord I cried for mercy: **9** "What is gained if I am silenced, if I go down to the pit? Will the dust praise you? Will it proclaim your faithfulness? **10** Hear, LORD, and be merciful to me; LORD, be my help." **11** You turned my wailing into dancing; you removed my sackcloth and clothed me with joy, **12** that my heart may sing your praises and not be silent. LORD my God, I will praise you forever.

OVERCONFIDENCE. We often stroll through life, thinking everything will be fine, until suddenly it isn't. Our unconscious or even verbalized thought is "I'm solid. I'm on top of things. I've got it nailed. I've planned well. I'm secure." Verses 6–7 show how even after a recent act of God's deliverance we can slip back into self-confidence, this time by thinking of God's favor as a right we earned. But God shakes our confidence in our earthly life so that we can yearn for our heavenly life, where our joy is truly unshakable and where our wailing will be turned into dancing.

Prayer: Lord, teach me, during all the stomach-churning ups and downs of life, how to fix my heart where true joys are to be found.[23] Amen.

February 25

READ Psalm 31:1–8. **1** In you, LORD, I have taken refuge; let me never be put to shame; deliver me in your righteousness. **2** Turn your ear to me, come quickly to my rescue; be my rock of refuge, a strong fortress to save me. **3** Since you are my rock and my fortress, for the sake of your name lead and guide me. **4** Keep me from the trap that is set for me, for you are my refuge. **5** Into your hands I commit my spirit; deliver me, LORD, my faithful God. **6** I hate those who cling to worthless idols; as for me, I trust in the LORD. **7** I will be glad and rejoice in your love, for you saw my affliction and knew the anguish of my soul. **8** You have not given me into the hands of the enemy but have set my feet in a spacious place.

INTO YOUR HANDS. Under great stress it is possible to journey from great "anguish of . . . soul" (verse 7) to confidence and being in "a spacious place" (verse 8). David makes this journey by being spiritually active, not passive. He cries in prayer, "Come quickly to my rescue" (verse 2). He repents in prayer of all idols (verse 6). He communes with God in prayer until his love and favor produce joy, compensating for all other losses (verse 7). These are all ways of committing ourselves into his hands (verse 5). Do this, and God will bring you also into a spacious place, despite your sins, because Jesus committed *his* spirit into God's hands (Luke 24:46) on the cross.

Prayer: Lord Jesus, on the cross you were being betrayed, denied, rejected, and forsaken by everyone. Yet you trusted and put yourself in your Father's hands. If you did all that for my sake, then I can trust and put myself into your hands, for your sake. Here I am. Amen.

READ Psalm 31:9–18. **9** Be merciful to me, LORD, for I am in distress; my eyes grow weak with sorrow, my soul and my body with grief. **10** My life is consumed by anguish and my years by groaning; my strength fails because of my affliction, and my bones grow weak. **11** Because of all my enemies, I am the utter contempt of my neighbors and an object of dread to my closest friends—those who see me on the street flee from me. **12** I am forgotten as though I were dead; I have become like broken pottery. **13** For I hear many whispering, "Terror on every side!" They conspire against me and plot to take my life. **14** But I trust in you, LORD; I say, "You are my God." **15** My times are in your hands; deliver me from the hands of my enemies, from those who pursue me. **16** Let your face shine on your servant; save me in your unfailing love. **17** Let me not be put to shame, LORD, for I have cried out to you; but let the wicked be put to shame and be silent in the realm of the dead. **18** Let their lying lips be silenced, for with pride and contempt they speak arrogantly against the righteous.

MY TIMES. David lives with "terror on every side" (verse 13). Life seems precarious and even capricious. Terrible things happen that make no sense to us. But, David knows, world history and our personal histories are not, ultimately, operating on chance. "My times are in your hands," he reminds himself and us (verse 15). The Bible's teaching on this is balanced. Many events are evil and grievous, yet God overrules them and works them all together, in the long run, for good (Romans 8:28). So in the end our lives cannot be derailed permanently. Learn how to say to God: "My times are in your hands."

Prayer: Lord, so many of the circumstances of my life make no sense to me, but they make sense to you. Help me, like David, to rest in that. My times are truly in your hands, and that is absolutely, infinitely better than if they were in my hands. Amen.

READ Psalm 31:19–24. **19** How abundant are the good things that you have stored up for those who fear you, that you bestow in the sight of all, on those who take refuge in you. **20** In the shelter of your presence you hide them from all human intrigues; you keep them safe in your dwelling from accusing tongues. **21** Praise be to the LORD, for he showed me the wonders of his love when I was in a city under siege. **22** In my alarm I said, "I am cut off from your sight!" Yet you heard my cry for mercy when I called to you for help. **23** Love the LORD, all his faithful people! The LORD preserves those who are true to him, but the proud he pays back in full. **24** Be strong and take heart, all you who hope in the LORD.

FEELINGS AND REALITY. When David was in trouble, he felt God was not with him—"I am cut off from your sight!" (verse 22). During success we can have the opposite feeling ("I will never be shaken," Psalm 30:6), which is just as wrong. We must live, then, on the basis of what God has revealed, not what we feel. Pilots who fly into clouds must follow their instruments even when those contradict their clear sense perceptions of which way is up, or they will inevitably die.[24] When we go through clouds of prosperity or adversity, we must not go on feelings of self-sufficiency or despair but rather should trust a gracious, wise God.

Prayer: Lord, if my heart doesn't learn to trust your Word when it tells me things I don't want to hear, then my heart won't accept it when it tells me things I desperately *do* want to hear—about your love and forgiveness. Teach me to trust your Word. Amen.

READ Psalm 32:1–5. **1** Blessed is the one whose transgressions are forgiven, whose sins are covered. **2** Blessed is the one whose sin the LORD does not count against them and in whose spirit is no deceit. **3** When I kept silent, my bones wasted away through my groaning all day long. **4** For day and night your hand was heavy on me; my strength was sapped as in the heat of summer. **5** Then I acknowledged my sin to you and did not cover up my iniquity. I said, "I will confess my transgressions to the LORD." And you forgave the guilt of my sin.

FORGIVENESS. Many insist that guilt is an imposition of society or religion, that people can define right and wrong for themselves. Nonetheless we have a sense of condemnation, of not being as we ought, that we can't shake. The liberation of forgiveness starts with honesty. It is only when we uncover and admit our sin (verse 5) that God is willing to cover it (verse 1). That is, he removes our objective guilt so it can't bring us into punishment (verse 5), and he removes our subjective shame so we don't remain in inner anguish (verse 3 and 4). The happiest (most "blessed") people in the world are those who not only know they need to be deeply forgiven but also have experienced it.

Prayer: Father, as great as my sins are, it is a great and additional sin to refuse to rest in your grace and accept your pardon. Give me the blessedness and release of knowing I am completely, absolutely, freely forgiven through Jesus. Amen.

March 1

READ Psalm 32:6–11. **6** Therefore let all the faithful pray to you while you may be found; surely the rising of the mighty waters will not reach them. **7** You are my hiding place; you will protect me from trouble and surround me with songs of deliverance. **8** I will instruct you and teach you in the way you should go; I will counsel you with my loving eye on you. **9** Do not be like the horse or the mule, which have no understanding but must be controlled by bit and bridle or they will not come to you. **10** Many are the woes of the wicked, but the LORD's unfailing love surrounds the one who trusts in him. **11** Rejoice in the LORD and be glad, you righteous; sing, all you who are upright in heart!

BIT AND BRIDLE. God calls us to go beyond forgiveness to real friendship with him. We usually live as we should only if we *have* to, out of self-interest, because there are consequences that keep us on the path. That is to heed God like a mule, controlled only by bit and bridle (verse 9). Instead we should obey because we *want* to, out of love for him, who counsels us personally through the Word and prayer (verse 8). Sometimes God allows a difficult season of "mighty waters" to be a kind of bit and bridle that pulls us back to him and shows us we need his friendship and love above all else. Be glad that he doesn't let us wander.

Prayer: Lord, I don't want to confess my sin only out of external compulsion. I want to look at the costly love of Jesus until I am sorry not just for the consequences of this sin but for the sin itself and how it grieves you. Only then will it lose its power over me. Amen.

March 2

READ Psalm 33:1–9. **1** Sing joyfully to the LORD, you righteous; it is fitting for the upright to praise him. **2** Praise the LORD with the harp; make music to him on the ten-stringed lyre. **3** Sing to him a new song; play skillfully, and shout for joy. **4** For the word of the LORD is right and true; he is faithful in all he does. **5** The LORD loves righteousness and justice; the earth is full of his unfailing love. **6** By the word of the LORD the heavens were made, their starry host by the breath of his mouth. **7** He gathers the waters of the sea into jars; he puts the deep into storehouses. **8** Let all the earth fear the LORD; let all the people of the world revere him. **9** For he spoke, and it came to be; he commanded, and it stood firm.

THE HEALTH OF WORSHIP. Praise is "fitting" (verse 1). It fits God because he is worthy and fits us because we were created for it. Thus, generous and happy people are prone to praise, while others are prone to complain. Praise is "inner health made audible."[25] But we were created not for praise in general but to worship something supremely, to have our thoughts and hearts captivated. We need to draw our hearts from fixation on other things and become enraptured with the beauty of the Lord. One of the main ways to do this is to use skillful music in our worship and private devotion (verse 3).

Prayer: Lord, I praise you that you *are* a praiseworthy God, both perfectly good and unimaginably glorious. And I thank you for how your praise heals me—clarifies my vision, changes my perspective, strengthens my heart, and produces joy upon joy. Help me to see you as you are so I will praise you as I ought.[26] Amen.

March 3

READ Psalm 33:10–17. **10** The LORD foils the plans of the nations; he thwarts the purposes of the peoples. **11** But the plans of the LORD stand firm forever, the purposes of his heart through all generations. **12** Blessed is the nation whose God is the LORD, the people he chose for his inheritance. **13** From heaven the LORD looks down and sees all mankind; **14** from his dwelling place he watches all who live on earth—**15** he who forms the hearts of all, who considers everything they do. **16** No king is saved by the size of his army; no warrior escapes by his great strength. **17** A horse is a vain hope for deliverance; despite all its great strength it cannot save.

THE NATIONS FOILED. Those in power have always had their plans and purposes. It says here they *all* come to nothing. They either get nothing that they want, or what they want only unwittingly serves God's purposes. So the people who sought to thwart God's salvation through Jesus only furthered it (Acts 4:28). God works out his plans to save us unaltered by the rise and fall of civilizations, nations, and powers. Putting our trust in earthly power and wealth is useless. We think our talent procured the award. But God says, "I gave you the talent and arranged who was in the competition. It was all my doing." In God we trust, not social power, political maneuvers, or economic clout.

Prayer: Lord, keep me from putting my hope too much in my knowledge, social connections, and ability to plan. The reality is that we are completely dependent on you for everything. Help me to not resist that truth but to derive the comfort and grateful joy that come from gladly accepting it. Amen.

March 4

HOPE THAT DOESN'T DISAPPOINT. If you love someone, you are "quick-eyed" with them.[27] You watch intently for the merest facial expression or gesture or tone of voice that hints at a need, so that you can meet it. Wonderfully, God loves us like that, his all-seeing eyes alert to both what threatens us and what nurtures us (verse 19). The psalm ends on a note of hope, but this is not a general optimism. The psalmist does not hope in God giving him this or that. He waits in hope for the Lord himself. He is focused "not on the gift (though there is a place for this: Romans 8:18–25) but on the Giver. Such hope will 'never disappoint us' (Romans 5:5)."[28]

Prayer: Lord, I can hardly believe that you, with your infinite power and glory, are watching me eagerly from heaven, filled with love, always attentive to my needs. You love me more—and infinitely more wisely—than I love myself. Help me to rejoice and rest in that enough not to worry. Amen.

March 5

READ Psalm 34:1–10. **1** I will extol the LORD at all times; his praise will always be on my lips. **2** I will glory in the LORD; let the afflicted hear and rejoice. **3** Glorify the LORD with me; let us exalt his name together. **4** I sought the LORD, and he answered me; he delivered me from all my fears. **5** Those who look to him are radiant; their faces are never covered with shame. **6** This poor man called, and the LORD heard him; he saved him out of all his troubles. **7** The angel of the LORD encamps around those who fear him, and he delivers them. **8** Taste and see that the LORD is good; blessed is the man who takes refuge in him. **9** Fear the LORD, you his holy people, for those who fear him lack nothing. **10** The lions may grow weak and hungry, but those who seek the LORD lack no good thing.

BOASTING IN THE LORD. How can we be delivered from all our fears (verse 4)? The answer is comprehensive. Build an identity that gets its significance ("glory")—makes its "boast" (Jeremiah 9:23–24)—not from your accomplishments or racial identity or talent or moral efforts or family but from God (verse 2). Then and only then is the foundation of your self-worth secure and not subject to fears or shame (verse 5). How can we get such an identity? By not just believing in God but "tasting" and experiencing God's goodness in prayer (verse 8). And by comforting afflicted people with the comfort we have received (verse 2; 2 Corinthians 1:3–4) until they can glorify God with us (verse 3). This is the mission of every believer.

Prayer: Lord, my anxieties, shame, and discouragement come when I try to make my boast in other things than your goodness and unfailing love toward me. Teach me how to look to you and seek you until I know the radiance of your joy. Amen.

March 6

READ Psalm 34:11–16. **11** Come, my children, listen to me; I will teach you the fear of the LORD. **12** Whoever of you loves life and desires to see many good days, **13** keep your tongue from evil and your lips from speaking lies. **14** Turn from evil and do good; seek peace and pursue it. **15** The eyes of the LORD are on the righteous and his ears are attentive to their cry; **16** but the face of the LORD is against those who do evil, blot out their name from the earth.

THE LIE. To enjoy a good life (verse 12) you must live a good life (verses 13–14). This challenges the lie of the serpent in Eden that if we obey God fully we will be miserable, that rich living lies outside God's will, not within it.[29] This lie has passed deeply into every human heart: that we would be happier if we, rather than God, were free to choose how our lives should be lived. But the ultimate good is knowing God personally, and the ultimate punishment is just as personal—to lose the face of God (verse 16), the only source of joy and love, to be "left utterly and absolutely *outside*—repelled, exiled, estranged, finally and unspeakably ignored."[30]

Prayer: Father, if I want to love life, I have to love you—and loving you means doing your will with gladness. Shine your face on me—let me know your love—so I can love you for who you are. Remind me that the only loss that is unbearable is to lose you and your presence. Amen.

March 7

READ Psalm 34:17–22. **17** The righteous cry out, and the LORD hears them; he delivers them from all their troubles. **18** The LORD is close to the brokenhearted and saves those who are crushed in spirit. **19** A righteous person may have many troubles, but the LORD delivers him from them all; **20** he protects all his bones, not one of them will be broken. **21** Evil will slay the wicked; the foes of the righteous will be condemned. **22** The LORD will rescue his servants; no one who takes refuge in him will be condemned.

HOW GOD KEEPS US SAFE. Verses 17 and 19 seem to promise believers exemption from troubles, but other psalms say God is with us *in* our troubles (Psalms 23:4 and 91:15). Indeed, verse 18 says we can be broken and crushed by life. But these sufferings bring God's presence near in a way nothing else can (verse 18). Afterward, sufferers come to realize that they could not have received their deeper joy in God any other way. Verse 22 says the Lord "will rescue his servants." Only the New Testament reveals what this promise cost God. On the cross Jesus secured "no condemnation" (Romans 8:1) for those who take refuge in him—to a degree David could not have imagined.

Prayer: Lord, it is not exactly right to thank you for my sorrows, for you did not create a world filled with evil, and my grief causes you grief. And yet I do thank you for the many riches I have found in these dark mines: patience, courage, self-understanding, and most of all your love and presence. Amen.

March 8

READ Psalm 35:1–10. **1** Contend, LORD, with those who contend with me; fight against those who fight against me. **2** Take up shield and armor; arise and come to my aid. **3** Brandish spear and javelin against those who pursue me. Say to me, "I am your salvation." **4** May those who seek my life be disgraced and put to shame; may those who plot my ruin be turned back in dismay. **5** May they be like chaff before the wind, with the angel of the LORD driving them away; **6** may their path be dark and slippery, with the angel of the LORD pursuing them. **7** Since they hid their net for me without cause and without cause dug a pit for me, **8** may ruin overtake them by surprise—may the net they hid entangle them, may they fall into the pit, to their ruin. **9** Then my soul will rejoice in the LORD and delight in his salvation. **10** My whole being will exclaim, "Who is like you, LORD? You rescue the poor from those too strong for them, the poor and needy from those who rob them."

WITHOUT CAUSE. David is wrestling with unfair treatment. People are attacking him "without cause" (verse 7). David's call for God to punish is not personal vindictiveness but a concern for justice to prevail in his kingdom. While psalms like this should make us profoundly sensitive to injustice, Christians have a resource that David did not have. We know that Jesus was also "hated . . . without cause" (John 15:25). Therefore mistreatment is an opportunity to follow in Christ's steps (1 Peter 2:19–24), to tell the truth about wrongdoing but with no ill will toward the wrongdoer (Matthew 5:44; 23:37). When we are being slandered, opposed, or criticized unfairly, we should say to our own soul, "The Lord is my salvation," (verse 3) not the opinions of others.

Prayer: Lord, what others think of me is far too important to my heart. At times when I am being criticized unfairly, I need you to send your Spirit and speak to my soul, saying, "I am your salvation—nothing else and no one else is." Amen.

March 9

READ Psalm 35:11–18. **11** Ruthless witnesses come forward; they question me on things I know nothing about. **12** They repay me evil for good and like one bereaved. **13** Yet when they were ill, I put on sackcloth and humbled myself with fasting. When my prayers returned to me unanswered, **14** I went about mourning as though for my friend or brother. I bowed my head in grief as though weeping for my mother. **15** But when I stumbled, they gathered in glee; assailants gathered against me without my knowledge. They slandered me without ceasing. **16** Like the ungodly they maliciously mocked; they gnashed their teeth at me. **17** How long, Lord, will you look on? Rescue me from their ravages, my precious life from these lions. **18** I will give you thanks in the great assembly; among the throngs I will praise you.

UNANSWERED PRAYER. What did David do when his prayers returned to him unanswered during his persecution (verse 13)? The delay caused him grief and he expressed it. He mourned and wept. There was no pietistic, forced cheerfulness such as "I'm fine, just trusting the Lord!" (verse 14). But his grieving was still being done before God; he didn't stop praying. He cried out "How long, Lord, will you look on?" And remarkably, even in the midst of his grief and the continued intrigues of his opponents (see verses 19–28), he was confident that someday he would give thanks to God (verse 18). This is close to Paul's exhortation: "In every situation, by prayer and petition, with thanksgiving [ahead of time], present your requests to God" (Philippians 4:6).

Prayer: Lord, it feels like you are just looking on passively. But I know that ultimately there is no unanswered prayer, that you hear the desires of my heart and respond to my needs in ways beyond my wisdom. So I wait for you in prayer, Lord. Amen.

March 10

READ Psalm 35:19–28. **19** Do not let those gloat over me who are my enemies without cause; do not let those who hate me without reason maliciously wink the eye. **20** They do not speak peaceably, but devise false accusations against those who live quietly in the land. **21** They sneer at me and say, "Aha! Aha! With our own eyes we have seen it." **22** LORD, you have seen this; be not silent. Do not be far from me, Lord. **23** Awake, and rise to my defense! Contend for me, my God and Lord. **24** Vindicate me in your righteousness, LORD my God; do not let them gloat over me. **25** Do not let them think, "Aha, just what we wanted!" or say, "We have swallowed him up." **26** May all who gloat over my distress be put to shame and confusion; may all who exalt themselves over me be clothed with shame and disgrace. **27** May those who delight in my vindication shout for joy and gladness; may they always say, "The LORD be exalted, who delights in the well-being of his servant." **28** My tongue will speak of your righteousness, your praises all day long.

GLOATING. One of the great spiritual dangers of persecution is that it can make you self-righteous. You feel noble and superior because of your unjust victimization. Here David asks God to prevent his enemies from gloating over him, yet he does not gloat in return. To be happy over bad things that happen to others is called schadenfreude. David commits himself to rejoicing in God's justice and greatness (verse 28) rather than his own moral superiority. While many bemoan the incivility that technology has made easy and anonymous, the cause is really the human heart that wants to fire back a defensive attack. Don't try to pay back but leave it to God, who alone knows what people deserve (verses 23–24.) Let God be your vindicator; one day all will be known.

Prayer: Lord, it is true that people are saying and doing things to me that I don't deserve. But you know that my heart is filled with selfish, foolish, unkind thoughts that *are* blameworthy. So protect me from becoming bitter or proud through this. I commit my reputation and cause to you. Amen.

March 11

READ Psalm 36:1–4. **1** I have a message from God in my heart concerning the sinfulness of the wicked: There is no fear of God before their eyes. **2** In their own eyes they flatter themselves too much to detect or hate their sin. **3** The words of their mouths are wicked and deceitful; they fail to act wisely or do good. **4** Even on their beds they plot evil; they commit themselves to a sinful course and do not reject what is wrong.

AN ANATOMY OF SIN. Fearing God (verse 1) is not mere belief in him. It is to be so filled with joyful awe before the magnificence of God that we tremble at the privilege of knowing, serving, and pleasing him. Sin shrugs at God. Its essence is failing to believe not that he exists but that he matters. This attitude is deadly. Fear of God and self-understanding grow or diminish together. Indifference toward God is a form of self-conceit (verse 2) and self-deception (verse 2). To feel no need for God is to be out of touch with reality—such people have "ceased to be wise" (verse 3). What starts as mere overconfidence can grow into dishonesty and cruelty (verse 4). Sin is spiritual cancer.

Prayer: Lord, I confess the foolishness of my thought life. Even when I am able to avoid overt thoughts of resentment, fear, and lust, my mind still does not fix itself on the most worthy and beautiful things, and on you. Get glory in my eyes, Lord, and incline my heart to yourself. Amen.

March 12

READ Psalm 36:5–12. **5** Your love, LORD, reaches to the heavens, your faithfulness to the skies. **6** Your righteousness is like the highest mountains, your justice like the great deep. You, LORD, preserve both people and animals. **7** How priceless is your unfailing love, O God! People take refuge in the shadow of your wings. **8** They feast on the abundance of your house; you give them drink from your river of delights. **9** For with you is the fountain of life; in your light we see light. **10** Continue your love to those who know you, your righteousness to the upright in heart. **11** May the foot of the proud not come against me, nor the hand of the wicked drive me away. **12** See how the evildoers lie fallen—thrown down, not able to rise!

THE SPACIOUSNESS OF HIS LOVE. In contrast to the claustrophobic, self-absorbed nature of sin, the love of God is as high as the heavens (verse 5), majestic as the mountains (verse 6), and inexhaustible as the ocean (verse 6). God's love is like a land of endless delights. Those who first eat of its bounty and drink from its river (verse 8) want to return to it again and again in prayer and worship. God is loving (verse 5) yet holy (verse 6). The cross reveals how he can be both. As a mother bird shelters her young by letting the rain and wind fall on her, so Jesus took our punishment. Verses 8 and 9 provide a glimpse of Eden restored. Light, joy, clarity, truth—all ours through Jesus.

Prayer: Lord, I so often live in a cramped world of self-pity, nursing hurt feelings, wondering why people don't treat me better. Let me explore the innumerable facets of your love. That's better than listening to the best music, better than standing on a mountaintop, better than gazing at a huge diamond. How priceless is your unfailing love! Amen.

March 13

READ Psalm 37:1-6. **1** Do not fret because of those who are evil or be envious of those who do wrong; **2** for like the grass they will soon wither, like green plants they will soon die away. **3** Trust in the LORD and do good; dwell in the land and enjoy safe pasture. **4** Take delight in the LORD, and he will give you the desires of your heart. **5** Commit your way to the LORD; trust in him and he will do this: **6** He will make your righteous reward shine like the dawn, your vindication like the noonday sun.

DON'T FRET. "Fretting" is a common activity of our age. It is composed of worry, resentment, jealousy, and self-pity. It is dominant online. It chews us up inside while accomplishing nothing. David gives three practical remedies. Look forward (verse 2)—those whose main happiness is found in this world are living on borrowed time. Look upward (verses 3–5)—neither repress nor vent your frustrations but redirect them to God. Leave your burdens in his hand ("commit") and learn to find your heart's deepest desires in who he is and what he has done ("delight"). Finally, get busy with the things that must be done—"do good" (verse 3). Self-pity can lead you to cut corners ethically. Don't add a bad conscience to a heavy heart.

Prayer: Father, I brood that I am getting a worse life than I deserve and others are getting better ones. But your son, Jesus, did not begrudge me a far better life than I deserve in your grace or his blood shed to secure it. Make me generous to others and content in your great love. Amen.

March 14

READ Psalm 37:7–11. **7** Be still before the LORD and wait patiently for him; do not fret when people succeed in their ways, when they carry out their wicked schemes. **8** Refrain from anger and turn from wrath; do not fret—it leads only to evil. **9** For those who are evil will be destroyed, but those who hope in the LORD will inherit the land. **10** A little while, and the wicked will be no more; though you look for them, they will not be found. **11** But the meek will inherit the land and enjoy peace and prosperity.

THE MEEK SHALL INHERIT. Who are the meek (verse 11)? The humble—who don't second-guess God's timing (verse 7). And the dependent—who leave vindication and vengeance to God (verse 9). David says they will possess the land, but Jesus speaks of meekness that inherits the whole earth (Matthew 5:5). Christians confess they have no power at all to save themselves and depend and rely wholly on the sheer grace of God. But how is that even possible? Because Jesus became meek and helpless (Matthew 11:29), like a lamb before his shearers. And why can Christians literally inherit the whole earth? Because he took our punishment Jesus was stripped of everything—they cast lots for his last possession, his garment. His amazing, loving meekness creates meekness in us.

Prayer: Lord, how I want the peace in my heart that comes from spiritual humility. I want the humility that rests in your wise dealings, the humility that makes bitterness impossible. You are "gentle and humble in heart," so teach me this "rest for [the] soul" (Matthew 11:29). Amen.

March 15

READ Psalm 37:12–20. **12** The wicked plot against the righteous and gnash their teeth at them; **13** but the Lord laughs at the wicked, for he knows their day is coming. **14** The wicked draw the sword and bend the bow to bring down the poor and needy, to slay those whose ways are upright. **15** But their swords will pierce their own hearts, and their bows will be broken. **16** Better the little that the righteous have than the wealth of many wicked; **17** for the power of the wicked will be broken, but the LORD upholds the righteous. **18** The blameless spend their days under the LORD's care, and their inheritance will endure forever. **19** In times of disaster they will not wither; in days of famine they will enjoy plenty. **20** But the wicked will perish: Though the LORD's enemies are like the flowers of the field, they will be consumed—they will go up in smoke.

THE PARADOXES OF FAITHFUL LIVING. Believers sometimes seem weak, but they are ultimately strong. We are "persecuted, but not abandoned" (2 Corinthians 4:9; verses 12–15). Those who live for their own power may have temporary success, but sin sets up strains in the fabric of life that will lead to breakdown. "Their swords" in various ways "will pierce their own hearts" (verse 15). Also, "having nothing," we "yet possess everything" (2 Corinthians 6:10; verses 16–20.) Righteousness is no guarantee of prosperity. It is possible to be faithful and hardworking and end with "little" (verse 16). Yet riches can erode quickly and can't help you in the next life, so only God himself—and his unfailing love for you—are investments that never lose their value.[31]

Prayer: Lord, how easy it is to put faith in power and money. If I know the right people and have plenty in the bank, I'm secure—an illusion! Through the cross my great debt has been paid, and through the Resurrection my future wealth is assured. Let me rest in that daily. Amen.

March 16

THE PARADOXES, CONTINUED. The faithful don't see their money as their own but give and lend freely in order to bring about blessing (verse 26), trusting God to provide for them (verse 25). While David had never seen believers' children impoverished, Habakkuk 3:17–19 famously tells us that even when we fall into poverty God is with us and is our true wealth. We may be "struck down, but not destroyed" (2 Corinthians 4:9). We may "stumble"—may sin or fail or suffer calamity—but God won't let us go into free fall (verse 24). He will use these troubles, if we trust him, to turn us into something great and beautiful (2 Corinthians 4:17).

Prayer: Lord, it is difficult for me to trust in your provision for me enough to be radically generous with my money. But if Jesus had been as grudging with his life and blood as I am with my money, then where would I be? Make me a joyful giver. Amen.

March 17

READ Psalm 37:27–34. **27** Turn from evil and do good; then you will dwell in the land forever. **28** For the LORD loves the just and will not forsake his faithful ones. Wrongdoers will be completely destroyed; the offspring of the wicked will perish. **29** The righteous will inherit the land and dwell in it forever. **30** The mouths of the righteous utter wisdom, and his tongue speaks what is just. **31** The law of their God is in their hearts; their feet do not slip. **32** The wicked lie in wait for the righteous, intent on putting them to death; **33** but the LORD will not leave them in the power of the wicked or let them be condemned when brought to trial. **34** Hope in the LORD and keep his way. He will exalt you to inherit the land; when the wicked are destroyed, you will see it.

THE LORD LOVES THE JUST. We are to "do good" (verse 27), and verse 28 shows that this means living a life of justice. The Hebrew word for "just" is *mishpat*. This means to treat people equitably, not having one standard for people of your own race and another for others (Leviticus 24:22). It also means caring for the rights and needs of the poor, immigrants, widows, and orphans (Zechariah 7:10–11). Many Christians think of social justice as an optional interest, but it is an essential characteristic of those the Lord loves and delights in. Jesus told his followers to have the poor and disabled in their homes regularly (Luke 14:12–13). Are we listening to these summonses to live justly?

Prayer: Lord, I praise you that you are a God who cares for the poor, weak, and helpless—otherwise I would still be lost! I confess the self-sufficiency, pride, and indifference that make it hard for me to love the poor. Change me and use me to help others. Amen.

March 18

READ Psalm 37:35–40. **35** I have seen a wicked and ruthless man flourishing like a luxuriant native tree, **36** but he soon passed away and was no more; though I looked for him, he could not be found. **37** Consider the blameless, observe the upright; a future awaits those who seek peace. **38** But all sinners will be destroyed; there will be no future for the wicked. **39** The salvation of the righteous comes from the LORD; he is their stronghold in time of trouble. **40** The LORD helps them and delivers them; he delivers them from the wicked and saves them, because they take refuge in him.

THERE IS A FUTURE. Living for yourself inevitably comes to nothing (verses 35–36), but for us "a future awaits" (verse 37). This doesn't necessarily mean a prosperous life. It does mean a future of increasing joy and love in this world and infinite amounts of both in the next. We will be resurrected (1 Corinthians 15:35–58). We will not go to nothing. We will not be just a floating consciousness. We will not become part of an impersonal cosmic force. Our future is a world of love (1 Corinthians 13:12–13). We will walk, eat, converse, embrace, sing, and dance—all in degrees of joy, satisfaction, and power that we cannot now imagine. We will eat and drink with the Son of Man "forever" (Psalm 23:6).

Prayer: O Lord, the future is beyond my imagining. Yet even my small efforts to do so give me a lightheartedness and hope I can get no other way. *"Till then I would thy love proclaim with every fleeting breath; and may the music of thy name refresh my soul in death."*[32] Amen.

March 19

READ Psalm 38:1–8. **1** LORD, do not rebuke me in your anger or discipline me in your wrath. **2** Your arrows have pierced me, and your hand has come down on me. **3** Because of your wrath there is no health in my body; there is no soundness in my bones because of my sin. **4** My guilt has overwhelmed me like a burden too heavy to bear. **5** My wounds fester and are loathsome because of my sinful folly. **6** I am bowed down and brought very low; all day long I go about mourning. **7** My back is filled with searing pain; there is no health in my body. **8** I am feeble and utterly crushed; I groan in anguish of heart.

COMPOUND SUFFERING. Here there is guilt (verse 4) as well as sickness (verse 5). The illness is linked to the psalmist's sin in some way, either as the physical effects of a tortured conscience or as the result of some foolish behavior or as a messenger sent to humble the psalmist and bring him to his senses about the way he is living. This illness in turn has isolated him from friends and given his opponents an opportunity to move against him (see verses 11–12). So he is suffering from guilt, bodily pain, and injustice. Suffering often comes in such overwhelmingly complex compounds that the only solution is to simply call out to God himself to forgive, protect, and heal.

Prayer: Lord, sometimes there's nothing to do but cry to you. I can feel so overwhelmed by the complexity of my troubles. Some are my fault, some are not—I feel angry and guilty and overwhelmed by it all. I confess my sin and my helplessness. Help me! Amen.

March 20

READ Psalm 38:9–14. **9** All my longings lie open before you, Lord; my sighing is not hidden from you. **10** My heart pounds, my strength fails me; even the light has gone from my eyes. **11** My friends and companions avoid me because of my wounds; my neighbors stay far away. **12** Those who want to kill me set their traps, those who would harm me talk of my ruin; all day long they scheme and lie. **13** I am like the deaf, who cannot hear, like the mute, who cannot speak; **14** I have become like one who does not hear, whose mouth can offer no reply.

ALL MY LONGINGS. The psalms are remarkable for recording with brutal honesty the cries of those who are sick and suffering. The Bible knows nothing of "Pain is an illusion" or "Just don't let it get to you" or "If you really believed with all your heart, you would get your deliverance." These views make human will the solution. But it is not "mind over matter"—it is God over matter. God alone can restore a body or a soul to health. Not a molecule of our bodies or a faculty of our soul does its appointed job without his upholding hand. If he removes his hand, even for a moment, we face the truth we so often ignore: Without his help, we perish.

Prayer: Lord, what a frail creature I am, in body and soul. Without your sustenance of both, I fall apart. So I come to you for both forgiveness and my health. *"Though I fail—I weep. Though I halt in pace—yet I creep, to the throne of grace."*[33] Amen.

March 21

READ Psalm 38:15–22. **15** LORD, I wait for you; you will answer, Lord my God. **16** For I said, "Do not let them gloat or exalt themselves over me when my feet slip." **17** For I am about to fall, and my pain is ever with me. **18** I confess my iniquity; I am troubled by my sin. **19** Many have become my enemies without cause; those who hate me without reason are numerous. **20** Those who repay my good with evil lodge accusations against me, though I seek only to do what is good. **21** LORD, do not forsake me; be not far from me, my God. **22** Come quickly to help me, my Lord my Savior.

RISING OUT OF THE DARKNESS. David does not merely admit his sin but is troubled by it (verse 18). If we only confess but do not also find the sin repellent—for how it grieves and dishonors God and destroys others—the sin will retain its power over us. We will find ourselves doing it again. Also, he seeks not just legal pardon but the restoration of loving fellowship with God (verses 21–22). This is possible because this God is *"my* God"—the God of covenant grace who is committed to him (Exodus 6:6–7). The depths of that commitment were seen fully only in the one who cried, *"My God, my God"* and was forsaken so we could be pardoned and brought in.

Prayer: *"Approach, my soul, the mercy seat, where Jesus answers prayer; there humbly fall before His feet, for none can perish there. Bowed down beneath a load of sin, by Satan sorely pressed, by war without and fears within, I come to Thee for rest."*[34] Amen.

March 22

READ Psalm 39. **1** I said, "I will watch my ways and keep my tongue from sin; I will put a muzzle on my mouth while in the presence of the wicked." **2** So I remained utterly silent, not even saying anything good. But my anguish increased; **3** my heart grew hot within me. While I meditated, the fire burned; then I spoke with my tongue: **4** "Show me, LORD, my life's end and the number of my days; let me know how fleeting is my life. **5** You have made my days a mere handbreadth; the span of my years is as nothing before you. Everyone is but a breath, even those who seem secure. **6** "Surely everyone goes around like a mere phantom; in vain they rush about, heaping up wealth without knowing whose it will finally be. **7** "But now, Lord, what do I look for? My hope is in you. **8** Save me from all my transgressions; do not make me the scorn of fools. **9** I was silent; I would not open my mouth, for you are the one who has done this. **10** Remove your scourge from me; I am overcome by the blow of your hand. **11** When you rebuke and discipline anyone for their sin, you consume their wealth like a moth—surely everyone is but a breath. **12** "Hear my prayer, LORD, listen to my cry for help; be not deaf to my weeping. I dwell with you as a foreigner, a stranger, as all my ancestors were. **13** Look away from me, that I may enjoy life again before I depart and am no more."

DESPERATION. Everything in life is eventually taken away from us after a tragically brief time of enjoyment (verses 4–5). The bleakness of this can lie heavy on the soul. The psalm ends without a note of hope, and that is instructive. It is remarkable that God not only allows his creatures to complain to him of their ills but actually records those wails in his Word. "The very presence of such prayers in Scripture is a witness to His understanding. He knows how men speak when they are desperate."[35] God is confident we will look back at *that* and close our mouths, lost in wonder at the spectacular love that planned even our darkest moments.

Prayer: Father, I can get so confused and angry at your dealings that I might also say, "Look away from me." But your Son lost your presence on the cross, so that now you patiently stay near me even when I don't deserve it. I praise you for being a God who understands. Amen.

March 23

READ Psalm 40:1–5. **1** I waited patiently for the LORD; he turned to me and heard my cry. **2** He lifted me out of the slimy pit, out of the mud and mire; he set my feet on a rock and gave me a firm place to stand. **3** He put a new song in my mouth, a hymn of praise to our God. Many will see and fear the LORD and put their trust in him. **4** Blessed is the one who trusts in the LORD, who does not look to the proud, to those who turn aside to false gods. **5** Many, LORD my God, are the wonders you have done, the things you planned for us. None can compare with you; were I to speak and tell of your deeds, they would be too many to declare.

WAIT, WAIT. Most translations of verse 1 say "I waited patiently," but the Hebrew literally says "I waited-waited." In Hebrew the doubling of a term conveys intensification and magnitude. This means not passivity but great concentration. Servants waiting on a great lord are not twiddling their thumbs but watching every expression and gesture to discern their master's will. Waiting on God, then, is to be busy in service to God and to others, all in full acceptance of his wisdom and timing. That kind of waiting may indeed be long and excruciating, as Psalms 37 through 39 have shown us. But finally it leads to a new song of praise to God (verse 3) and joy (verse 4).

Prayer: Lord, I remember with deep gratitude some of those slimy pits you lifted me from and those firm rocks you put me upon. And that helps me wait for you again now. Amen.

March 24

READ Psalm 40:6–10. **6** Sacrifice and offering you did not desire—but my ears you have opened—burnt offerings and sin offerings you did not require. **7** Then I said, "Here I am, I have come—it is written about me in the scroll. **8** I desire to do your will, my God; your law is within my heart." **9** I proclaim your saving acts in the great assembly; I do not seal my lips, LORD, as you know. **10** I do not hide your righteousness in my heart; I speak of your faithfulness and your saving help. I do not conceal your love and your faithfulness from the great assembly.

FROM DUTY TO PLEASURE. Waiting for God (see yesterday's entry) changed David from the inside out. He no longer obeyed God's laws under compulsion but joyfully from the heart (verse 7–8). "Our pleasure and our duty, though opposite before, since we have seen his beauty, are joined to part no more."[36] David seems to say his eager self-offering ends all sacrifices for sin (verse 6). The New Testament quotes these words to tell of a greater David, who told his Father that he would willingly live the obedient life we should have lived and die the death we should have died in order to bring us to God (Hebrews 10:5–10). Let yourself be moved by what he did for you until your duty becomes a joy.

Prayer: Father, how wonderful it is in these verses to overhear the ancient conversation between you and your Son and to know that from all eternity you have been loving us and planning our salvation at infinite cost to yourself. I can only bow in grateful awe before this love from before the foundation of the world. Amen.

March 25

READ Psalm 40:11–17. 11 Do not withhold your mercy from me, Lord; may your love and faithfulness always protect me. **12** For troubles without number surround me; my sins have overtaken me, and I cannot see. They are more than the hairs of my head, and my heart fails within me. **13** Be pleased to save me, Lord; come quickly, Lord, to help me. **14** May all who want to take my life be put to shame and confusion; may all who desire my ruin be turned back in disgrace. **15** May those who say to me, "Aha! Aha!" be appalled at their own shame. **16** But may all who seek you rejoice and be glad in you; may those who love your saving help always say, "The Lord is great!" **17** But as for me, I am poor and needy; may the Lord think of me. You are my help and my deliverer; you are my God, do not delay.

PRAYING FOR GLORY. The first part of Psalm 40 is a great thanksgiving for God's help, together with powerful testimony about the changes of character that patient waiting brings. Verses 11–17 show, however, that situations that require waiting on God will always return, sometimes with startling suddenness. David is back under pressure, but this time he has a deeper sense of God's unmerited grace (verses 16–17). The final verses also give us an abiding spiritual principle. "To compare what *I am* [verse 17] with what *You are* [verse 17] is a steadying thing; but to pray for God's glory [*The Lord be exalted*, verse 16] is a liberation, the way of victory, and, as John 12:27f. shows, the way of Christ himself."[37]

Prayer: Lord, praying for your glory is indeed the way of liberation. If I pray, "Glorify yourself in my needs," that frees me to receive whatever you send as your wise will. For I know that your glory includes your love. In my life, Lord, be glorified. Amen.

March 26

READ Psalm 41:1–4. **1** Blessed are those who have regard for the weak; the LORD delivers them in times of trouble. **2** The Lord protects and preserves them—they are counted among the blessed in the land—he does not give them over to the desire of their foes. **3** The LORD sustains them on their sickbed and restores them from their bed of illness. **4** I said, "Have mercy on me, LORD; heal me, for I have sinned against you."

BLESSED ARE THE MERCIFUL. To "have regard for the weak" (verse 1) means giving sustained reflection to the poor. This is far more than donating to charity. The call is to think hard about what keeps the poor down and work to help them. Those who do this will be blessed—spiritual health and favor will come to them. When they sin they get mercy as they have shown mercy (verse 4). This also works in reverse. It is because we have received radical spiritual generosity that we can be radically generous with those in need (Matthew 18:28–33; 2 Corinthians 8:7–9). A sign that I have been saved by grace is that I care about the poor. Do I have that sign?

Prayer: Lord, my culture and my heart tell me that it is wholly due to my hard work that I am not poor. If I believe that lie, I will be ungenerous. I praise you that you are a God with a heart for the poor. Give me the same kind of heart. Amen.

March 27

READ Psalm 41:5–8. **5** My enemies say of me in malice, "When will he die and his name perish?" **6** When one of them comes to see me, he speaks falsely, while his heart gathers slander; then he goes out and spreads it around. **7** All my enemies whisper together against me; they imagine the worst for me, saying, **8** "A vile disease has afflicted him; he will never get up from the place where he lies."

SLANDER. These verses bring up the sin of gossip. People come to see David in his sickness (see verses 3–4) only to spread news that puts him in the worst possible light (verse 6). His opponents impute the worst motives to everything he does (verse 7). Gossip is not necessarily spreading untruths. It is revealing information that should be kept confidential (Proverbs 11:13, 20:19). It is giving news about a person intended to lower him or her in the regard of the listener. Gossip can do its work with tones of voice or a roll of the eye. While we may think of gossip as a harmless diversion, the New Testament lists it along with envy, murder, strife, and hating God (Romans 1:28–30).

Prayer: Lord, I pass along a bad report about someone because it makes me look better than they are. Lord, you lost your reputation in order to give me an everlasting name. How can I hurt the good name of anyone else? Forgive me and help me. Amen.

March 28

READ Psalm 41:9–13. **9** Even my close friend, someone I trusted, one who shared my bread, has turned against me. **10** But you may have mercy on me, LORD; raise me up, that I may repay them. **11** I know that you are pleased with me, for my enemy does not triumph over me. **12** Because of my integrity you uphold me and set me in your presence forever. **13** Praise be to the LORD, the God of Israel, from everlasting to everlasting. Amen and Amen.

BETRAYAL. David asks God's help to "repay" evildoers within his own intimate circle ("one who shared my bread," verse 9) not as an act of personal vengeance but because as king he must promote public justice. How should we respond to betrayal by a friend—the cruelest kind? Centuries later Jesus applied this verse to himself (John 13:18) as he was reaching out to Judas, gently giving him every opportunity to repent. Judas was, of course, not the only person disloyal and untrue to Jesus that night. And Christians, though we break bread at the Lord's table with him, regularly let him down. Yet he forgives us. So we should forgive those who betray us.

Prayer: Father, there are persons who wronged me in the past whom, I realize, I have not fully forgiven. I hold their actions against them. I avoid them or I'm unusually hard on them. Let your costly grace to me through Jesus Christ so melt my icy heart that I can forgive fully and freely. Amen.

March 29

READ Psalm 42:1–5. **1** As the deer pants for streams of water, so my soul pants for you, my God. **2** My soul thirsts for God, for the living God. When can I go and meet with God? **3** My tears have been my food day and night, while people say to me all day long, "Where is your God?" **4** These things I remember as I pour out my soul: how I used to go to the house of God under the protection of the Mighty One with shouts of joy and praise among the festive throng. **5** Why, my soul, are you downcast? Why so disturbed within me? Put your hope in God, for I will yet praise him, my Savior and my God.

LOSING GOD. The psalmist has lost not belief in God but the experience of meeting with the *living* God (verse 2). Human beings need the sense of God's presence and love as much as the body pants after water (verse 1). His first response to this dryness is to simply remind himself that it will not last (verse 5). "This too shall pass" is a fact about any condition in this changeful world. While often painful, the truth can be used for comfort too. Though our good things will inevitably be shaken, a believer's difficult times will always end as well. Only when we are safe in heaven, surrounded forever by love unshakable, will all fear of change be gone. Hope in God, for we shall again praise him.

Prayer: Lord, I praise you for being not just a remote, nebulous force but a living, personal God who can be known. I need your presence and love to sometimes soften my hard heart, strengthen my fainting heart, and humble my proud heart. Amen.

March 30

READ Psalm 42:6–11. **6** My soul is downcast within me; therefore I will remember you from the land of the Jordan, the heights of Hermon—from Mount Mizar. **7** Deep calls to deep in the roar of your waterfalls; all your waves and breakers have swept over me. **8** By day the LORD directs his love, at night his song is with me—a prayer to the God of my life. **9** I say to God my Rock, "Why have you forgotten me? Why must I go about mourning, oppressed by the enemy?" **10** My bones suffer mortal agony as my foes taunt me, saying to me all day long, "Where is your God?" **11** Why, my soul, are you downcast? Why so disturbed within me? Put your hope in God, for I will yet praise him, my Savior and my God.

SELF-COMMUNION. As the psalm proceeds we see that the phrase "I will yet praise him" (verses 5 and 11; Psalm 43:5) is not a mere prediction of change but an active exercise. When we are discouraged, we listen to the fearful speculations of our hearts. "What if this happens?" "Maybe it's because of that!" Here instead we see the psalmist not merely listening to his troubled heart but addressing it, taking his *soul* in hand, saying, "Remember this, O soul!" He reminds his heart of the loving things God has done (verse 6–8). He also tells his heart that God is working within the troubles—the waves sweeping over him are *"your"* waves (verse 7). This self-communion is a vital spiritual discipline.

Prayer: Lord, I need to learn how to preach to my own heart, rather than just listening to its foolish or panicky chatter. Help me learn how to effectively say to my unruly inward being, "Put your hope in God!" Amen.

March 31

READ Psalm 43. **1** Vindicate me, my God, and plead my cause against an unfaithful nation. Rescue me from those who are deceitful and wicked. **2** You are God my stronghold. Why have you rejected me? Why must I go about mourning, oppressed by the enemy? **3** Send me your light and your faithful care, let them lead me; let them bring me to your holy mountain, to the place where you dwell. **4** Then I will go to the altar of God, to God, my joy and my delight. I will praise you with the lyre, O God, my God. **5** Why, my soul, are you downcast? Why so disturbed within me? Put your hope in God, for I will yet praise him, my Savior and my God.

FINDING GOD. Psalms 42 and 43 share the same refrain: "Why, my soul, are you downcast? . . . Put your hope in God" (Psalm 42:5,11; Psalm 43:5). Change and hope come as we, in effect, argue with ourselves. But the psalmist also makes God his "stronghold" (verse 2), a safe shelter. When we put our trust in the living God, we know that nothing can come into that stronghold without God's permission, limitation, and purpose. He also rests in God for his vindication, not looking either to human approval or to personal vengeance (verse 1). By doing all this, slowly but surely, the psalmist raises his spirits. The final refrain has a ringing confidence that the earlier ones did not (verses 4–5).

Prayer: Lord, *you* are my vindication and reputation—it doesn't matter what anyone else says. *You* are my stronghold—nothing else can protect me from every danger, even death. *You* are my joy and delight—all others will desert me. If *you* are my God, why should I be downcast? Amen.

April 1

READ Psalm 44:1–8. **1** We have heard it with our ears, O God; our ancestors have told us what you did in their days, in days long ago. **2** With your hand you drove out the nations and planted our ancestors; you crushed the peoples and made our ancestors flourish. **3** It was not by their sword that they won the land, nor did their arm bring them victory; it was your right hand, your arm, and the light of your face, for you loved them. **4** You are my King and my God, who decrees victories for Jacob. **5** Through you we push back our enemies; through your name we trample our foes. **6** I do not trust in my bow, my sword does not bring me victory; **7** but you give us victory over our enemies, you put our adversaries to shame. **8** In God we make our boast all day long, and we will praise your name forever.

IN AGES PAST. The psalmist remembers the times of the "ancestors" (verse 1) as a period of national flourishing. We have a direct link to the mighty deeds of the past, because they were the exploits not of our ancestors but of God himself, and that God is still with us. Christians should never look at church history as if it contained some great race of heroes that has vanished irretrievably. Their God is our God. Nor should we look at earlier times of spiritual ministry in our lives and think that we'll never be capable of that again. You weren't capable of it the first time. It was God. And he is still there.

Prayer: "O God our help in ages past"[38]—you are still with me now. I thank you that you are eternal, unchanging in your person, character, and attributes. Let me remember that with excited anticipation for the things you will be doing today through me. Amen.

April 2

READ Psalm 44:9–16. **9** But now you have rejected and humbled us; you no longer go out with our armies. **10** You made us retreat before the enemy, and our adversaries have plundered us. **11** You gave us up to be devoured like sheep and have scattered us among the nations. **12** You sold your people for a pittance, gaining nothing from their sale. **13** You have made us a reproach to our neighbors, the scorn and derision of those around us. **14** You have made us a byword among the nations; the peoples shake their heads at us. **15** I live in disgrace all day long, and my face is covered with shame **16** at the taunts of those who reproach and revile me, because of the enemy, who is bent on revenge.

LAMENT. When we think of the essential forms of prayer, we think of adoration and thanksgiving, confession, and supplication. Learning to do these three kinds of prayer in the midst of suffering—and about our suffering—is so critical for spiritual growth (and for survival) that it should be considered a spiritual skill on its own. Most of us in suffering stop praying or put up a brief petition for help. Here the psalmist nearly shouts his pain, frustration, and even anger to God, but the significant thing is that he does so before God, processing his grief in sustained prayer. God understands us so well that he permits, even encourages, us to speak to him with uncensored hearts.

Prayer: Lord, I praise you for being a God who invites us to give you long lists of complaints! How patient, loving, and caring you are to all your children. Thank you for the invitation to unburden myself fully, without the need to say everything in the "right way." Amen.

April 3

READ Psalm 44:17–26. **17** All this came upon us, though we had not forgotten you; we had not been false to your covenant. **18** Our hearts had not turned back; our feet had not strayed from your path. **19** But you crushed us and made us a haunt for jackals; you covered us over with deep darkness. **20** If we had forgotten the name of our God or spread out our hands to a foreign god, **21** would not God have discovered it, since he knows the secrets of the heart? **22** Yet for your sake we face death all day long; we are considered as sheep to be slaughtered. **23** Awake, Lord! Why do you sleep? Rouse yourself! Do not reject us forever. **24** Why do you hide your face and forget our misery and oppression? **25** We are brought down to the dust; our bodies cling to the ground. **26** Rise up and help us; rescue us because of your unfailing love.

WHY DOES GOD SLEEP? Everything is going wrong (verses 9–16) though Israel has *not* been unfaithful to its covenant (verses 17–21). God seems to be asleep (verse 23). "Awake, Lord!" is the daring but honest cry. Ultimately, however, we always and only suffer under God's loving care (verse 26). God may seem to be asleep in the storms of our lives the way Jesus was (Mark 4:38, "Teacher, don't you care if we drown?"). However, God is not asleep, but he won't be rushed. He knows what he's doing. He has a plan and it's a plan of love.

Prayer: Lord Jesus, in the boat during the storm your disciples accused you of not caring—but you were never out of control and you saved them. I confess that to me also you seem to not care, to be doing nothing. That is wrong. The cross proves incontrovertibly, eternally, that you do care. I praise you and rest in you for that. Amen.

April 4

READ Psalm 45:1–9. **1** My heart is stirred by a noble theme as I recite my verses for the king; my tongue is the pen of a skillful writer. **2** You are the most excellent of men and your lips have been anointed with grace, since God has blessed you forever. **3** Gird your sword on your side, you mighty one; clothe yourself with splendor and majesty. **4** In your majesty ride forth victoriously in the cause of truth, humility and justice; let your right hand achieve awesome deeds. **5** Let your sharp arrows pierce the hearts of the king's enemies; let the nations fall beneath your feet. **6** Your throne, O God, will last for ever and ever; a scepter of justice will be the scepter of your kingdom. **7** You love righteousness and hate wickedness; therefore God, your God, has set you above your companions by anointing you with the oil of joy. **8** All your robes are fragrant with myrrh and aloes and cassia; from palaces adorned with ivory the music of the strings makes you glad. **9** Daughters of kings are among your honored women; at your right hand is the royal bride in gold of Ophir.

THE LORD'S BEAUTY. This describes a royal wedding (the bride and ceremony will be described in tomorrow's text). The king is humble yet majestic, gracious yet terrible, but the language runs to shocking extremes. In verses 6–7 the king is called *God*. The book of Hebrews (1:8–9) says this is Christ himself, the ultimate King, infinitely high yet humble (verse 4). And in verse 7 we have a glimpse of the ascension, when Jesus, after accomplishing our salvation, is given the throne of the world by the Father, to rule and direct all things until evil and suffering are destroyed (Ephesians 1:20–23; 1 Corinthians 15:25). We should be as smitten with his beauty as a new spouse—for that is what we are (Ephesians 5:25–32).

Prayer: Lord, Isaiah 33:17 says, "Your eyes will see the king in his beauty"—and in this psalm, with the eyes of faith, I can indeed see your Son humble and weak yet powerful and majestic. Only because he was both divine and human could your Son save me, and for that I am grateful forever. Amen.

April 5

READ Psalm 45:10–17. **10** Listen, daughter, and pay careful attention: Forget your people and your father's house. **11** Let the king be enthralled by your beauty; honor him, for he is your lord. **12** The city of Tyre will come with a gift, people of wealth will seek your favor. **13** All glorious is the princess within her chamber; her gown is interwoven with gold. **14** In embroidered garments she is led to the king; her virgin companions follow her—those brought to be with her. **15** Led in with joy and gladness, they enter the palace of the king. **16** Your sons will take the place of your fathers; you will make them princes throughout the land. **17** I will perpetuate your memory through all generations; therefore the nations will praise you for ever and ever.

OUR BEAUTY. The bride is led to the king (verses 10–15). If the king is Jesus (see yesterday's discussion), we are his spouse. He is enthralled with us (verse 11), but Ephesians 5:25–27 teaches that he doesn't love us because we are lovely but in order to make us so, by grace. On the last day we will be united with him, as will all others, in love forever. Christian marriages can display a small bit of the joy that awaits us in heaven. But idolatry is a temptation. We must let our marriages reveal Christ, not replace Christ. And if we are not married but wish to be, we should remember that we already have the only spousal love that will truly fulfill.

Prayer: Lord Jesus, you look on us as a spouse and lover, with passionate love and delight. I praise you that you can love like that, but I confess that I do not live like someone who is loved like that. Make it a truth that controls how I act every day. Amen.

April 6

THE ULTIMATE STRONGHOLD. Until recently no one imagined the possibility of the world itself being destroyed, but today our films are filled with ways it could happen. But if you have this God as your God, you can face even such cataclysms without any fear. It doesn't say here that God will help you if you get into a strong refuge. It says he *is* that refuge. God is a stronghold or city that cannot be bombed or destroyed. Though earthquakes and tidal waves dissolve the solid world and civilizations melt, his rule is unshaken. If God is with you, even the worst thing that happens to you—death—only makes you infinitely happier and greater.

Prayer: Lord, I feel so vulnerable—to disease and injury, to financial loss, to political betrayal, to professional failure. But in this psalm you say that even earthquakes and mountains melting can't take away my inheritance of infinite love, resurrection, new heavens, and new earth. As I praise you for this, my anxiety ebbs. Thank you. Amen.

April 7

READ Psalm 46:6–11. 6 Nations are in uproar, kingdoms fall; he lifts his voice, the earth melts. 7 The LORD Almighty is with us; the God of Jacob is our fortress. 8 Come and see what the LORD has done, the desolations he has brought on the earth. 9 He makes wars cease to the ends of the earth. He breaks the bow and shatters the spear; he burns the shields with fire. 10 "Be still, and know that I am God; I will be exalted among the nations, I will be exalted in the earth." 11 The LORD Almighty is with us; the God of Jacob is our fortress.

THE PROPER RESPONSE. Nothing is truly solid, trustworthy, and lasting but God. Nor can anything thwart him. Even the rage and assaults of others against God and his people and his cause will only be ultimately used by him for redemptive purposes (Acts 4:24–28). No matter how bleak the prospects seem or how overwhelming the opposition, the city of God—the heavenly community and reality (Psalm 48:2; Galatians 4:25–29; Hebrews 12:18–24)—cannot be harmed but can only triumph. Why? Because that reality and community are in God himself (verse 7). There is no more proper response to really seeing God as he is—transcendent beyond all imagination—than to be still and adore.

Prayer: Lord, to "be still" means not to be anxious or fretting or complaining or boasting. So show me who you are—your absolute power and infinite love for me—until I am still. Amen.

April 8

READ Psalm 47:1–3. **1** Clap your hands, all you nations; shout to God with cries of joy. **2** For the LORD Most High is awesome, the great King over all the earth. **3** He subdued nations under us, peoples under our feet.

THE JOY OF SUBMISSION. God is the powerful King of the whole earth and is subduing people to his rule. But because God is the *rightful* King—the one we were created to know, serve, and love—the result of his conquest of their hearts is joy. They clap their hands because of his rule over them (verse 1). God is the fuel that our souls were designed to run on. So the greater the submission to the true King, the greater the pleasure. Rather than thinking of ourselves as an embattled political minority or persecuted underdogs, Christians should be so overflowing with the joy of our salvation that we feel the privilege of singing his praises to those who do not know him.

Prayer: Lord, "sharing my faith" feels like a threatening duty, but it should not be that. If I urge people to believe in you, I am summoning them into joy. I should not do such a thing with a long face. Open my lips, that my mouth can speak your praise with winsomeness. Amen.

April 9

READ Psalm 47:4–9. **4** He chose our inheritance for us, the pride of Jacob, whom he loved. **5** God has ascended amid shouts of joy, the LORD amid the sounding of trumpets. **6** Sing praises to God, sing praises; sing praises to our King, sing praises. **7** For God is the King of all the earth; sing to him a psalm of praise. **8** God reigns over the nations; God is seated on his holy throne. **9** The nobles of the nations assemble as the people of the God of Abraham, for the kings of the earth belong to God; he is greatly exalted.

THE JOY OF GRACE. The song of the nations someday will be about how God saved the world through his grace. He chose and loved Israel ("Jacob," verse 4) not because its people were wiser or better but simply because he loved them (Deuteronomy 7:8). So as we speak to others about God, there is no place for condescension or superiority. Every last one of us has been saved by grace alone, and so shall all his people be. The final verse reveals an astonishing vision. Eventually God's people, the children of Abraham, will include people from every tongue, tribe, people, and nation (verse 9). This was promised to Abraham (Genesis 12:3), but only in Jesus Christ, in the ultimate ascension to the greatest throne (Ephesians 1:20–23), will it be realized (Revelation 7:9).

Prayer: Lord, I often look at some people and think, "That type of person would never believe the Christian faith"—but to think that is to forget that *no* one is a Christian "type." The only reason I believe or anyone believes is because of a miracle of your grace. So let me tell the gospel to all with confidence and hope. Amen.

April 10

READ Psalm 48:1–8. **1** Great is the LORD, and most worthy of praise, in the city of our God, his holy mountain. **2** Beautiful in its loftiness, the joy of the whole earth, like the heights of Zaphon is Mount Zion, the city of the Great King. **3** God is in her citadels; he has shown himself to be her fortress. **4** When the kings joined forces, when they advanced together, **5** they saw her and were astounded; they fled in terror. **6** Trembling seized them there, pain like that of a woman in labor. **7** You destroyed them like ships of Tarshish shattered by an east wind. **8** As we have heard, so have we seen in the city of the LORD Almighty, in the city of our God: God makes her secure forever.

THE BEAUTY OF COMMUNITY. When this psalm was written, the city of God was Jerusalem, containing the hill of Zion with the Temple, the place for the atonement of sin. But after Jesus, who was the final temple and sacrifice for sin, the city of God becomes a community of the faithful both in heaven and on earth (Galatians 4:25–29; Hebrews 12:18–24). The community of God's people is to be "the joy of the whole earth" (verse 2)—an alternate human society based on love and justice rather than on power and exploitation. The earthly Jerusalem never did draw in the nations, but the transformed community of believers in Christ did (Acts 2:41, 4:32–35). Do our churches do that today?

Prayer: Lord, too many of our Christian communities are ingrown and invisible at best or unattractive at worst. Help me become one small but important part of making my church beautiful to all around it. Amen.

April 11

READ Psalm 48:9–14. **9** Within your temple, O God, we meditate on your unfailing love. **10** Like your name, O God, your praise reaches to the ends of the earth; your right hand is filled with righteousness. **11** Mount Zion rejoices, the villages of Judah are glad because of your judgments. **12** Walk about Zion, go around her, count her towers, **13** consider well her ramparts, view her citadels, that you may tell of them to the next generation. **14** For this God is our God for ever and ever; he will be our guide even to the end.

GUIDE TO THE END. Jesus is the true temple (John 2:21), and when we unite with him by faith we receive his Spirit and become a living temple in which God dwells (Ephesians 2:19–22). When Christians "count [Zion's] towers," they thank God for the church and joyfully wonder at what they have become in Christ. When they "tell of them to the next generation," they show inquirers the way of salvation through Jesus. And the Lord is "our guide even to the end" (verse 14). The end of what? There are many endings in life, the greatest one being death. Its mystery and terror are made bearable by the knowledge that Jesus will be with us, into death and out the other side.

Prayer: Lord, I need to be melted by spiritual understanding of the greatness of what we have become in you. We are your flock, your dwelling, your body, your kingdom, your people, your love. Teach me how to love your church and fully participate in its life and mission. Amen.

April 12

READ Psalm 49:1–4. **1** Hear this, all you peoples; listen, all who live in this world, **2** both low and high, rich and poor alike: **3** My mouth will speak words of wisdom; the meditation of my heart will give understanding. **4** I will turn my ear to a proverb; with the harp I will expound my riddle.

WISDOM. All people share a common humanness, whatever their race, social class, or even beliefs (verses 1–2). God created us, so there is a "fabric" or "grain" to the universe. It is foolish to go against the grain of how God made things. That is why to be greedy, unkind, unjust, and dishonest not only violates God's law but also ruins you and all around you. To be wise is not just to comply with rules but to perceive God's will for human life. It means to change not just behavior but also attitudes, and to make wise choices in the many not specifically regulated by God's Word. This psalm calls out especially the foolishness and futility of trusting in wealth.

Prayer: Lord, I face crucial decisions in which both alternatives are morally permitted but are probably not equally wise. How I need wisdom to discern the best path, the best choice! Educate my heart and mind to make me wiser and a better steward of the resources you have given me. Amen.

April 13

READ Psalm 49:5–12. **5** Why should I fear when evil days come, when wicked deceivers surround me— **6** those who trust in their wealth and boast of their great riches? **7** No man can redeem the life of another or give to God a ransom for them— **8** the ransom for a life is costly, no payment is ever enough— **9** so that they should live on forever and not see decay. **10** For all can see that the wise die, that the foolish and the senseless also perish, leaving their wealth to others. **11** Their tombs will remain their houses forever, their dwellings for endless generations, though they had named lands after themselves. **12** People, despite their wealth, do not endure; they are like the beasts that perish.

NO SECURITY. The ordinary way to deal with the fear of the future is to "trust in . . . wealth." (verse 6). But that is to put your confidence in something that will fail. Neither wealth nor any kind of human ingenuity can save you from bereavement, ill health, financial reversals, or relational betrayals—and finally, it cannot hold off your mortality. There is no "ransom" that can buy you out of death (verses 7–12). It is coming, and it will strip you of everything dear to you. It is, then, utterly foolish to live your life as if economic prosperity could keep you truly safe, or as if you will never die. Only God can give you things of value that death cannot touch but only enhance.

Prayer: Lord, I often catch myself imagining how much greater life would be if I had more. I also quietly "boast" in my heart when I see myself able to afford certain goods and inhabit certain places. Save my heart from such shallowness and foolishness. Amen.

April 14

READ Psalm 49:13–20. **13** This is the fate of those who trust in themselves, and of their followers, who approve their sayings. **14** They are like sheep and are destined to die; death will be their shepherd (but the upright will prevail over them in the morning). Their forms will decay in the grave, far from their princely mansions. **15** But God will redeem me from the realm of the dead; he will surely take me to himself. **16** Do not be overawed when others grow rich, when the splendor of their houses increases; **17** for they will take nothing with them when they die, their splendor will not descend with them. **18** Though while they live they count themselves blessed—and men praise you when you prosper—**19** they will join those who have gone before them, who will never again see the light of life. **20** People who have wealth but lack understanding are like the beasts that perish.

THE ULTIMATE RANSOM. In ancient times a king might attack another country but be defeated, captured, and imprisoned. A ransom (verse 7) was owed for his release. Every human being owes God a death. Our sins mean we belong to death (verse 14). But God, instead of demanding a ransom from us, pays it himself (verse 15). The psalmist doesn't know how this can be done, but he is confident. The missing piece is Jesus, who by his death killed death and set us free. Only at the cross do we discover how much it cost God to redeem us "from the realm of the dead." So don't resent, fear, or envy the rich (verse 16). Pity those who have nothing more than their riches.

Prayer: Lord, the wealthiest and most powerful are so only by your leave and at your disposal. Instill in me this understanding of things (verse 20) so I will be neither too puffed up nor too cast down by how much or little money I have. Steady me with the knowledge of where true riches can be found. Amen.

April 15

READ Psalm 50:1–6. **1** The Mighty One, God, the LORD, speaks and summons the earth from the rising of the sun to where it sets. **2** From Zion, perfect in beauty, God shines forth. **3** Our God comes and will not be silent; a fire devours before him, and around him a tempest rages. **4** He summons the heavens above, and the earth, that he may judge his people: **5** "Gather to me this consecrated people, who made a covenant with me by sacrifice." **6** And the heavens proclaim his righteousness, for he is a God of justice.

JUDGMENT BEGINS. The nations are summoned around Zion to hear God speak (verses 1–2). We expect God will be judging the heathens, but instead we are startled to find that he is assembling the nations to witness as he brings testimony against his own people (verses 5–7). God's judgment "begin[s] with God's household" (1 Peter 4:17). While our salvation in Christ assures us that our sins can't bring us into ultimate condemnation (Romans 8:1), it also means that with our greater spiritual resources God holds us *more* responsible for living as he prescribes. To whom much is given much will be required (Luke 12:48). Christians are more loved and pardoned—and yet called to a stricter account at the same time.

Prayer: Lord, I praise you that, like a good father, you love your children far more than others, yet you hold them to far stricter standard. It is only when I grasp *both* of these truths that I change for the better, escaping both self-hate and self-indulgence. Infuse them deep into my heart by your Spirit. Amen.

April 16

READ Psalm 50:7–15. 7 "Listen, my people, and I will speak; I will testify against you, Israel: I am God, your God. 8 I bring no charges against you concerning your sacrifices or concerning your burnt offerings, which are ever before me. 9 I have no need of a bull from your stall or of goats from your pens, 10 for every animal of the forest is mine, and the cattle on a thousand hills. 11 I know every bird in the mountains, and the insects in the fields are mine. 12 If I were hungry I would not tell you, for the world is mine, and all that is in it. 13 Do I eat the flesh of bulls or drink the blood of goats? 14 "Sacrifice thank offerings to God, fulfill your vows to the Most High, 15 and call on me in the day of trouble; I will deliver you, and you will honor me."

SUPERFICIAL RELIGION. God rebukes his people for two things. The first is external religiosity without inward heart change. Verses 8–13 show people who think their worship offerings are somehow doing God a favor. This is moralism, the idea that with our ethical life and religious observance we can put God in our debt, so that he owes us things. On the contrary, grateful joy for our undeserved, free salvation should be motivating all we do (verses 14–15). Examine your heart. Do you feel God owes you a better life? Do you obey him because you feel you have to in order to get what you want, or out of loving wonder for what he has done?

Prayer: Lord, I cannot give you anything without remembering that both the thing I am giving you and even the desire to give it to you are both from you anyway! I can never put you in my debt. Because of what Jesus did, I am not my own—I'm bought with a price (1 Corinthians 6:19–20). Let that insight rid me of all grumbling and self-pity. Amen.

April 17

READ Psalm 50:16–23. 16 But to the wicked person, God says: "What right have you to recite my laws or take my covenant on your lips? 17 You hate my instruction and cast my words behind you. 18 When you see a thief, you join with him; you throw in your lot with adulterers. 19 You use your mouth for evil and harness your tongue to deceit. 20 You sit and testify against your brother and slander your own mother's son. 21 When you did these things and I kept silent, you thought I was exactly like you. But I now arraign you and set my accusations before you. 22 "Consider this, you who forget God, or I will tear you to pieces, with no one to rescue you: 23 Those who sacrifice thank offerings honor me, and to the blameless I will show my salvation."

HYPOCRITICAL RELIGION. The second thing God rebukes is doctrinal profession of belief without life change (verses 16–21). Some worship weekly and profess an orthodox faith, but they engage in theft, adultery, slander, and gossip (verses 18–20) based on too small a concept of God ("you thought I was exactly like you," verse 21). The judgment is terrible—but Jesus took it for us. He was torn to pieces (verse 22)—scourged, speared, nailed, crowned with thorns. Those who trust in him respond with a life of gratitude that honors God and reveals salvation to the world (verse 23). No one who is truly saved by faith and grace can fail to live a changed life of love for God and others (James 2:14–17).

Prayer: Lord, I may not be committing theft or adultery, but my tongue does gossip and shades the truth. I confess that I am simply not changed enough by the great truths of the Gospel that I profess to believe with all my heart. Show me the specific gaps between my faith and my practice, and empower me to close them. Amen.

April 18

READ Psalm 51:1–4. **1** Have mercy on me, O God, according to your unfailing love; according to your great compassion blot out my transgressions. **2** Wash away all my iniquity and cleanse me from my sin. **3** For I know my transgressions, and my sin is always before me. **4** Against you, you only, have I sinned and done what is evil in your sight; so you are right in your verdict and justified when you judge.

SIN AS TREASON. King David had fallen into an adulterous affair and resorted to murder to cover it up (2 Samuel 11). After Nathan the prophet preached one of the most powerful sermons ever recorded (2 Samuel 12), David's confession to God is radical and intense: "Against you, you only, have I sinned" (verse 4). How can he say that when he has killed someone? It is because sin is like treason. If you try to overthrow your own country you may harm or kill individuals in the process, but you will be tried for treason because you have betrayed the entire country that nurtured you. So every sin is cosmic treason—it is overthrowing the rule of the one to whom you owe everything.

Prayer: Lord, when I sin against others—and even against myself—I am ultimately sinning against you because we are all your possessions whom you love. When I sin I don't just break your laws but trample on your heart. Help me to grasp that, because it helps me not just admit my sins but forsake them. Amen.

April 19

READ Psalm 51:5–9. **5** Surely I was sinful at birth, sinful from the time my mother conceived me. **6** Yet you desired faithfulness even in the womb; you taught me wisdom in that secret place. **7** Cleanse me with hyssop, and I will be clean; wash me, and I will be whiter than snow. **8** Let me hear joy and gladness; let the bones you have crushed rejoice. **9** Hide your face from my sins and blot out all my iniquity.

SIN CREATES A RECORD. In verses 1 and 9 David asks that his sins be "blotted out." This means literally to wipe the writing out of a book. Sin creates an objective record—a debt, an offense against justice—that calls for punishment. If someone is found guilty, a judge cannot ignore the record. A criminal's record can be wiped clean only if he or she pays the penalty. How, then, can God blot out David's sin without striking him dead—the just penalty for all he has done? Only in the New Testament do we learn what it cost Jesus to "cancel the charge of our legal indebtedness, which stood against us" (Colossians 2:14).

Prayer. Father, you can hide your face from my sins because you hid your face from Jesus on the cross. Yet I despise his sacrifice when I try to add to his work by beating myself up. Help me to honor you by believing in my forgiveness. Amen.

April 20

READ Psalm 51:10–13. **10** Create in me a pure heart, O God, and renew a steadfast spirit within me. **11** Do not cast me from your presence or take your Holy Spirit from me. **12** Restore to me the joy of your salvation and grant me a willing spirit, to sustain me. **13** Then I will teach transgressors your ways, so that sinners will turn back to you.

THE IMPORTANCE OF JOY. "Restore to me the joy of your salvation" is a prayer we should pray frequently. The Bible commands us to rejoice in God (Philippians 4:4). This is a command not simply to have an emotion but to remind ourselves in such a disciplined way about all we have in Christ that the greatness of it breaks in on our hearts. It is a sin to be less than joyful at what God has done in our lives. Furthermore, we cannot minister to others except out of our own joy. Our words will be hard, harsh, indifferent, or absent unless we are overflowing with the joy of knowing that we are God's precious possessions, bought at great cost.

Prayer: Lord, I don't want my heart to be too cast down by my disappointments and losses—but it is hard. Send your Spirit to speak to my heart of the astonishing goods and glories I have and will have in you. Amen.

April 21

READ Psalm 51:14–19. **14** Deliver me from the guilt of blood-shed, O God, you who are God my Savior, and my tongue will sing of your righteousness. **15** Open my lips, Lord, and my mouth will declare your praise. **16** You do not delight in sacrifice, or I would bring it; you do not take pleasure in burnt offerings. **17** My sacrifice, O God, is a broken spirit; a broken and contrite heart you, God, will not despise. **18** May it please you to prosper Zion, to build up the walls of Jerusalem. **19** Then you will delight in the sacrifices of the righteous, in burnt offerings offered whole; then bulls will be offered on your altar.

THE ELOQUENCE OF BROKENNESS. What is the broken and contrite heart God wants so much (verse 17)? It is a heart that knows how little it deserves yet how much it has received. To know only the first truth is to be self-loathing, to know only the second is to be self-satisfied—and both kinds of hearts will be self-absorbed. David is talking instead about hearts broken by costly, free grace—knowing both how lost and how loved we are. This gets us out of ourselves, freeing us from the need to be constantly looking at ourselves. When our lips are opened, we do not speak of ourselves but of God's praise (verse 15).

Prayer: Lord, create in me true brokenness—not the counterfeit ones of discouragement, bitterness, or despair. Let me know liberation from always needing to defend myself, always standing on my dignity, always smarting because I've been snubbed. Give me the quiet peace of a broken spirit. Amen.

April 22

READ Psalm 52:1–4. **1** Why do you boast of evil, you mighty hero? Why do you boast all day long, you who are a disgrace in the eyes of God? **2** You who practice deceit, your tongue plots destruction; it is like a sharpened razor. **3** You love evil rather than good, falsehood rather than speaking the truth. **4** You love every harmful word, you deceitful tongue!

DISORDERED LOVES. Doeg the Edomite had ingratiated himself with King Saul by informing on David and causing the slaughter of a whole community of priests (1 Samuel 22:6–19). David confronts Doeg with a critique of his character. "Boast" is not necessarily outward bragging but smugness, despising others as unsophisticated, naive fools. Arrogance always leads to cruelty. His tongue has become like a sharpened razor (verse 2) that destroys people. But the source of all the evil is the disordered love of his heart. Repeatedly verses 3–4 say that what he *loves*—what his imagination is filled with, what delights and attracts him—is harming people and accruing power. Look at your daydreams. They tell you what you are living for, who you really are.

Prayer: Lord, let me know my own heart. Help me nip any budding self-satisfaction, all tendencies to despise people. Let me spend my free moments praying to you rather than fantasizing about my success. Cast the boasting out of me with a humbling vision of your costly love. Amen.

April 23

HOW TO LAST. The sure downfall of those who trust in great wealth and who grow strong by destroying others (verse 7) is not a plot invented by Hollywood, nor is it wishful thinking. We know deep down that judgment will eventually come to those who ruin others for their own gain. . . . Why else do those books and movies that depict the victory of the underdog over the oppressor ring so true? Success due to pride and ruthlessness never lasts. But to trust in God's steadfast, gracious love (verse 8) and know him in prayer (verse 9) and be rooted in the community of believers (verse 9) is to be like an olive tree, one of the longest-living trees (verse 8). This is how to last.

Prayer: Lord, the only safety and protection is in you—anyone relying on their own schemes and ingenuity will fail. Give me the courage and the skill to warn my friends who are living as if they didn't need you. Let me speak a word that witnesses to your unfailing love. Amen.

April 24

READ Psalm 53. 1 The fool says in his heart, "There is no God." They are corrupt, and their ways are vile; there is no one who does good. 2 God looks down from heaven on all mankind to see if there are any who understand, any who seek God. 3 Everyone has turned away, all have become corrupt; there is no one who does good, not even one. 4 Do all these evildoers know nothing? They devour my people as though eating bread; they never call on God. 5 But there they are, overwhelmed with dread, where there was nothing to dread. God scattered the bones of those who attacked you; you put them to shame, for God despised them. 6 Oh, that salvation for Israel would come out of Zion! When God restores his people, let Jacob rejoice and Israel be glad!

OVERCOMING DREAD. Psalms 14 and 53 are virtually identical until verses 5 and 6. Psalm 14 is a warning to unbelievers to fear because God really exists. But Psalm 53 is a call to believers. God has defeated their enemies (verse 5), so why are they overwhelmed with dread where there is nothing to dread (verse 5)? There are seasons when we feel almost smothered by fears for our health, our families, our jobs, even for the overall state of the world. *Dread* is less specific than *fear*. It is an attitude that something is sure to go wrong, if it hasn't already. Besides often being untrue, as the psalm says, it is an insult to our loving Savior, who will walk with us even if the worst *does* happen.

Prayer: Lord, worry and fear come because I forget what you've accomplished for me in Jesus Christ. You have defeated sin (so it can't condemn me) and death (so I can be assured of my resurrection). Meanwhile you are working things out for good. Remind me, remind me of all this, so I can rest in you. Amen.

April 25

READ Psalm 54. **1** Save me, O God, by your name; vindicate me by your might. **2** Hear my prayer, O God; listen to the words of my mouth. **3** Arrogant foes are attacking me; ruthless people are trying to kill me—people without regard for God. **4** Surely God is my help; the Lord is the one who sustains me. **5** Let evil recoil on those who slander me; in your faithfulness destroy them. **6** I will sacrifice a freewill offering to you; I will praise your name, LORD, for it is good. **7** You have delivered me from all my troubles, and my eyes have looked in triumph on my foes.

THE RECOIL OF EVIL. The most basic prayer is: "Save me, O God" (verse 1). David leaves his vindication to God (verse 1) and to the natural outworking of evil's self-destructive tendencies (verse 5). The self-defeating nature of evil is depicted nowhere better than in *Perelandra,* the second book of C. S. Lewis's space trilogy. The character possessed by the devil gloats over the death of the Son of God until Ransom, the Christian, asks him, essentially, "And how did that work out for you?" The demon throws back his head and howls, because he remembers that in killing Christ he defeated himself and ended death. Evil is not locked in a battle with good. . . . The good has already triumphed and evil everywhere recoils on itself.[39]

Prayer: Lord, evil destroys itself because you are sovereign and this is your world. Deep in my heart I don't believe that, and so I get tempted to do wrong myself, and I get too discouraged when I see others "getting away with it." I praise you that because of who you are evil cannot prevail! Amen.

April 26

READ Psalm 55:1–8. **1** Listen to my prayer, O God, do not ignore my plea; **2** hear me and answer me. My thoughts trouble me and I am distraught **3** because of what my enemy is saying, because of the threats of the wicked; for they bring down suffering upon me and assail me in their anger. **4** My heart is in anguish within me; the terrors of death have fallen on me. **5** Fear and trembling have beset me; horror has overwhelmed me. **6** I said, "Oh, that I had the wings of a dove! I would fly away and be at rest— **7** I would flee far away and stay in the desert; **8** I would hurry to my place of shelter, far from the tempest and storm."

THE TEMPTATION TO FLEE. David's impulse is to flee the trouble and pain and go elsewhere . . . anywhere (verses 6–8). In his case this would mean abdicating as king and letting someone else assume the stresses of leadership. In other cases it might mean giving in to temptation—by taking the way of least resistance, by lying, by undermining someone else to save yourself. It might entail falling into some addiction that numbs your pain. But there is no shelter apart from God. We *must* continue to trust in him, because all other "shelters" will prove to be places of greater danger. There is no other place to go. He has the words of eternal life (John 6:66–69).

Prayer: Lord, I often want to just check out. Being the friend, the family member, and the Christian I should be seems so hard! But in your presence I realize that while living that way *is* hard, all the alternatives are harder, infinitely so. Be my support and keep me on the path of life. Amen.

April 27

READ Psalm 55:9–19. **9** Lord, confuse the wicked, confound their words, for I see violence and strife in the city. **10** Day and night they prowl about on its walls; malice and abuse are within it. **11** Destructive forces are at work in the city; threats and lies never leave its streets. **12** If an enemy were insulting me, I could endure it; if a foe were raising himself against me, I could hide. **13** But it is you, a man like myself, my companion, my close friend, **14** with whom I once enjoyed sweet fellowship at the house of God, as we walked about among the worshipers. **15** Let death take my enemies by surprise; let them go down alive to the realm of the dead, for evil finds lodging among them. **16** As for me, I call to God, and the LORD saves me. **17** Evening, morning and noon I cry out in distress, and he hears my voice. **18** He rescues me unharmed from the battle waged against me, even though many oppose me. **19** God, who is enthroned from of old, who does not change—he will hear them and humble them—because they have no fear of God.

THE PRAYER-HEARING GOD. David has been betrayed not just by a colleague but by a close friend (verses 12–14). How do we survive similar experiences of extraordinary inward pain and distress? David prays three times a day—morning, noon, and evening (verse 7). Many churches and Christians have adopted this as their daily schedule of prayer. They did it because God is a prayer-hearing God (verses 18–19). The more we ask, the more we receive (James 4:3).

Prayer: Lord, there are many things you are willing to give me. But only if I ask you for them are they spiritually safe to give me. So lead me and strengthen me to come to you more often with my needs. I praise you that you invite us to do so—through Jesus. Amen.

April 28

READ Psalm 55:20–23. **20** My companion attacks his friends; he violates his covenant. **21** His talk is smooth as butter, yet war is in his heart; his words are more soothing than oil, yet they are drawn swords. **22** Cast your cares on the LORD and he will sustain you; he will never let the righteous be shaken. **23** But you, God, will bring down the wicked into the pit of decay; the bloodthirsty and deceitful will not live out half their days. But as for me, I trust in you.

CASTING YOUR CARES ON HIM. You must "cast your cares" on the Lord (verse 22). The result is not that God takes all troubles away but that he sustains you, gives you strength to handle them. If we are in a storm and we pray to him, he may still the storm (Mark 4:39), or he may instead help us, as he did Peter, to walk through the storm without sinking (Matthew 14:27–31). As Peter had to keep his eyes on Jesus (Matthew 14:30), so we should look at our Savior, suffering betrayal and rejection patiently in order to save us. If he did that for us, we can endure betrayals patiently, trusting in him.

Prayer: Lord, so much of my worry stems from a proud belief that I may know better than you what needs to happen. Teach me to cast my burdens on you—leaving them to your power and wisdom. Amen.

April 29

READ Psalm 56:1–7. **1** Be merciful to me, my God, for my enemies are in hot pursuit; all day long they press their attack. **2** My adversaries pursue me all day long; in their pride many are attacking me. **3** When I am afraid, I put my trust in you. **4** In God, whose word I praise—in God I trust and am not afraid. What can mere mortals do to me? **5** All day long they twist my words; all their schemes are for my ruin. **6** They conspire, they lurk, they watch my steps, hoping to take my life. **7** Because of their wickedness do not let them escape; in your anger, God, bring the nations down.

WHAT CAN MORTALS DO TO ME? Fearfulness and faith in God can coexist in us even as trust slowly wins out. Faith is not a vague sense that "God will work it out." It comes from prayerful immersion in the Scripture, the Word of God (verses 3–4). Jesus answers David's question "What can mere mortals do to me?" in Matthew 10:28. We should not fear those who can kill our bodies, because if we are safe in Jesus, who has already taken our sentence of death, then our real, eternal lives are safe. David still prays to be delivered from his attackers, and we can and should cry out to God for deliverance, whether from wicked people or stubborn diseases, but in the end we are safe in Jesus.

Prayer: Lord, I need not merely read but praise your Word—to relish and rejoice in what it tells me about your glory and grace. Help me calm and silence my fearful heart with the promises and claims of the Scripture. Amen.

April 30

READ Psalm 56:8–13. **8** Record my misery; list my tears on your scroll—are they not in your record? **9** Then my enemies will turn back when I call for help. By this I will know that God is for me. **10** In God, whose word I praise, in the LORD, whose word I praise— **11** in God I trust and am not afraid. What can man do to me? **12** I am under vows to you, my God; I will present my thank offerings to you. **13** For you have delivered me from death and my feet from stumbling, that I may walk before God in the light of life.

IF GOD IS FOR ME. David asks, "What can man do?" again (verse 11), but only after saying that he knows God is for him (verse 9). God has such detailed, tender care for us that he keeps a record of every tear (verse 8). How can we be sure of this? Paul asks the same question—"If God is for us, who can be against us?" (Romans 8:31)—and grounds his confidence in the work of Jesus Christ (Romans 8:37–39). Christians overcome their fears by looking not only at the written Word, the Bible, but also at the incarnate Word, Jesus Christ. Through his sovereign and creative power, God is able to give us his saving Word, human and divine, written and writhing on the cross.

Prayer: Lord, you *have* delivered me from death through the cross and guaranteed my resurrection and eternal life. If you truly love me so much that you notice and record every tear of mine, why am I afraid of anything? Sink this truth deep into my heart till I fear no one. Amen.

May 1

1 Have mercy on me, my God, have mercy on me, for in you I take refuge. I will take refuge in the shadow of your wings until the disaster has passed. **2** I cry out to God Most High, to God, who vindicates me. **3** He sends from heaven and saves me, rebuking those who hotly pursue me—God sends forth his love and his faithfulness. **4** I am in the midst of lions; I am forced to dwell among ravenous beasts—men whose teeth are spears and arrows, whose tongues are sharp swords. **5** Be exalted, O God, above the heavens; let your glory be over all the earth. **6** They spread a net for my feet—I was bowed down in distress. They dug a pit in my path—but they have fallen into it themselves.

IN THE LIONS' DEN. David is surrounded by danger, as if standing in the midst of roaring beasts (verse 4). He cries for help (verses 1–2) but suddenly simply praises God, "Be exalted, O God, above the heavens; let your glory be over all the earth" (verse 5). Deeper than disaster, danger, and distress is the desire for God to be glorified. If that can be accomplished by saving us from our circumstances, then praise God! If it is better accomplished by our circumstances remaining unchanged while we continue to show our confidence in God before the watching world, praise God as well. Either way, God fulfills his purpose for you as you delight to honor him.

Prayer: Father, your Son taught us to pray, "Hallowed be thy name" before "Give us this day our daily bread." Help me pray not "You've *got* to do this, God!" but "Be glorified in my life." That is hard at first; then it is freedom itself. Amen.

May 2

READ Psalm 57:7–11. **7** My heart, O God, is steadfast, my heart is steadfast; I will sing and make music. **8** Awake, my soul! Awake, harp and lyre! I will awaken the dawn. **9** I will praise you, Lord, among the nations; I will sing of you among the peoples. **10** For great is your love, reaching to the heavens; your faithfulness reaches to the skies. **11** Be exalted, O God, above the heavens; let your glory be over all the earth.

SONGS IN THE NIGHT. How do we handle times of great danger, when we are surrounded by predatory forces (see verses 1–4)? David continues to sing praise to God's glory, right in the deep darkness, with a fierce, joyful buoyancy (verses 7–8). He sees God's greatness in the skies and heavens (verses 9–11). There's light and high beauty forever beyond the reach of any evil shadows in this world.[40] This is not mere stoic defiance ("I won't let it get me down") but theological hope. The universe is an endless ocean of God's joy and glory. We are caught temporarily in a little drop of sadness here on earth. But eventually it will be removed. Regardless of what happens immediately to believers, eventually it will be all right.

Prayer: Lord, help me gain perspective. Someday your glory will rise as the ultimate dawn to end all nighttimes and darkness. I will be resurrected and will live with you in the unimaginable pleasures of infinite love. Lift up the eyes of my heart to see this horizon. Amen.

May 3

READ Psalm 58:1–5. **1** Do you rulers indeed speak justly? Do you judge people with equity? **2** No, in your heart you devise injustice, and your hands mete out violence on the earth. **3** Even from birth the wicked go astray; from the womb they are wayward, spreading lies. **4** Their venom is like the venom of a snake, like that of a cobra that has stopped its ears, **5** that will not heed the tune of the charmer, however skillful the enchanter may be.

EVIL IN THE CORRIDORS OF POWER. Political corruption is not a new phenomenon. Men and women were commissioned to rule the world and cultivate its riches as stewards, seeing all they have as belonging to God (Genesis 1:26–30). But under sin they rule out of self-interest, exploiting others to increase their assets and power. David rightly denounces them, but his description of the wicked in verse 3 is striking, because in Psalm 51:5 he admits that he too has been "sinful from the time my mother conceived me." Whenever we confront a wrongdoer, no matter how evil, we are looking in a mirror. If you, unlike the people you see, have been "granted repentance that leads to life" (Acts 11:18) or to "a knowledge of the truth (2 Timothy 2:25), you have "only God to thank."[41]

Prayer: Lord, put into authority honest, wise, and generous leaders. And when I see those who are not so, do not let me fall into the error of thinking that I would be impervious to the temptations of power. Establish justice in our land. Amen.

May 4

READ Psalm 58:6–11. **6** Break the teeth in their mouths, O God; LORD, tear out the fangs of those lions! **7** Let them vanish like water that flows away; when they draw the bow, let their arrows fall short. **8** May they be like a slug that melts away as it moves along, like a stillborn child that never sees the sun. **9** Before your pots can feel the heat of the thorns—whether they be green or dry—the wicked will be swept away. **10** The righteous will be glad when they are avenged, when they dip their feet in the blood of the wicked. **11** Then people will say, "Surely the righteous still are rewarded; surely there is a God who judges the earth."

THE CRY FOR JUSTICE. Those leading comfortable lives may be troubled by verses 6–10, but the psalms refuse to "allow us to get used to the scandal of evil in high places."[42] They give voice to the anger of the oppressed. Notice, however, the request is not "Help *me* break the teeth of the wicked"—that is left to God (verse 6). The New Testament uses similarly intense language for what will happen on Judgment Day (Revelation 19:11–13), but in the meantime we do not war against evil with literal swords but with the Gospel (Revelation 12:11). If we have known real evil, we will *want* a divine judge who will take up the sword, so that we can refrain from doing so.

Prayer: Lord, make me an agent of reconciliation, forgiving from the heart those who do wrong yet at the same insisting on truth and responsibility. That is a life shaped by the cross, honoring both mercy and justice at the same time. Amen.

May 5

READ Psalm 59:1–7. **1** Deliver me from my enemies, O God; be my fortress against those who are attacking me. **2** Deliver me from evildoers and save me from those who are after my blood. **3** See how they lie in wait for me! Fierce men conspire against me for no offense or sin of mine, LORD. **4** I have done no wrong, yet they are ready to attack me. Arise to help me; look on my plight! **5** You, LORD God Almighty, you who are the God of Israel, rouse yourself to punish all the nations; show no mercy to wicked traitors. **6** They return at evening, snarling like dogs, and prowl about the city. **7** See what they spew from their mouths—the words from their lips are sharp as swords, and they think, "Who can hear us?"

SPEWING. Today's media make it easier than ever to "spew . . . words . . . sharp as swords" (verse 7). Unlike in writing letters, we dash e-mails and text messages off without weighing them. Unlike in face-to-face confrontation, we blurt things out without fear of seeing the hurt or anger in the other person's face. Because of anonymity we think no one can identify us. Words are thus more weaponized now than in David's day. But every word— even an offhanded careless one (Matthew 12:36)—is an indicator of what is in the heart (Matthew 12:34) and will be judged by God. More often than ever we are saying, "I didn't really mean what I said." But you did. Watch and control words to know and shape your heart (James 3:1–12).

Prayer: Lord, save me from the sins of my tongue and the flaws of character that fuel them. Make my words honest (by taking away my fear), few (by taking away my self-importance), wise (by taking away my thoughtlessness), and kind (by taking away my indifference and irritability). Amen.

May 6

READ Psalm 59:8–13. **8** But you, laugh at them, Lord; you scoff at all those nations. **9** You are my strength, I watch for you; you, God, are my fortress, **10** my God on whom I can rely. God will go before me and will let me gloat over those who slander me. **11** But do not kill them, Lord our shield, or my people will forget. In your might uproot them and bring them down. **12** For the sins of their mouths, for the words of their lips, let them be caught in their pride. For the curses and lies they utter, **13** consume them in your wrath, consume them till they are no more. Then it will be known to the ends of the earth that God rules over Jacob.

THE LAUGHTER OF GOD. We are intimidated by the world but God is not. He laughs at all forces that oppose him (verse 8). Yet God's laughter is not the whole story. While he is not impressed by sinful rebellion, he is not indifferent to it. Sin also causes him grief. Genesis 6:6 says God looked on the evil of the world and "his heart was deeply troubled." He ties his heart so much to us that our sin causes him suffering. Only on the cross do we learn how much. If we see Jesus both weeping over sin (Luke 19:41–44) and denouncing it (Luke 19:45–47), then we can follow God in neither being overawed by wrongdoers nor hardening our hearts toward them.

Prayer: Lord, give me a sense of your undeserved but preserving grace, so that when I look at those who are rejecting you and your ways I will not disdain them, fear them, or simply not care about them. Teach me to speak the truth in love. Amen.

May 7

READ Psalm 59:14–17. **14** They return at evening, snarling like dogs, and prowl about the city. **15** They wander about for food and howl if not satisfied. **16** But I will sing of your strength, in the morning I will sing of your love; for you are my fortress, my refuge in times of trouble. **17** You are my Strength, I sing praise to you; you, God, are my fortress, my God on whom I can rely.

YOU CAN SNARL—I WILL SING. In contrast to the snarling, howling dogs is the singing, praising psalmist. Though still under attack (the dogs are still howling), he praises God in his heart for being his fortress and refuge. "Rock of Ages, cleft for me, let me hide myself in Thee," is a line from Augustus Toplady's famous hymn. Jesus is the place we run to when under any kind of attack, and we can hide in him for safety. The psalmist calls God "my God on whom I can rely" and, literally, "my unconditional love" (Psalm 144:2). Christians know that love must be unconditional, not based on our worthiness, but because Jesus was "cleft," split apart, to make a hiding place for us.

Prayer: Lord, teach me how to regularly sing about your love. That will mean not just thinking about you but rejoicing in you and to you under my breath, in my thoughts, throughout the day. Help me do this, my loving God. Amen.

May 8

READ Psalm 60:1–5. **1** You have rejected us, God, and burst upon us; you have been angry—now restore us! **2** You have shaken the land and torn it open; mend its fractures, for it is quaking. **3** You have shown your people desperate times; you have given us wine that makes us stagger. **4** But for those who fear you, you have raised a banner to be unfurled against the bow. **5** Save us and help us with your right hand, that those you love may be delivered.

HOW TO PRAY A DISASTER. Israel had been attacked.[43] David discerns that the real threat to his people is not military force but the judgment of God (verses 1–3). Therefore the only "banner" of defense is prayer (verse 4–5). To pray is to unfurl the ultimate royal colors. In prayer David says they have been "rejected" (verse 1) yet at the same time are "those you love" (verse 5). God's anger is that of a father who is unconditionally committed to his children but *because of that* is furious at their sin. There is nothing that affects us like the displeasure of one we love and adore. This fatherly anger, full of unfailing love, when understood, is a transforming motivation that makes us willing and able to change.

Prayer: Lord, if you were only a God of holy perfection, I'd be too crushed under a sense of my inadequacy to change. If you were only a general spirit of love, I'd be complacent in my sin. But you are a God of holy love—help me respond with repentance through Jesus. Amen.

May 9

READ Psalm 60:6–12. **6** God has spoken from his sanctuary: "In triumph I will parcel out Shechem and measure off the Valley of Sukkoth. **7** Gilead is mine, and Manasseh is mine; Ephraim is my helmet, Judah is my scepter. **8** Moab is my washbasin, on Edom I toss my sandal; over Philistia I shout in triumph." **9** Who will bring me to the fortified city? Who will lead me to Edom? **10** Is it not you, God, you who have now rejected us and no longer go out with our armies? **11** Give us aid against the enemy, for human help is worthless. **12** With God we will gain the victory, and he will trample down our enemies.

SPIRITUAL WARFARE. Israel used literal weapons to visit God's wrath on evil nations. But Jesus bore the divine wrath against sin on the cross (Romans 3:24–26) and will return to put down all evil (Revelation 19:11–13). Meanwhile Christians fight not flesh-and-blood enemies but spiritual ones (Ephesians 6:1–20).[44] To fight discouragement, doubt, suffering, temptation, uncontrollable emotions, pride, guilt, shame, loneliness, persecution, false doctrine, spiritual dryness, and darkness—Paul says we must "put on" the armor of salvation, of the Gospel, of faith. Like David, we are to remind ourselves in prayer of who we are in Christ—accepted, pardoned, and adopted into the family—given the Spirit, access in prayer, and assurance of resurrection. With this "aid against the enemy" we will gain the victory (verses 11–12).

Prayer: Lord, life is a battle with forces in the world that oppose you, with the residual sin and rebellion of my heart, and with the devil himself. Like David, let me look to your promises and sense your presence with me so I can face these spiritual enemies with confidence. Amen.

May 10

READ Psalm 61. **1** Hear my cry, O God; listen to my prayer. **2** From the ends of the earth I call to you, I call as my heart grows faint; lead me to the rock that is higher than I. **3** For you have been my refuge, a strong tower against the foe. **4** I long to dwell in your tent forever and take refuge in the shelter of your wings. **5** For you, God, have heard my vows; you have given me the heritage of those who fear your name. **6** Increase the days of the king's life, his years for many generations. **7** May he be enthroned in God's presence forever; appoint your love and faithfulness to protect him. **8** Then will I ever sing in praise of your name and fulfill my vows day after day.

PROTECTION. David piles up images: God is his rock, a secure place where he can see things from God's perspective. God is his fortified tower, where he can take refuge from attackers. God dwells in the tabernacle, where he can be met in worship. God is like a mother bird, protecting her chicks under her wings. Jesus claims each of them for himself: He is the temple (John 2:12–21), where we can come face to face with God; he is the mother bird, protecting his loved ones by sheltering them and enduring danger and pain while keeping them unharmed (Luke 13:34–35). He is the rock (1 Corinthians 10:4), struck for us, so in Jesus we are kept safe from every enemy, even death.

Prayer: Lord, I praise you that I am truly, only, and finally *safe* in you. You are sovereignly working all things out for your glory and my good. You have removed my sin in Christ so my ultimate future is bliss. You hear my prayers and care for me. I thank you for being the rock that is higher than me. Amen.

May 11

READ Psalm 62:1–4. **1** Truly my soul finds rest in God; my salvation comes from him. **2** Truly he is my rock and my salvation; he is my fortress, I will never be shaken. **3** How long will you assault me? Would all of you throw me down—this leaning wall, this tottering fence? **4** Surely they intend to topple me from my lofty place; they take delight in lies. With their mouths they bless, but in their hearts they curse.

THE LESSON LEARNED. This is a psalm for those under stress, and the first verse is the key to facing it. Literally it says, "Only toward God my soul is silence." When we are in trouble our soul chatters to us, "We *have* to have this, or we won't make it. This *must* happen, or all is lost." The assumption is that God alone will not be enough— some other circumstance or condition or possession is necessary to be happy and secure. David, however, learned to tell his soul, "I need only one thing to survive and thrive—and I have it. I need only God and his all-powerful fatherly love and care—everything else is expendable." When this realization sinks in, you will "never be shaken."

Prayer: Lord, I praise you for your all-sufficiency—that you are enough for my heart, my life, my joy. Forgive me for not praising and treasuring you and your salvation until I come to the place of rest. Help me do so now. Amen.

May 12

READ Psalm 62:5–8. **5** Yes, my soul, find rest in God; my hope comes from him. **6** Truly he is my rock and my salvation; he is my fortress, I will not be shaken. **7** My salvation and my honor depend on God; he is my mighty rock, my refuge. **8** Trust in him at all times, you people; pour out your hearts to him, for God is our refuge.

THE LESSON REMEMBERED. In verse 5 David counsels himself with the lesson of verse 1. The battle to shape our hearts with the truths our minds know is never over. And here indeed is *the* great truth of the Bible, the Gospel—salvation comes from God alone, not from ourselves or any effort we can produce (Jonah 2:9). "To the one who does not work but trusts [rests in] God who justifies the ungodly, their faith is credited as righteousness" (Romans 4:5). David talks not just to himself but to "you people" (verse 8). We can best help others with their fears and distress when we have been through our own and found God faithful, our rock and our refuge.

Prayer: Lord, the deepest impulse of my heart is to *do* things to secure your blessing rather than rest in what Christ has done for me. This only makes me anxious and in turn insecure and self-righteous. Teach me to *"cast my deadly 'doing' down—down at Jesus feet"* and to *"stand in him, in him alone, gloriously complete."*[45] Amen.

May 13

READ Psalm 62:9–12. **9** Surely the lowborn are but a breath, the highborn are but a lie. If weighed on a balance, they are nothing; together they are only a breath. **10** Do not trust in extortion or put vain hope in stolen goods; though your riches increase, do not set your heart on them. **11** One thing God has spoken, two things I have heard: "Power belongs to you, God, **12** and with you, Lord, is unfailing love"; and, "You reward everyone according to what they have done."

HEALTHY SKEPTICISM. If we trust God alone, we no longer fully trust anything else. We don't trust either "the people" or the elites (verse 9). Neither socialism nor capitalism will bring a better world. We don't trust in any career path—respectable or otherwise—to fulfill us. What is the one thing you can depend on? That God is both strong and loving (verse 11). But how can he be both loving *and* fair, since justice demands punishment? God passed the required sentence of death on our sin and then took that punishment himself on the cross. We can never question his love or wisdom in our life circumstances when we see the lengths to which he has gone in order to demonstrate both his justice and his love.

Prayer: Lord, help me prosper in my work, but don't let career ups and downs have power over me. Provide for my family's financial needs, but don't let wealth have dominion over me. I need not to love these good things less, but to love you far more than them. Give me the freedom that comes only through loving you intensely. Amen.

May 14

SPIRITUAL LONGING. David wrote when he was in a literal desert, driven there by the betrayal of his son Absalom. Despite the pain of physical thirst and lost love, David knows that his deepest longings are for God (verse 1)—they can be met only by God's presence and by experiencing his love, which is *better* than good circumstances and even than life itself (verse 3). This spiritual thirst, unrecognized as such in nonbelievers (John 4:7–21), is in all of us. Beholding God's power and glory and worship should be our first care, not only because it is right but also because only a relationship with God lasts "as long as [we] live" (verse 4)—and beyond—and satisfies our deepest need.

Prayer: Lord Jesus, when you met the woman at the well, you told her that what she was looking for in male affection could be found only in you and the eternal life you give. Let me realize that my longings for professional success, social acceptance, and even family affection are functioning the same way. Give me the love that is better than life! Amen.

May 15

READ Psalm 63:5–8. **5** I will be fully satisfied as with the richest of foods; with singing lips my mouth will praise you. **6** On my bed I remember you; I think of you through the watches of the night. **7** Because you are my help, I sing in the shadow of your wings. **8** I cling to you; your right hand upholds me.

THE WATCHES OF THE NIGHT. Sleepless nights, tossing and turning, filled with anxiety and fear . . . Who has not had that experience? David puts his sleeplessness to a different use—he sings to God, praising him and thinking about his love, his goodness, and above all his protection. The "watches of the night" refer to military changes of the guard, and David is awake through all of them, so he has time for his mind to wander. But instead he *clings* to God, staying close enough to him to feel his presence helping him, as close as a baby chick under its mother's wing. Training our hearts to spend our sleepless nights in praise and fellowship with God will redeem our frustration, turning it into a cherished intimacy with our Savior.

Prayer: Lord, I praise you that you are a God who *satiates.* Teach me how to praise you with such joy and wonder and love that when I am finished I feel full, satisfied with you. And teach me how to cling to you in prayer with such tenacity that when I am finished I feel utterly safe. Amen.

May 16

READ Psalm 63:9–11. **9** Those who want to kill me will be destroyed; they will go down to the depths of the earth. **10** They will be given over to the sword and become food for jackals. **11** But the king will rejoice in God; all who swear by God will glory in him, while the mouths of liars will be silenced.

SPIRITUAL EXPERIENCE. David longs not just for belief but for experience of God. It is possible to "see" the Lord, not with our physical eyes but by faith (verse 2; 1 Corinthians 13:12; 2 Corinthians 3:18, 5:7). This is delighting in God not for what he gives us in life but for who he is in himself (verse 3).[46] The result of David's experience is the reassertion of his identity. "But [I] *the king* will rejoice in God" (verse 11). This joyful, strengthened grounding in who we are in him is always the fruit of spiritual experience (Romans 8:16). Christians too are all kings and priests in Jesus (Revelation 1:6). "If David's faith in his kingly calling was well-founded, still more is the Christian's."[47]

Prayer: Lord, I praise you that you are not just my King but my Father—and that the child of a royal sovereign is also royal! All the language of "ruling" and "reigning" with you staggers me. But help me grasp it enough that I no longer easily feel hurt or snubbed or dependent on the approval of others. Amen.

May 17

READ Psalm 64:1–6. **1** Hear me, my God, as I voice my complaint; protect my life from the threat of the enemy. **2** Hide me from the conspiracy of the wicked, from the plots of evildoers. **3** They sharpen their tongues like swords and aim cruel words like deadly arrows. **4** They shoot from ambush at the innocent; they shoot suddenly, without fear. **5** They encourage each other in evil plans, they talk about hiding their snares; they say, "Who will see it?" **6** They plot injustice and say, "We have devised a perfect plan!" Surely the human mind and heart are cunning.

VOICING COMPLAINT. David voices his "complaint" to God. Complaint departments have staff persons whose job it is to listen to you and who are empowered within the institution to do something for you. God is the ultimate complaint department—he invites us to pour out our frustrations to him so he can act for us (verse 1). But this aspect of God's nature is not just a comfort to victims; it is a severe warning to those who do wrong. Don't think "no one sees" (verse 5), for Hagar, herself a victim of Sarah's malice, calls God "the One who sees" (Genesis 16:13). How would you live, speak, and act differently if you remembered that the Lord God was always observing you?

Prayer: O Lord, help me remember that you hear and see everything. Let it infuse my daily life with comfort and accountability, so that when I see people seeming to get away with terrible things, I'll remember, "God sees," and when I am tempted to lie or cut corners, I'll also remember, "God sees." Amen.

May 18

READ Psalm 64:7–10. **7** But God will shoot them with his arrows; they will suddenly be struck down. **8** He will turn their own tongues against them and bring them to ruin; all who see them will shake their heads in scorn. **9** All people will fear; they will proclaim the works of God and ponder what he has done. **10** The righteous will rejoice in the LORD and take refuge in him; all the upright in heart will glory in him!

THE COMFORT OF JUDGMENT. David's comfort again is the self-defeating nature of evil and the fact that in God's world there are natural consequences to sin. We become trapped in our own lies; our slander recoils on us (verse 7–8). God is a God of reaping and sowing (Galatians 6:7; Luke 6:38). Even in this life the greedy will be at least spiritually poor, while the generous will have a rich life whether they are wealthy or not. In the end, all will be amazed at God's judgment on sin (verses 9–10). David didn't know what we know, that all the ends of the earth will wonder and rejoice at how God judged sin in Jesus Christ, so that at the end of time he can end evil without ending us.

Prayer: Lord, many recoil from a God of judgment. But I could not live in such an evil world if I didn't know that you will judge all things in your wisdom and with your justice. And I would have no hope if I did not know all the judgment I deserved was borne in love by your Son. Amen.

May 19

READ Psalm 65:1–4. **1** Praise awaits you, our God, in Zion; to you our vows will be fulfilled. **2** You who answer prayer, to you all people will come. **3** When we were overwhelmed by sins, you forgave our transgressions. **4** Blessed are those you choose and bring near to live in your courts! We are filled with the good things of your house, of your holy temple.

CHOSEN BY GRACE. God hears and forgives us, though we do not deserve it (verses 1–3). And those who choose him realize that it was originally he who chose them and drew them near (verse 4; John 6:44; 15:16). Only in the New Testament do we see how radical that grace was. God brings us near to live in his courts not simply as guests but as his children and heirs (John 1:12–13). God's highest praise is from those who know they have been brought home to live with him through Jesus, God's true son, who died to make us his brothers (Hebrews 2:10–18). Our salvation is absolutely free to us but infinitely costly to him. That is amazing grace.

Prayer: Lord, because your grace is undeserved I should be humble; because it is costly I should be holy and loving; because it is unconditional I should be at peace. O let your tender, loving grace cleanse me of all these sinful, wrongful frames of heart, and give me joy. Amen.

May 20

READ Psalm 65:5–8. **5** You answer us with awesome and righteous deeds, God our Savior, the hope of all the ends of the earth and of the farthest seas, **6** who formed the mountains by your power, having armed yourself with strength, **7** who stilled the roaring of the seas, the roaring of their waves, and the turmoil of the nations. **8** The whole earth is filled with awe at your wonders; where morning dawns, where evening fades, you call forth songs of joy.

THE ENDS OF THE EARTH. David is again speaking prophetically about a time when "all people will come" (see verse 2) and when all the "turmoil of the nations" (verse 7)—all the war, strife, conflict, oppression—will be ended. God is the Savior and hope of even those who live at the farthest ends of the earth (verse 5). God's salvation began with Abraham's family, who then became the nation of Israel, and now has burst all boundaries of nation, race, language, ethnic origin, or geographical location. We must prepare our hearts for the rich diversity of heaven (Revelation 7:9) by showing love for all, and especially those of God's people on earth who are far from us socially, economically, racially, politically, or any other way.

Prayer: Lord, I am so absorbed in my own troubles I don't see and praise you for what you are doing across the world. Help me to escape the defense mechanism of racial superiority so I can embrace, learn from, and rejoice in my brothers and sisters across the boundaries of race, class, and nationality. Amen.

May 21

READ Psalm 65:9–13. **9** You care for the land and water it; you enrich it abundantly. The streams of God are filled with water to provide the people with grain, for so you have ordained it. **10** You drench its furrows and level its ridges; you soften it with showers and bless its crops. **11** You crown the year with your bounty, and your carts overflow with abundance. **12** The grasslands of the wilderness overflow; the hills are clothed with gladness. **13** The meadows are covered with flocks and the valleys are mantled with grain; they shout for joy and sing.

GOD OF BOUNTY. God himself cares for the world he has made (verse 9). He waters it and fertilizes it—the cycles of growth and fertility are grounded in his own life-giving nature. He is the author of *all* life—from the life of a flower to the new birth that saves eternally (1 Timothy 6:13). Since God's Spirit both preaches to hearts (John 16:8–10) and cultivates the soil (Psalm 104:30), the work of both the preacher and the farmer have divine dignity. God's people should be at the forefront of those who care for creation. In the final verses we get a vision of a great Spring, when through Christ all the world shakes off not just winter cold but sin and death (Psalm 96:11–13).

Prayer: Lord, help me receive the beauty and richness of nature as gifts from you that reflect your own abundance and life. Teach me how to glory in it so I rob neither you of your due nor myself of joy. Amen.

May 22

READ Psalm 66:1–5. **1** Shout for joy to God, all the earth! **2** Sing the glory of his name; make his praise glorious! **3** Say to God, "How awesome are your deeds! So great is your power that your enemies cringe before you. **4** All the earth bows down to you; they sing praise to you, they sing the praises of your name." **5** Come and see what God has done, his awesome deeds for mankind!

MAKE HIS PRAISE GLORIOUS. Everyone is called to praise God (verse 1). The content of this praise is God's name (verse 2)—all the things he is and has done. The character of this praise is to be *glorious* (verse 2). What is glorious praise? "Glory" has connotations of weightiness, dignity, magnificence, and beauty. Glorious worship is exuberant, never halfhearted. It is attractive, not off-putting. It is awesome, never sentimental. It is brilliant, not careless. It points to God, not to the speakers. It fits its great object—it seeks to be as glorious as the one it praises. So worship should be "never trivial, never pretentious."[48] There is nothing more evangelistic, nothing that will win the world more than glorious worship (Psalm 100, 105:1–2).

Prayer: Lord, so much of the public worship of your church is indeed trivial and pretentious. Let my church—and churches across the world—begin to praise you "in Spirit and in truth" (John 4:24). Grant us anointed worship—so beautiful that it attracts even those whose hearts are hardened toward you. Amen.

May 23

READ Psalm 66:6–12. **6** He turned the sea into dry land, they passed through the waters on foot—come, let us rejoice in him. **7** He rules forever by his power, his eyes watch the nations—let not the rebellious rise up against him. **8** Praise our God, all peoples, let the sound of his praise be heard; **9** he has preserved our lives and kept our feet from slipping. **10** For you, God, tested us; you refined us like silver. **11** You brought us into prison and laid burdens on our backs. **12** You let people ride over our heads; we went through fire and water, but you brought us to a place of abundance.

ROUGH HANDLING. Strikingly, the psalmist praises God for letting so many bad things happen to him and the people of God (verse 10–12). God is seen as present in every one of the sufferings that are listed in these verses. He "preserved our lives and kept our feet from slipping" in the midst of affliction (verse 9). He is the one behind the prison, the burdens, the oppression, all summed up as going "through fire and water." But God allows them in order to refine us into something precious, great, and beautiful (verse 10). Just as Joseph seemed to be handling his brothers roughly—but only as a way of breaking the ice over their hearts and saving them (Genesis 42)—so God's seeming rough handling is always a grace.

Prayer: Lord God, let me know deep down that when I suffer, even if it breaks your heart to see me so, you have allowed it, in infinite love and wisdom, because it is profitable for me. Amen.

May 24

READ Psalm 66:13–16. **13** I will come to your temple with burnt offerings and fulfill my vows to you— **14** vows my lips promised and my mouth spoke when I was in trouble. **15** I will sacrifice fat animals to you and an offering of rams; I will offer bulls and goats. **16** Come and hear, all you who fear God; let me tell you what he has done for me.

HIS LOVE IN TIMES PAST. The psalmist has spent the earlier part of this hymn of praise recounting great deeds of God in the past. He is now filled with gratitude and confidence. It is our part to remember these deeds and praise God, so that our hearts remain confident and trusting in all circumstances. As John Newton put it in one of his hymns, "His love in times past forbids me to think he'll leave me at last in troubles to sink."[49] These deeds are not just the things he has done for you personally but preeminently include Jesus's sacrifice of his own life for you. Remembering God's past love is the only way to face present stress with confidence and poise.

Prayer: Lord: *"Since all that I meet shall work for my good, the bitter is sweet, the medicine is food; Though painful at present, wilt cease before long, And then, O! how pleasant, the conqueror's song!"*[50] Amen.

May 25

READ Psalm 66:17–20. **17** I cried out to him with my mouth; his praise was on my tongue. **18** If I had cherished sin in my heart, the Lord would not have listened; **19** but God has surely listened and has heard my prayer. **20** Praise be to God, who has not rejected my prayer or withheld his love from me!

TWO PRINCIPLES FOR PRAYER. Praise must accompany petition. The psalmist "cried out" when he was in trouble (verse 17, cf. verse 14), but at the very same time "his praise was on [his] tongue" (verse 17). Expressions of need should go along with confession of God's greatness (2 Chronicles 20:12) and thanks to him ahead of any answer for whatever his wise response and timing will be. This settles the heart even before you get any answer. The other requirement for prayer is not perfect holiness but a sincere willingness to turn away from sin (verse 18). "Purity of heart is to will one thing."[51] As Joshua learned (Joshua 7:12–13), there's no use asking God for things when you are being disobedient.

Prayer: Lord, show me my "cherished" sins—the ones I confess but into which I keep falling. This is because I want to stop but I don't want to stop. Don't let me dishonor you by being divided in my loyalties. Amen.

May 26

READ Psalm 67. **1** May God be gracious to us and bless us and make his face shine on us— **2** so that your ways may be known on earth, your salvation among all nations. **3** May the peoples praise you, God; may all the peoples praise you. **4** May the nations be glad and sing for joy, for you rule the peoples with equity and guide the nations of the earth. **5** May the peoples praise you, God; may all the peoples praise you. **6** The land yields its harvest; God, our God, blesses us. **7** May God bless us still, so that all the ends of the earth will fear him.

BLESSED TO BLESS. Like Abraham, we are blessed (verse 1) only that we might *be* a blessing to all the peoples of the earth (verse 2; Genesis 12:2–3). If you truly enjoy something, you instinctively want to help others to praise it too. Praising it to others "completes the enjoyment."[52] So true enjoyment of God must lead naturally to mission—to helping others see the beauty you see. God never draws us in except to send us out—to serve and reach others. We want a multiethnic, international church of worshippers and a world of justice (verses 3–4). We must not take credit for our own blessings but point beyond ourselves to God.

Prayer: Lord, "the praise of the praiseworthy is above all rewards."[53] If you—in all your lofty beauty—have delighted in us and blessed us by grace, it should remove all fear and all lethargy so that we can speak to others of your glory and goodness. Make me a witness. Amen.

May 27

READ Psalm 68:1–6. **1** May God arise, may his enemies be scattered; may his foes flee before him. **2** May you blow them away like smoke—as wax melts before the fire, may the wicked perish before God. **3** But may the righteous be glad and rejoice before God; may they be happy and joyful. **4** Sing to God, sing in praise of his name, extol him who rides on the clouds; rejoice before him—his name is the LORD. **5** A father to the fatherless, a defender of widows, is God in his holy dwelling. **6** God sets the lonely in families, he leads out the prisoners with singing; but the rebellious live in a sun-scorched land.

HE SETS THE LONELY IN FAMILIES. In this world "the strong eat the weak," as the saying goes. But God's strength is seen in his care for the weak (verse 5), so we should be famous for sacrificially loving the poor and marginalized. This reflects the Gospel itself, for God does not call people to earn salvation by strength. He came in weakness to die for us, to save only those who admit their spiritual helplessness. God also created people to thrive best in families (Genesis 2:21–25). But for those without spouse, parent, or children there is God's family, the church (Mark 3:31–35), united by the common "life blood" of the Spirit (Galatians 4:4–6), providing fathers and mothers and brothers and sisters and children (1 Timothy 5:1–2) for the lonely (verse 6).

Prayer: Lord, I praise you that you created us in your image—to live well only in deep, loving relationships. Thank you for your great gift of the church, your family. Help me make my church not merely a club or association but a band of brothers and sisters, especially for those who are otherwise alone. Amen.

READ Psalm 68:7–18. **7** When you, God, went out before your people, when you marched through the wilderness, **8** the earth shook, the heavens poured down rain, before God, the One of Sinai, before God, the God of Israel. **9** You gave abundant showers, O God; you refreshed your weary inheritance. **10** Your people settled in it, and from your bounty, God, you provided for the poor. **11** The Lord announces the word, and the women who proclaim it are a mighty throng: **12** "Kings and armies flee in haste; the women at home divide the plunder. **13** Even while you sleep among the sheep pens, the wings of my dove are sheathed with silver, its feathers with shining gold." **14** When the Almighty scattered the kings in the land, it was like snow fallen on Mount Zalmon. **15** Mount Bashan, majestic mountain, Mount Bashan, rugged mountain, **16** why gaze in envy, you rugged mountain, at the mountain where God chooses to reign, where the LORD himself will dwell forever? **17** The chariots of God are tens of thousands and thousands of thousands; the Lord has come from Sinai into his sanctuary. **18** When you ascended on high, you took many captives; you received gifts from people, even from the rebellious—that you, LORD God, might dwell there.

GOD FIGHTS FOR US. This commemorates the exodus and the journey to the promised land (verse 10). God fought for his people (verses 12–16) and ascended his throne (verse 18) when the Ark of the Covenant was placed in the tabernacle on Mount Zion (2 Samuel 6:12,17). Paul saw this as a picture of a greater ascension in which Christ delivers us from sin and death and then shares with us the gifts of the Spirit (Ephesians 4:7–16; Acts 2:33).[54] We activate these gifts by using the Bible as a weapon in our warfare with temptation and doubt (Ephesians 6:10–20). If we do, we will find that God still fights for us.

Prayer: Lord, sometimes I feel so weak—all I can do is ask: "Fight for me." Amen.

May 29

READ Psalm 68:19–23. **19** Praise be to the Lord, to God our Savior, who daily bears our burdens. **20** Our God is a God who saves; from the Sovereign LORD comes escape from death. **21** Surely God will crush the heads of his enemies, the hairy crowns of those who go on in their sins. **22** The Lord says, "I will bring them from Bashan; I will bring them from the depths of the sea, **23** that your feet may wade in the blood of your foes, while the tongues of your dogs have their share."

THE GREAT ESCAPE. Here is a God we long to hear more about: who "daily bears our burdens" and provides a way to escape death (verses 19–20). To bear someone else's burdens is to sympathize, identify with, and become involved in the person's life so they do not have to face it alone. In Christ, God literally identified with us, becoming human, bearing not only the sufferings of mortality but also the judgment we deserve for sin (described chillingly in verses 21–23), a weight that literally crushed him (Isaiah 53:4–5; Luke 22:41–44). Death used to be just an executioner, but for those in Christ it is now a gardener, "an usher to convey our souls beyond the utmost stars and poles."[55]

Prayer: Lord, you have removed the one burden that can crush me—the effort to save myself, to achieve my own significance and security. Thank you for coming to me when I was "heavy laden" and giving me your wonderful rest (Matthew 11:28–30, King James Version). Amen.

May 30

READ Psalm 68:24–31. **24** Your procession, God, has come into view, the procession of my God and King into the sanctuary. **25** In front are the singers, after them the musicians; with them are the young women playing the timbrels. **26** Praise God in the great congregation; praise the LORD in the assembly of Israel. **27** There is the little tribe of Benjamin, leading them, there the great throng of Judah's princes, and there the princes of Zebulun and of Naphtali. **28** Summon your power, God; show us your strength, our God, as you have done before. **29** Because of your temple at Jerusalem kings will bring you gifts. **30** Rebuke the beast among the reeds, the herd of bulls among the calves of the nations. Humbled, may the beast bring bars of silver. Scatter the nations who delight in war. **31** Envoys will come from Egypt; Cush will submit herself to God.

ALL NATIONS PRAYER. Our God will one day be worshipped by people from all nations (verses 27 and 31), not because we vanquished them but because God overcame their rebellious hearts. This international assembly never happened at the physical temple in Jerusalem (verse 24). Only in Jesus—the final temple uniting a holy God with sinful humanity (John 2:18–22) through his final sacrifice—have people from all nations been drawn together. Jesus says that prayer in his house should unite all nations (Mark 11:17), and indeed, as depicted in this psalm, nothing unites people across racial and cultural barriers like prayer and praise. Even language differences can be overcome in such assemblies. God's worship is the key to healing the divisions of the human race.

Prayer: Lord, may your church never become beholden to any particular human culture, but let it grow more and more international, multiracial, and culturally, richly diverse. And may we strengthen the unity we have in you and display it to the world through glorious worship and prayer together. Amen.

May 31

READ Psalm 68:32–35. **32** Sing to God, you kingdoms of the earth, sing praise to the Lord, **33** to him who rides across the highest heavens, the ancient heavens, who thunders with mighty voice. **34** Proclaim the power of God, whose majesty is over Israel, whose power is in the heavens. **35** You, God, are awesome in your sanctuary; the God of Israel gives power and strength to his people. Praise be to God!

GOD OF AWE AND INTIMACY. This final chorus of praise is characterized by almost uncontainable excitement, one of the marks of true worship. It also exhibits the two poles between which biblical worship incessantly moves—awe and intimacy. "While it reasserts the cosmic power of God (verses 33–34), it names him still *the God of Israel* (verse 35), no diffused and faceless deity. The psalm . . . bears witness to its grasp of this reality, this union of immense power and intense care, in the God *whose majesty is over Israel* [and] *his power is in the skies*."[56] If our prayer life discerns God only as lofty, it will be cold and fearful—if it discerns God only as a spirit of love, it will be sentimental.

Prayer: Lord, you are immeasurably high, intimidatingly great, and beyond my comprehension. Yet you became a human baby and offer me your friendship through Jesus Christ. I can only wonder at your glory and grace! Let my life be marked by *both* holy awe before you and glad intimacy with you. Amen.

June 1

READ Psalm 69:1–6. **1** Save me, O God, for the waters have come up to my neck. **2** I sink in the miry depths, where there is no foothold. I have come into the deep waters; the floods engulf me. **3** I am worn out calling for help; my throat is parched. My eyes fail, looking for my God. **4** Those who hate me without reason outnumber the hairs of my head; many are my enemies without cause, those who seek to destroy me. I am forced to restore what I did not steal. **5** You, God, know my folly; my guilt is not hidden from you. **6** Lord, the LORD Almighty, may those who hope in you not be disgraced because of me; God of Israel, may those who seek you not be put to shame because of me.

HATED WITHOUT REASON. Here is a man deeply wounded by slander (verses 1–3). The false accusation (verse 4) leads to self-accusation (verse 5), because he knows his genuine sins. But rather than thinking only of his own reputation, he is concerned that other believers might become disgraced because of him (verse 6). Ironically, a more self-absorbed and hard man would not have cared as much. The more holy we are, the more our heart is bound up with others and with God and so the more we feel the sadness of the world. Jesus, the perfect man, was "a man of sorrows." Godliness leads us to be both far happier and far sadder at the same time, though the final note is always joy (Psalm 30:5).

Prayer: Lord, when people fall into trouble, I see myself afraid to get involved lest I be swallowed by their grief. But when you loved me you got eternally involved, and it cost you infinite grief. Strengthen me with your grace so that I can be available and open to the needs of others around me. Amen.

June 2

READ Psalm 69:7–12. **7** For I endure scorn for your sake, and shame covers my face. **8** I am a foreigner to my own family, a stranger to my own mother's children; **9** for zeal for your house consumes me, and the insults of those who insult you fall on me. **10** When I weep and fast, I must endure scorn; **11** when I put on sackcloth, people make sport of me. **12** Those who sit at the gate mock me, and I am the song of the drunkards.

MISUNDERSTOOD. David is being scorned for his zealous devotion to God (verse 9). When he prays and repents, he is laughed at (verses 10–11). His world is not so different from ours. Even when Christianity was taken for granted by Western society, the most devoted believers were silently laughed at. Today they are also despised. The world does not understand the Gospel of grace, in which holy living is the result of humble, grateful joy, not a way to earn heaven. The world therefore sees all righteous living as *self*-righteousness and bigotry. We should not be surprised at this (2 Timothy 3:12), but we should also undermine this false narrative by living lives of humility, forgiveness, and sacrificial service to others.

Prayer: Lord, you have said that anyone who lives a godly life will be persecuted. Don't let me be so cowardly that I never take any heat for my faith. But don't let me actually fall into the self-righteousness and hypocrisy that merits disdain. Amen.

June 3

READ Psalm 69:13–18. **13** But I pray to you, LORD, in the time of your favor; in your great love, O God, answer me with your sure salvation. **14** Rescue me from the mire, do not let me sink; deliver me from those who hate me, from the deep waters. **15** Do not let the floodwaters engulf me or the depths swallow me up or the pit close its mouth over me. **16** Answer me, LORD, out of the goodness of your love; in your great mercy turn to me. **17** Do not hide your face from your servant; answer me quickly, for I am in trouble. **18** Come near and rescue me; deliver me because of my foes.

GOD'S TIMING. David continues to pray, begging God to hear him not because of his own goodness but because of God's goodness and mercy (verse 16). He asks God to deliver him quickly (verse 17) and uses highly emotional language ("Do not let the . . . pit close its mouth over me. . . . Rescue me."). However, he recognizes that God will answer "in the time of [his] favor" (verse 13). Whenever we pray, it is appropriate for us to be passionate and desperate but also willing to wait for God's timing. Nothing makes us dependent on God's sovereign love and wisdom like having to persevere in prayer and wait for the time of his favor. "Unbelief talks of delays; faith knows that properly there can be no such thing."[57]

Prayer: Lord, you let Abraham, Joseph, and David wait decades before you answered their prayers, and your delays were always perfect in their wisdom. Help me as—I must admit—I struggle mightily to trust and rest in your judgment and your timing. Amen.

READ Psalm 69:19–21. **19** You know how I am scorned, disgraced and shamed; all my enemies are before you. **20** Scorn has broken my heart and has left me helpless; I looked for sympathy, but there was none, for comforters, but I found none. **21** They put gall in my food and gave me vinegar for my thirst.

UNANSWERED PRAYER. David is suffering without relief despite his prayers. Suddenly there is a startling reminder of Jesus—how on the cross *he* was scorned, disgraced, and shamed, helpless, friendless, and offered vinegar to drink (verse 21; John 19:28–29). Jesus knew—and knows still—the pain of unanswered prayer when he asked if another way could be found to save us besides the agony of the cross (Luke 22:42). God answered that prayer by saying, in effect, "There *is* no other way to save them. . . . If they are to be saved, I must not save *you*." This not only answers the question: Is there any other way to be saved besides Jesus? (No.) It is also the ultimate comfort when we sense no answer to our prayers.

Prayer: Lord, if you patiently bore the pain of unanswered prayer for my sake, then I can be patient with what seems to be unanswered prayer for your sake. The cross proves that you love me and so I can trust that you are listening to me and handling my request the way I would want if I had your wisdom. Amen.

June 5

READ Psalm 69:22–28. **22** May the table set before them become a snare; may it become retribution and a trap. **23** May their eyes be darkened so they cannot see, and their backs be bent forever. **24** Pour out your wrath on them; let your fierce anger overtake them. **25** May their place be deserted; let there be no one to dwell in their tents. **26** For they persecute those you wound and talk about the pain of those you hurt. **27** Charge them with crime upon crime; do not let them share in your salvation. **28** May they be blotted out of the book of life and not be listed with the righteous.

CHARGE THEM WITH CRIME. The psalmist prays that his betrayers be damned (verses 22–28). How do we read this? First, this "startles us into feeling something of the desperation that produced" it—keeping us from being complacent about injustice in the world.[58] But the foreshadowing of Jesus's suffering (verses 4, 7, and 21) reminds us we stand in a different place from the psalmists—on the other side of the cross. Stephen looked to Jesus for vindication, not retribution, and prayed for his enemies as they killed him (Acts 7:54–60), as did Jesus himself (Luke 23:34). The psalmist is right to want judgment on evil, but Jesus takes it himself. This forever changes our view of our own deserts and the way we seek justice.

Prayer: Lord, again I am reminded that I must neither abandon seeking justice nor do it with an ounce of vengefulness or ill will. Help me to forgive anyone who wrongs me or those I care about, remembering my own undeserved pardon in Jesus. Yet let me still have the courage and passion necessary to right wrongs where I can. Amen.

June 6

READ Psalm 69:29–33. **29** But as for me, afflicted and in pain—may your salvation, God, protect me. **30** I will praise God's name in song and glorify him with thanksgiving. **31** This will please the LORD more than an ox, more than a bull with its horns and hooves. **32** The poor will see and be glad—you who seek God, may your hearts live! **33** The LORD hears the needy and does not despise his captive people.

DON'T WASTE YOUR SORROWS. What do we do when we are afflicted and in pain? Usually we give in to self-pity, bitterness, fear, or envy. It is because "everything difficult indicates something more than our theory of life yet embraces."[59] David, however, does not fall into these things because he has an understanding of life that encompasses suffering—he uses it to glorify God (verses 29 and 30). Praise to God is an antidote to the self-absorption that can overtake us when we suffer. This not only honors God but also encourages others (verse 32). When suffering, don't get sucked down into yourself—turn outward in praise to God and minister to those in need.

Prayer: Lord, help me to see trouble and suffering as things not merely to be endured but to be invested. Serving you and serving others when I don't want to at all is the greatest act of love possible. Help me to see and thank you for the privilege of suffering patiently. Amen.

June 7

READ Psalm 69:34–36. **34** Let heaven and earth praise him, the seas and all that move in them, **35** for God will save Zion and rebuild the cities of Judah. Then people will settle there and possess it; **36** the children of his servants will inherit it, and those who love his name will dwell there.

USING THE FUTURE ON THE PRESENT. There's no indication that David's pain or circumstances have changed, so this final burst of praise is astonishing. David looks forward to a time when there will be no sickness, evil, or oppression, when all things will be put right. And Paul says that in some inexplicable but wonderful way our sufferings now are going to make that eventual glory even more brilliant and wonderful (2 Corinthians 4:16–18). If we believe in Christ this is a guaranteed inheritance that can't be eaten by moths or stolen by time (Matthew 6:19–25). When we receive healings and deliverances now, they are small windows into the great things to come. Learn to look through those windows, cling to his promised salvation, and praise him.

Prayer: Lord, I *must* learn to praise you—it is the only thing that will honor you and will fulfill me. *"Therefore with my utmost art I will sing thee; And the cream of all my heart, I will bring thee."*[60] Amen.

June 8

READ Psalm 70. **1** Hasten, O God, to save me; come quickly, LORD, to help me. **2** May those who want to take my life be put to shame and confusion; may all who desire my ruin be turned back in disgrace. **3** May those who say to me, "Aha! Aha!" turn back because of their shame. **4** But may all who seek you rejoice and be glad in you; may those who love your saving help always say, "The Lord is great!" **5** But as for me, I am poor and needy; come quickly to me, O God. You are my help and my deliverer; LORD, do not delay.

THE SECRET. There is a place in prayer for a godly urgency. Jesus himself approves of "audacity" (Luke 11:8), an almost shameless relentlessness in petitioning God. Yet in the midst of even this kind of prayer, David uses his need to stimulate praise (verse 4). Circumstances can drive us to seek God, yet even before they change (verse 5) we can say, "The Lord is great!" when we find that God himself and his salvation (verse 4) are enough. As Elisabeth Elliot said, "The secret is Christ in me, not me in a different set of circumstances."[61]

Prayer: Lord, how poorly I pray! Either I pray vaguely and halfheartedly or I pray heatedly, accusingly telling you exactly what you *have* to do. Teach me to pray with discipline and passion and yet also contentment with your love and will. Then through my prayers you will do much good in the world and in my heart. Amen.

June 9

READ Psalm 71:1–6. **1** In you, LORD, I have taken refuge; let me never be put to shame. **2** In your righteousness, rescue me and deliver me; turn your ear to me and save me. **3** Be my rock of refuge, to which I can always go; give the command to save me, for you are my rock and my fortress. **4** Deliver me, my God, from the hand of the wicked, from the grasp of those who are evil and cruel. **5** For you have been my hope, Sovereign LORD, my confidence since my youth. **6** From birth I have relied on you; you brought me forth from my mother's womb. I will ever praise you.

DELIVER ME IN YOUR RIGHTEOUSNESS. The psalmist asks for help because God is righteous (verse 2). But shouldn't that lead him to punish rather than aid us? "If you, Lord, kept a record of sins [and he does], Lord, who could stand?" (Psalm 130:3). How can God love us and still be true to his own righteousness? The Bible is one long, great answer to that question. It happens only through Jesus. Who else completely relied on God from birth and always praised him (verse 6)? He earned the blessing of salvation we don't deserve and took the curse for sin that we do deserve (Galatians 3:10–14). If we are in Christ, the confidence David had (verse 5) becomes ours by grace.

Prayer: O Lord—you are more ready to hear than I am to pray, and you are inclined to give me more than I desire or deserve. Because I have taken refuge in Jesus's saving work on my behalf, give me the protection and joy for which it would be presumptuous otherwise to ask.[62] *Amen.*

June 10

READ Psalm 71:7–18. **7** I have become like a sign to many; you are my strong refuge. **8** My mouth is filled with your praise, declaring your splendor all day long. **9** Do not cast me away when I am old; do not forsake me when my strength is gone. **10** For my enemies speak against me; those who wait to kill me conspire together. **11** They say, "God has forsaken him; pursue him and seize him, for no one will rescue him." **12** Do not be far from me, my God; come quickly, God, to help me. **13** May my accusers perish in shame; may those who want to harm me be covered with scorn and disgrace. **14** As for me, I will always have hope; I will praise you more and more. **15** My mouth will tell of your righteous deeds, of your saving acts all day long—though I know not how to relate them all. **16** I will come and proclaim your mighty acts, Sovereign LORD; I will proclaim your righteous deeds, yours alone. **17** Since my youth, God, you have taught me, and to this day I declare your marvelous deeds. **18** Even when I am old and gray, do not forsake me, my God, till I declare your power to the next generation, your might to all who are to come.

WHEN I AM OLD. In old age strength ebbs (verse 9) and we cannot accomplish what we once did (verses 10–11). But our value is based on our status not in society but in God's eyes (verse 7). When the nineteenth-century Anglican preacher Charles Simeon retired after fifty-four years of ministry, a friend discovered he still got up at 4:00 A.M. each day to pray and study Scripture. When it was suggested he take it easier, he retorted, "Shall I not now run with all my might when the winning post is in sight?"[63]

Prayer: Lord, help me get ready for old age now by showing me by your Spirit that my value is not based on income, productivity, or popularity. It is based on being a member of the people and family of God. Amen.

June 11

READ Psalm 71:19–24. **19** Your righteousness, God, reaches to the heavens, you who have done great things. Who is like you, God? **20** Though you have made me see troubles, many and bitter, you will restore my life again; from the depths of the earth you will again bring me up. **21** You will increase my honor and comfort me once more. **22** I will praise you with the harp for your faithfulness, my God; I will sing praise to you with the lyre, Holy One of Israel. **23** My lips will shout for joy when I sing praise to you—I, whom you have delivered. **24** My tongue will tell of your righteous acts all day long, for those who wanted to harm me have been put to shame and confusion.

YOU WILL RESTORE MY LIFE. In the middle of this psalm is a phrase that goes by quickly but that should make us stop and think: "Though you have made me see troubles, many and bitter, you will restore my life again" (verse 20). The psalmist trusts God's sovereign wisdom and love, even when he has sent bitter trouble into his life. He knows that in the end everything that happens is for the ultimate purpose of restoring our life— by deepening the love, wisdom, and joy of our spiritual life and by eventually resurrecting our bodies in the new world, wiped clean of all death and darkness (Romans 8:18–25). Indeed, then, "everything is needful that he sends; nothing can be needful that he withholds."[64]

Prayer: Lord, do not let advancing age increase either pride or worry in me. Instead let me grow in humility as I see the increasing number of sins from which you have forgiven me and from which you have protected me. And let me grow in patience as I see how patient you have been with me. Amen.

June 12

READ Psalm 72:1–7. **1** Endow the king with your justice, O God, the royal son with your righteousness. **2** May he judge your people in righteousness, your afflicted ones with justice. **3** May the mountains bring prosperity to the people, the hills the fruit of righteousness. **4** May he defend the afflicted among the people and save the children of the needy; he will crush the oppressor. **5** May he endure as long as the sun, as long as the moon, through all generations. **6** May he be like rain falling on a mown field, like showers watering the earth. **7** In his days may the righteous flourish and prosperity abound till the moon is no more.

GOOD GOVERNMENT. Only if you have experienced life in a country in which the state is corrupt and the rule of law has failed can you appreciate the blessing of good government. The great king depicted here brings social justice to the poor and marginalized (verses 2–4). The economy thrives because of good stewardship of assets and the deep trust among people that is necessary for commerce (verses 3 and 6–7). God is a God who is deeply concerned about these things. But the heading says this is a psalm "of Solomon," and even he, David's son, became an oppressor of his people (1 Kings 12:4). So the psalm provokes us to long for a better king than the best government has ever provided.

Prayer: Grant, O Lord, that the course of this world may be so peaceably ordered by your governance, that your people may joyfully serve you in all godly quietness.[65] Amen.

June 13

READ Psalm 72:8–14. 8 May he rule from sea to sea and from the River to the ends of the earth. 9 May the desert tribes bow before him and his enemies lick the dust. 10 May the kings of Tarshish and of distant shores bring tribute to him. May the kings of Sheba and Seba present him gifts. 11 May all kings bow down to him and all nations serve him. 12 For he will deliver the needy who cry out, the afflicted who have no one to help. 13 He will take pity on the weak and the needy and save the needy from death. 14 He will rescue them from oppression and violence, for precious is their blood in his sight.

HEALING THE NATIONS. The races and nations—always at war with one another—now offer themselves in service (verses 10–11), not because they have been conquered but rather because they have been attracted like a magnet by the perfect justice and compassion of this king (verses 12–14). No earthly king has ever been like this. This healing of racial strife and the elimination of poverty and injustice are the marks of God's kingdom, but governments, even the best ones, don't come close. Yet when Jesus was born, gifts were offered from afar (Matthew 2:1–12), and when the church was established, the races began to be unified (Ephesians 2:11–22) and the needy helped (Acts 2:44–45, 4:32–36). The kingdom of God had entered history.

Prayer: Lord, empower your church to win the world by not just proclaiming your Word but also embodying it. Make our congregations places where we see the races and classes reconciled in ways that they are in no other place on the face of the earth. Amen.

June 14

READ Psalm 72:15–20. **15** Long may he live! May gold from Sheba be given him. May people ever pray for him and bless him all day long. **16** May grain abound throughout the land; on the tops of the hills may it sway. May the crops flourish like Lebanon and thrive like the grass of the field. **17** May his name endure forever; may it continue as long as the sun. Then all nations will be blessed through him, and they will call him blessed. **18** Praise be to the LORD God, the God of Israel, who alone does marvelous deeds. **19** Praise be to his glorious name forever; may the whole earth be filled with his glory. Amen and Amen. **20** This concludes the prayers of David son of Jesse.

THE TRUE KING. This king's reign is endless (verse 5) and boundless (verse 8), but was that just ancient hyperbole? No. Here the claims could not possibly be said of any earthly king. The image of full harvests on the tops of hills and mountains, where soil cannot support such growth (verse 16), indicates a supernaturally renewed world. This king can only be Jesus. Putting ourselves under his reign brings supernatural life and growth now (Galatians 5:22–26). We were created to need to obey him as grass needs rain (verse 6). And Christ will eventually heal and unite everything (Colossians 1:15–20; Romans 8:18–21). All the old legends of a great king returning to put all things right find their fulfillment in him.

Prayer: Lord, I live in a culture that demands I cede authority over myself to no one. But it would violate your glory and my nature to *not* give you the Lordship over my life. Henceforth I will willingly obey whatever you say and accept whatever you send, whether I understand it or not. Amen.

June 15

READ Psalm 73:1–3. **1** Surely God is good to Israel, to those who are pure in heart. **2** But as for me, my feet had almost slipped; I had nearly lost my foothold. **3** For I envied the arrogant when I saw the prosperity of the wicked.

THE EVIL OF ENVY. The psalmist confesses that he is in the grip of envy (verse 3). To envy is to want someone else's life. It's to feel not just that they don't deserve their good life but that you *do* and God hasn't been fair. This spiritual self-pity—which forgets your sin and what you truly deserve from God—drains all the joy out of your life, making it impossible to enjoy what you have. The power of envy is such that it made even the Garden of Eden feel like it was not enough. No wonder the psalmist almost "slipped" and turned from God (verse 2). Don't let yourself slip into envy, or you will destroy your own joy.

Prayer: Lord, the goods of this world are spread so unevenly! Yet I confess that if *I* had more prosperity I would not be as upset about the injustices. My envy is filled with self-righteousness, and it robs me of contentment. Forgive me and change me. Amen.

June 16

READ Psalm 73:4–9. **4** They have no struggles; their bodies are healthy and strong. **5** They are free from common human burdens; they are not plagued by human ills. **6** Therefore pride is their necklace; they clothe themselves with violence. **7** From their callous hearts comes iniquity; their evil imaginations have no limits. **8** They scoff, and speak with malice; with arrogance they threaten oppression. **9** Their mouths lay claim to heaven, and their tongues take possession of the earth.

SELF-SUFFICIENCY. The psalmist's description of the elites of his day is almost timeless. They have healthy, sleek bodies; today we might call them the beautiful people (verse 4). They have the powerful connections to avoid the burdensome responsibilities most people face (verses 5 and 12). They have been what we call fortunate, but they take full credit, feeling superior to all beneath them (verses 6 and 8). The root of it all is that they see no need for God. If there is a heaven, they feel they have earned it (verses 9 and 11). Believers should remember we also have this spiritual self-sufficiency deep within us. Why do we pray less when things in life are going better? And why do we secretly feel that *we* deserve the lives that *they* have?

Prayer: Lord, there has never been a human society without overweening pride at the top and bitter envy at the bottom. That is why if the "have-nots" ever overthrow the "haves" they become the same. Father, give our culture your grace, humbling both leaders and followers and giving us peace. Amen.

June 17

READ Psalm 73:10–14. **10** Therefore their people turn to them and drink up waters in abundance. **11** They say, "How would God know? Does the Most High know anything?" **12** This is what the wicked are like—always free of care, they go on amassing wealth. **13** Surely in vain have I kept my heart pure and have washed my hands in innocence. **14** All day long I have been afflicted, and every morning brings new punishments.

WHAT HAVE I GOTTEN OUT OF IT? The psalmist concludes that a good life has not brought him wealth or freedom from troubles (verse 12) and therefore has been "in vain" (verse 13). But this unmasks his heart. His obedience was not a way of pleasing God but rather a means of getting God to please him. When we say to God, "I'll serve you only if X happens," then it is X that we love, and God is just a necessary apparatus for obtaining it. The shock of this admission begins to clear his mind. In every difficult circumstance we may hear God saying to us: "Now we will see if you came to me to get me to serve you or so that you could serve me."

Prayer: Lord, I resent my service to you when my life isn't going as I wish. I don't love you as much as I love the good things I hope to get from you. Oh, illumine my mind and heart to see your beauty and love you for yourself alone. That is not only right to do but also my real joy. Amen.

June 18

READ Psalm 73:15–20. **15** If I had spoken out like that, I would have betrayed your children. **16** When I tried to understand all this, it troubled me deeply **17** till I entered the sanctuary of God; then I understood their final destiny. **18** Surely you place them on slippery ground; you cast them down to ruin. **19** How suddenly are they destroyed, completely swept away by terrors! **20** They are like a dream when one awakes; when you arise, Lord, you will despise them as fantasies.

THE DREAM OF THE WORLD. The first step out of the sinkhole of resentment and envy is worship. The psalmist enters the sanctuary, and in the presence of the true God his sight clears and he begins to get the long-term perspective (verses 16–17). He realizes that the rich without God are on their way to being eternally poor; the celebrities without God are on their way to being endlessly ignored (verses 18–19). Within the confines of a dream, you may be very intimidated by some powerful being, but as soon as you wake, you laugh at its impotence to harm your real life. All the world's power and wealth are like a dream. They can neither enhance nor ruin a Christian's deepest identity, happiness, and inheritance.

Prayer: Lord, I praise you for being more real than the mountains, and in you I am richer than if I had all the jewels that lie beneath the earth. In my eyes, by your Spirit's power, let *"the things of the world grow strangely dim in the light of your glory and grace."*[66] Amen.

June 19

READ Psalm 73:21–23. **21** When my heart was grieved and my spirit embittered, **22** I was senseless and ignorant; I was a brute beast before you. **23** Yet I am always with you; you hold me by my right hand.

ELECTRIFYING GRACE. The antitoxin for envy and self-pity is humility. The psalmist first saw that his sin hurt him (verse 2) and then that it hurt others (verse 15), but finally he sees he has been as arrogant toward *God* as the people he despised. There is in us a fierce, instinctive self-will as unthinking and inhuman as that of a wild beast (verse 22). Augustine remembered stealing pears only because it was forbidden.[67] Deep in us something snarls, "*No* one tells *me* what to do." Only by admitting this darkness within can the glorious word of grace—"yet" (verse 23)—dawn on him. God never let him go. Only when we see the depth of our sin will we be electrified by the wonder of grace.

Prayer: Lord, the deeper the darkness, the more visible and beautiful the stars. And the more I admit my sin, the more your grace becomes a reality rather than an abstract idea. Only then does your grace humble me and affirm me, cleanse me and shape me. Make your grace amazing to my heart. Amen.

June 20

READ Psalm 73:24–28. **24** You guide me with your counsel, and afterward you will take me into glory. **25** Whom have I in heaven but you? And earth has nothing I desire besides you. **26** My flesh and my heart may fail, but God is the strength of my heart and my portion forever. **27** Those who are far from you will perish; you destroy all who are unfaithful to you. **28** But as for me, it is good to be near God. I have made the Sovereign LORD my refuge; I will tell of all your deeds.

NOTHING BUT YOU. The psalmist breaks through. "Whom have I in heaven but you?" (verse 25) means "If I don't have you I have nothing—nothing else will satisfy or last." We rightly want to be reunited with loved ones in heaven. What makes heaven *heaven*, however, is that God is there. Those who have gone before are not looking down at us fondly but rather are caught up in a never-ending fountain of joy, delight, and adoration. Augustine writes: "God alone is the place of peace that cannot be disturbed— and He will not withhold Himself from your love unless you withhold your love from him."[68] Life in glory with God (verse 24) will suffice for the healing of all wounds, the answering of all questions. Jesus has promised.

Prayer: Lord, I thank you for how suffering drives me like a nail deeper into your love. It is not my earthly joys but my griefs that show me your grace is enough. *"I live to show your power, who once did bring first my joys to weep, and now my griefs to sing."*[69] Amen.

June 21

READ Psalm 74:1–8. **1** O God, why have you rejected us forever? Why does your anger smolder against the sheep of your pasture? **2** Remember the nation you purchased long ago, the tribe of your inheritance, whom you redeemed—Mount Zion, where you dwelt. **3** Turn your steps toward these everlasting ruins, all this destruction the enemy has brought on the sanctuary. **4** Your foes roared in the place where you met with us; they set up their standards as signs. **5** They behaved like men wielding axes to cut through a thicket of trees. **6** They smashed all the carved paneling with their axes and hatchets. **7** They burned your sanctuary to the ground; they defiled the dwelling place of your Name. **8** They said in their hearts, "We will crush them completely!" They burned every place where God was worshiped in the land.

FACING COMPLETE COLLAPSE. The psalmist surveys the complete destruction of Jerusalem and the Temple (verses 3 and 7) by the Babylonian army. It is generally assumed that while God might allow some difficulties, he would never let horrendous, cataclysmic tragedies happen to people who have faith in him. But the Bible shows that this particular disaster was not total, that God was not deserting them. And the most faithful person who ever lived, Jesus Christ, also suffered horrendously for redemptive purposes. So remember, "God is God. If He is God, He is worthy of my worship and my service. I will find rest nowhere but in His will, and that will is infinitely, immeasurably, unspeakably beyond my largest notions of what He is up to."[70]

Prayer: Lord, I praise you that you not only bring glory out of darkness, strength out of weakness, and joy out of sorrow but often make good things richer and more powerful *through* those bad things. Help me so that my mind and heart rests in this truth. Amen.

June 22

READ Psalm 74:9–17. **9** We are given no signs from God; no prophets are left, and none of us knows how long this will be. **10** How long will the enemy mock you, God? Will the foe revile your name forever? **11** Why do you hold back your hand, your right hand? Take it from the folds of your garment and destroy them! **12** But God is my king from long ago; he brings salvation upon the earth. **13** It was you who split open the sea by your power; you broke the heads of the monster in the waters. **14** It was you who crushed the heads of Leviathan and gave it as food to the creatures of the desert. **15** It was you who opened up springs and streams; you dried up the ever-flowing rivers. **16** The day is yours, and yours also the night; you established the sun and moon. **17** It was you who set all the boundaries of the earth; you made both summer and winter.

PRAYING COMPLETE COLLAPSE. Now the psalmist begins to process this disaster in prayer. There are two things he does *not* do. He does not passively resign himself to the evil status quo, but neither does he angrily turn away from God, assuming he knows better. Instead he expresses his sorrow and complaints, but always toward God. He remembers that God has all power (verses 13–17). He is saying, "Lord, to whom shall we go? You have the words of eternal life" (John 6:68). If we believe in God only when he is doing great things for us, we are not really serving him; we are only using him.

Prayer: Lord, in dark times I feel I get little out of going to the throne of grace in prayer—but give me strength to go and stay there nonetheless. Amen.

June 23

READ Psalm 74:18–23. **18** Remember how the enemy has mocked you, LORD, how foolish people have reviled your name. **19** Do not hand over the life of your dove to wild beasts; do not forget the lives of your afflicted people forever. **20** Have regard for your covenant, because haunts of violence fill the dark places of the land. **21** Do not let the oppressed retreat in disgrace; may the poor and needy praise your name. **22** Rise up, O God, and defend your cause; remember how fools mock you all day long. **23** Do not ignore the clamor of your adversaries, the uproar of your enemies, which rises continually.

REMEMBER YOUR COVENANT. The destroyed temple, the place of sacrifice and atonement, was the place where the people could approach the holy God despite their sin. This provision was part of the covenant he made with them through Moses, that he would be their God. In the end the psalmist rests in the knowledge that God will not forget this covenant (verse 20). We can also lay down our fears, knowing that God *has* upheld his covenant in Jesus Christ, whose ultimate sacrifice for sin and mediation is the new, final temple.[71] Now we know that the covenant promise "I will be your God" really means "no matter what," because in Christ we see the lengths to which he will go to love us.

Prayer: Lord, our lives are filled with both darkness and light, sin and grace. So help me respond as I should in prayer—both complaining and praising, both lamenting and trusting—but sweetened with the knowledge that ultimately all will end in joy and glory. Amen.

June 24

READ Psalm 75:1–5. **1** We praise you, God, we praise you, for your Name is near; people tell of your wonderful deeds. **2** You say, "I choose the appointed time; it is I who judge with equity. **3** When the earth and all its people quake, it is I who hold its pillars firm. **4** To the arrogant I say, 'Boast no more,' and to the wicked, 'Do not lift up your horns. **5** Do not lift your horns against heaven; do not speak so defiantly.'"

HUMBLING THE PROUD. Today our public discourse is filled with language about how technologies or policies or ideas will be "game changing" or will "change the world." From our viewpoint it is the most brilliant, powerful, and wealthy who set the course of events. God, however, says it is *he* who "hold[s the] pillars firm" (verse 3), who literally holds the world together (Acts 17:28; Hebrews 1:3). All human talent (James 1:17) and wisdom (Romans 2:14–15) and success (Matthew 5:45) are only gifts from him. He is in control of everything that happens in history, and even the most powerful end up only fulfilling God's purposes (verse 2; cf. John 19:11). Therefore we should not arrogantly think we are competent to run our own lives. We are not.

Prayer: Lord, I praise you that you are sovereign over all. How threatening this is—I have no control over my life. Yet how comforting this is—I cannot keep my life together but must rest in you. Clear my vision to see this truth and to receive its challenge and comfort every day. Amen.

June 25

READ Psalm 75:6–10. **6** No one from the east or the west or from the desert can exalt themselves. **7** It is God who judges: He brings one down, he exalts another. **8** In the hand of the LORD is a cup full of foaming wine mixed with spices; he pours it out, and all the wicked of the earth drink it down to its very dregs. **9** As for me, I will declare this forever; I will sing praise to the God of Jacob, **10** who says, "I will cut off the horns of all the wicked, but the horns of the righteous will be lifted up."

THE CUP. In biblical imagery a cup was an ordeal. The cup "full of foaming wine" is the cup of divine wrath on evildoers (verse 8), the ultimate ordeal of infinite punishment that made even the heart of the Son of God quail (Matthew 26:42). Yet on the cross Jesus embraced God's will and drank this cup on our behalf, knowing that no matter how dreadful, on the other side would lie the joy of being with us. We are his reward (Isaiah 40:10). When faced with an aspect of God's will in our life that we want to run from, we must cling closely to Jesus and whisper, "Thy will be done." Then we can expect the joy of being with him.

Prayer: Father, I cannot begin to praise and thank you for your inestimable gift. *For Christ, my loving Savior, hath / drunk up the wine of Thy fierce wrath. What bitter cups were due to be / had he not drank them up for me.*[72] Amen.

June 26

READ Psalm 76:1–6. **1** God is renowned in Judah; in Israel his name is great . **2** His tent is in Salem, his dwelling place in Zion. **3** There he broke the flashing arrows, the shields and the swords, the weapons of war. **4** You are radiant with light, more majestic than mountains rich with game. **5** The valiant lie plundered, they sleep their last sleep; not one of the warriors can lift his hands. **6** At your rebuke, God of Jacob, both horse and chariot lie still.

THE GOD WHO FIGHTS FOR US. The horse and chariot represented the latest technology in modern warfare. No foot soldier could stand against them and win. But God is infinitely more powerful than any human force (verse 5). One of the great themes of the Bible is that God fights for us against our foes. When it says God merely has to rebuke an army and it is stilled (verse 6), we think of Christ stilling a hurricane with a word (Mark 4:39). Christians know that Jesus came to fight our ultimate enemies—sin and death—by going to the cross. In all danger he protects us, and either he will be with us or we will be with him, so all will be well.

Prayer: Lord, I praise you for being a majestic, resplendent God. You are infinitely important and all else peripheral; you are eternally solid and everything else fleeting. Don't let me be dazzled by human power and beauty. Amen.

June 27

READ Psalm 76:7–12. **7** It is you alone who are to be feared. Who can stand before you when you are angry? **8** From heaven you pronounced judgment, and the land feared and was quiet— **9** when you, God, rose up to judge, to save all the afflicted of the land. **10** Surely the wrath of mankind brings you praise, and with the remainder of wrath you arm yourself.[73] **11** Make vows to the LORD your God and fulfill them; let all the neighboring lands bring gifts to the One to be feared. **12** He breaks the spirit of rulers; he is feared by the kings of the earth.

YOU MAKE THE WRATH OF MEN PRAISE YOU. Verse 10 is full of interest. Not only will all efforts to rebel or defeat God in the end only fulfill God's plan (Genesis 50:20; Acts 4:27–28), but they will only make the ultimate joy and glory of the renewed world and God's people greater. That will be the ultimate defeat of evil. The greatest example is the death of Jesus. "This man was handed over to you by God's deliberate plan and foreknowledge; and you, with the help of wicked men, put him to death by nailing him to the cross" (Acts 2:23). This does indeed lead us to fear him, to wonder at his greatness, and to submit to his lordship (verse 7).

Prayer: *"Lord, make us to have a perpetual fear and love of thy holy name; for thou never failest to help and govern them whom thou dost bring up in thy steadfast love."*[74] Grant this through Jesus Christ our Lord. Amen.

READ Psalm 77:1–4. **1** I cried out to God for help; I cried out to God to hear me. **2** When I was in distress, I sought the Lord; at night I stretched out untiring hands, and I would not be comforted. **3** I remembered you, God, and I groaned; I meditated, and my spirit grew faint. **4** You kept my eyes from closing; I was too troubled to speak.

THE IMPORTANCE OF MEDITATION. The psalmist faces some unnamed suffering and distress (verse 2). In response he meditates (verses 3, 6, 11, and 12). The word "meditate" can be translated as "to muse," a word related to "music." When we put words to music, they go right to the heart. When we meditate, we work the truth down until it affects the heart. This is the key to handling difficulty. The psalmist is not just being a stoic and gritting his teeth till the storm passes. Nor is he simply venting his feelings. He redirects his thoughts and feelings toward the truth about God. His first effort, here in verses 1–4, doesn't seem to have helped much. So this is not the work of a moment, and learning it takes a lifetime.

Prayer: Lord, your disciples asked you to teach them to pray— but I also ask you to teach me how to meditate on your Word. Give me the patience and habits of mind that can mark and notice, savor and relish, and inwardly digest your words. Let them dwell in me richly. Amen.

June 29

READ Psalm 77:5–9. 5 I thought about the former days, the years of long ago; 6 I remembered my songs in the night. My heart meditated and my spirit asked: 7 "Will the Lord reject forever? Will he never show his favor again? 8 Has his unfailing love vanished forever? Has his promise failed for all time? 9 Has God forgotten to be merciful? Has he in anger withheld his compassion?"

ASKING QUESTIONS. Another important phrase for meditation is "my spirit asked" (verse 6). Meditation consists in large part of asking the right questions. To meditate is to ask oneself questions about the truth, such as "What difference does this make? Am I taking this seriously? If I forget this, how will that affect me? Have I forgotten it? Am I living in light of this?" The psalmist's questions about "unfailing love" begin to suggest their own answers (verse 8). While we count every minute of sorrow as an eon, God's mercies remain new every morning that we wake up breathing. He will not forget or fail us, and though we may cry to him and tell him of our feelings of abandonment, he will never leave us.

Prayer: Lord, thank you for being a God who takes questions! And keep my mind clear as I pose them, because questions asked honestly in the face of your holiness always lead back to trust in you. Whom should I trust more than you? Myself? That would be the most foolish thing of all. Amen.

June 30

READ Psalm 77:10–15. **10** Then I thought, "To this I will appeal: the years when the Most High stretched out his right hand. **11** I will remember the deeds of the LORD; yes, I will remember your miracles of long ago. **12** I will consider all your works and meditate on all your mighty deeds." **13** Your ways, God, are holy. What god is as great as our God? **14** You are the God who performs miracles; you display your power among the peoples. **15** With your mighty arm you redeemed your people, the descendants of Jacob and Joseph.

ARGUING YOUR CASE. Finally the psalmist decides to conduct a sustained meditation (verse 12). He "appeals" (verse 10) to the account of the redemptive miracles of God during the exodus. Lawyers appeal a case when they hope for a different conclusion from the one they received from the lower court. The psalmist is then arguing against his own heart, which had "ruled" that things were hopeless. His case: "If a God with power like this (verse 14) loves us, then what am I afraid of?" He muses on the might and love of God as shown in the past, in order to overwhelm his fears in the present.

Prayer: Lord, I praise you that the greatest displays of your power in history have been in showing mercy and saving love. So now open my eyes and stir up my heart to trust every one of your promises, so that I can live in the peace you have for all who know you. Amen.

July 1

THE SUPREME EXODUS. Verses 13–20 are an example of a successful meditation, in which the psalmist preaches to his own heart about God's grace revealed in the exodus. The result is that his heart believes afresh and he can face his problems. Christians have a far better way to assure ourselves that God will never abandon us or leave us. Jesus accomplished the greatest exodus of all, liberating us not just from social or political bondage but from sin and death (Luke 9:31). Also, his death on the cross is a model for how God often works his gracious purposes out through what looks like a defeat. When we meditate on *that,* we will have a resource for facing anything at all.

Prayer: Lord, I thank you that you are a God of infinite power, so that even the oceans and hurricanes do your bidding, yet you are a tender shepherd to us. If the infinite power in the universe is our loving shepherd, then we can live fearlessly. Amen.

July 2

READ Psalm 78:1–8. **1** My people, hear my teaching; listen to the words of my mouth. **2** I will open my mouth with a parable; I will utter hidden things, things from of old— **3** things we have heard and known, things our ancestors have told us. **4** We will not hide them from their descendants; we will tell the next generation the praise-worthy deeds of the LORD, his power, and the wonders he has done. **5** He decreed statutes for Jacob and established the law in Israel, which he commanded our ancestors to teach their children, **6** so the next generation would know them, even the children yet to be born, and they in turn would tell their children. **7** Then they would put their trust in God and would not forget his deeds but would keep his commands. **8** They would not be like their ancestors—a stubborn and rebellious generation, whose hearts were not loyal to God, whose spirits were not faithful to him.

A RELIGION OF THE HEART. This psalm recounts the history of Israel from its deliverance from Egypt to the kingship of David. Its negative lesson is that this history not be repeated in the lives of the listeners (verse 8). The positive lesson is that believers be marked by true faith (verse 7). We should not just know the truth about who God is (verse 7) but must trust him from the heart (verses 7 and 8) and show this saving faith through a changed life of obedience (verse 7). Throughout history many have honored God with external behavior but failed to have converted hearts (Isaiah 29:13; Jeremiah 4:4). Are you just going through the motions of religion, or have you been born again (John 3:1–16)?

Prayer: Lord, I can obey you dutifully, but that will not satisfy you. You want my heart. But like Paul I see impulses within me that resist you. Replace my still-stony heart with a heart of flesh. Help me love you and want you. Amen.

July 3

READ Psalm 78:9–16. **9** The men of Ephraim, though armed with bows, turned back on the day of battle; **10** they did not keep God's covenant and refused to live by his law. **11** They forgot what he had done, the wonders he had shown them. **12** He did miracles in the sight of their ancestors in the land of Egypt, in the region of Zoan. **13** He divided the sea and led them through; he made the water stand up like a wall. **14** He guided them with the cloud by day and with light from the fire all night. **15** He split the rocks in the wilderness and gave them water as abundant as the seas; **16** he brought streams out of a rocky crag and made water flow down like rivers.

DON'T FORGET. The "men of Ephraim" are the northern tribes of Israel (verses 9–10) that fell into idolatry (1 Kings 12) and were deported and lost to history (2 Kings 17). The root of their problem was spiritual forgetting (verse 11). Christians too can stagnate because they "forget that they have been cleansed from their past sins" (2 Peter 1:9). The key is to have a heart constantly vitalized by deliberate remembering of the costly sacrifice of Jesus. We must remember that for our sins Jesus was, as it were, forgotten ("Why have you forsaken me?" Matthew 27:46) so that God can now no more forget us than a mother her nursing infant (Isaiah 49:14–16). Remembering that will make you a great heart.

Prayer: Lord, I worry because I forget your wisdom, I resent because I forget your mercy, I covet because I forget your beauty, I sin because I forget your holiness, I fear because I forget your sovereignty. You always remember me; help me to always remember you. Amen.

July 4

READ Psalm 78:17–25. **17** But they continued to sin against him, rebelling in the wilderness against the Most High. **18** They willfully put God to the test by demanding the food they craved. **19** They spoke against God; they said, "Can God really spread a table in the wilderness? **20** True, he struck the rock, and water gushed out, streams flowed abundantly, but can he also give us bread? Can he supply meat for his people?" **21** When the LORD heard them, he was furious; his fire broke out against Jacob, and his wrath rose against Israel, **22** for they did not believe in God or trust in his deliverance. **23** Yet he gave a command to the skies above and opened the doors of the heavens; **24** he rained down manna for the people to eat, he gave them the grain of heaven. **25** Human beings ate the bread of angels; he sent them all the food they could eat.

TESTING GOD. In the wilderness the people demanded more signs and proofs of God's love for them, as if the deliverance from Egypt hadn't been enough. "Put[ting] God to the test" (verse 18) is one of the essential impulses of the human heart. No matter what God has done for us, our heart says, "But what have you done for me *lately*?" The evil of this is that we reverse places with God. We put him on probation, making our relationship conditional on how well we think he performs. But God created the universe with a word of his power, and even the galaxies are like dust before him. Is this the kind of person you ask into your life to be your personal assistant?

Prayer: Lord Jesus, how can I obey and love you conditionally when you loved me unconditionally? You looked down from the cross and saw us betraying, denying, forsaking you, and yet you stayed. Help me to cling to you and obey you no matter what. Amen.

July 5

READ Psalm 78:26–31. **26** He let loose the east wind from the heavens and by his power made the south wind blow. **27** He rained meat down on them like dust, birds like sand on the seashore. **28** He made them come down inside their camp, all around their tents. **29** They ate till they were gorged—he had given them what they craved. **30** But before they turned from what they craved, even while the food was still in their mouths, **31** God's anger rose against them; he put to death the sturdiest among them, cutting down the young men of Israel.

SIN AS BOREDOM. This psalm refers to Numbers 11, where the Israelites complained that they had become tired of God's provision of manna for their daily food. They craved meat. God sent them a flock of quail but rightly predicted that they would come to loathe what they had so desired (Numbers 11:20). One of the marks of addiction is the "tolerance effect," in which an addict needs greater and greater doses of a drug to get the same sensation. Similarly, anything besides God that we get our meaning from or put our hopes in will, after an initial "rush," increasingly bore us. Only God and his love become more and more engaging, absorbing, and satisfying forever.

Prayer: Lord, I confess I often find prayer to be boring and sin to be fascinating. But that is because my mind is distorted by sin. You alone can satisfy the deepest longings of my soul. Only you are eternally interesting. I commit myself to encountering you afresh in prayer and the Word. Help me keep this promise. Amen.

July 6

READ Psalm 78:32–37. **32** In spite of all this, they kept on sinning; in spite of his wonders, they did not believe. **33** So he ended their days in futility and their years in terror. **34** Whenever God slew them, they would seek him; they eagerly turned to him again. **35** They remembered that God was their Rock, that God Most High was their Redeemer. **36** But then they would flatter him with their mouths, lying to him with their tongues; **37** their hearts were not loyal to him, they were not faithful to his covenant.

THE LIFE OF SELFISH FEAR. Some seem very eager to follow God (verse 34). They speak eloquently of their faith (Hosea 6:1–3) and exhibit much joy in believing (Matthew 13:20–21). Yet their faith never lasts. They turn to God only when their sin has painful consequences ("Whenever God slew them, they would seek him," verse 34). For example, they may be honest, but only out of fear of being found out or from of a desire to appear moral and upright. Ironically, all their morality is based on deep selfishness. They come to God to avoid pain for themselves, not to give honor and joy to him. They flatter him but do not love him (verse 36). Are you living a moral, decent life? Why?

Prayer: Lord, your Word says that the heart is deceitful and no one can know it (Jeremiah 17:9) without the radical help of your Spirit. Give me that help now. Lay bare the motivations at my foundation. Show me your love and glory in prayer so my obedience becomes more and more a grateful, willing gift. Amen.

July 7

READ Psalm 78:38–43. **38** Yet he was merciful; he forgave their iniquities and did not destroy them. Time after time he restrained his anger and did not stir up his full wrath. **39** He remembered that they were but flesh, a passing breeze that does not return. **40** How often they rebelled against him in the wilderness and grieved him in the wasteland! **41** Again and again they put God to the test; they vexed the Holy One of Israel. **42** They did not remember his power—the day he redeemed them from the oppressor, **43** the day he displayed his signs in Egypt, his wonders in the region of Zoan.

THE PATIENCE OF GOD. The history recounted in this psalm shows how patient God is (verses 38–39). He is "slow to anger" (Exodus 34:6; Psalm 86:15). He says, "I take no pleasure in the death of anyone. . . . Repent and live!" (Ezekiel 18:32, cf. Romans 2:4). It is only because he bears with us patiently, never fully giving anyone what they deserve when they deserve it, that anyone is saved (2 Peter 3:15). When we read that he "remember[s] that [we are] but flesh" (verse 39), we hear Jesus looking at his disciples, falling asleep in Gethsemane in his hour of greatest need and saying, "The spirit is willing, but the flesh is weak." In other words, "I know you meant well." What a patient Savior!

Prayer: Lord Jesus, the old meaning of patience is "long suffering," and you indeed suffered infinitely rather than give me the punishment my sins deserved. You have been unspeakably patient with me. Let that truth make me patient with people around me, and with my circumstances, and with your every disposal of my life. Amen.

July 8

READ Psalm 78:44–53. **44** He turned their rivers into blood; they could not drink from their streams. **45** He sent swarms of flies that devoured them, and frogs that devastated them. **46** He gave their crops to the grasshopper, their produce to the locust. **47** He destroyed their vines with hail and their sycamore-figs with sleet. **48** He gave over their cattle to the hail, their livestock to bolts of lightning. **49** He unleashed against them his hot anger, his wrath, indignation and hostility—a band of destroying angels. **50** He prepared a path for his anger; he did not spare them from death but gave them over to the plague. **51** He struck down all the firstborn of Egypt, the firstfruits of manhood in the tents of Ham. **52** But he brought his people out like a flock; he led them like sheep through the desert. **53** He guided them safely, so they were unafraid; but the sea engulfed their enemies.

THE PLAGUE OF PLAGUES. The plagues God inflicted on Egypt were natural disasters. He made the Nile River undrinkable. That forced frogs out of the marshes, where they died. Their carcasses led to a plague of flies and gnats, which in turn led to epidemics. The unraveling of nature in Egypt points to a crucial truth. God created the world, so when we disobey him we unleash forces of chaos and disorder. When you, a being created to live for God, live instead for yourself, you violate your design. The ultimate plague is sin, and it will disintegrate you without the antidote—the grace of God in Jesus Christ.

Prayer: Lord, the plague of sin infects every part of me. It makes me miserably and cruelly self-absorbed. It makes me spiritually impotent to change without your grace and intervention. Give me that help: show me myself, free me from my besetting sins, and let me *love* to obey you. Amen.

July 9

READ Psalm 78:54–58. **54** And so he brought them to the border of his holy land, to the hill country his right hand had taken. **55** He drove out nations before them and allotted their lands to them as an inheritance; he settled the tribes of Israel in their homes. **56** But they put God to the test and rebelled against the Most High; they did not keep his statutes. **57** Like their ancestors they were disloyal and faithless, as unreliable as a faulty bow. **58** They angered him with their high places; they aroused his jealousy with their idols.

IDOLATRY. The epitome of Israel's failure is that the people turned from the living God to worship idols (verse 58). Idolatry is foundational to what is wrong with the human race (Romans 1:21–25). Anything that is functionally more important to you than God is an idol. Anything you love more than God—even a good thing like a spouse or child or social cause—is a false god. Because we love them too much, we are wracked with uncontrollable fears and anger when they are threatened and inconsolable despair when we lose them. Until you can identify your idols you cannot understand yourself. Until you turn from them you can't know and walk with God.

Prayer: Lord, I am prone to turn good things into idols. Things I should merely receive with thanks I look to for the contentment and safety that only you can give. *"The dearest idol I have known, whate'er that idol be—Help me to tear it from thy throne, and worship only thee."*[75] Amen.

July 10

READ Psalm 78:59–64. **59** When God heard them, he was furious; he rejected Israel completely. **60** He abandoned the tabernacle of Shiloh, the tent he had set up among humans. **61** He sent the ark of his might into captivity, his splendor into the hands of the enemy. **62** He gave his people over to the sword; he was furious with his inheritance. **63** Fire consumed their young men, and their young women had no wedding songs; **64** their priests were put to the sword, and their widows could not weep.

ICHABOD. Israel became so indifferent to the things of God that he allowed the Ark of the Covenant—the sign of his presence with them—to be captured by the Philistines (verse 61). A child born that day was named Ichabod—meaning "the Glory has departed" (1 Samuel 4:21). Because God is holy, sin separates us from the presence of God (Isaiah 59:2). Even in Christians whose sins are pardoned, Jesus finds spiritual halfheartedness as nauseating to him as uncooked food. "Because you are . . . neither hot nor cold . . . I . . . spit you out of my mouth" (Revelation 3:16). Have you become nonchalant toward sin in your life because you say, "God is love"? God *does* love you, and that is why he will not support you in living apart from him.

Prayer: Lord, I have drifted from you. *What peace with you I once enjoyed! How sweet its memory still! But it has left an aching void the world can never fill. Return, O Spirit, please return—sweet messenger of rest. I hate the sins that made thee mourn and drove thee from my breast.*[76] Amen.

July 11

READ Psalm 78:65–72. **65** Then the Lord awoke as from sleep, as a warrior wakes from the stupor of wine. **66** He beat back his enemies; he put them to everlasting shame. **67** Then he rejected the tents of Joseph, he did not choose the tribe of Ephraim; **68** but he chose the tribe of Judah, Mount Zion, which he loved. **69** He built his sanctuary like the heights, like the earth that he established forever. **70** He chose David his servant and took him from the sheep pens; **71** from tending the sheep he brought him to be the shepherd of his people Jacob, of Israel his inheritance. **72** And David shepherded them with integrity of heart; with skillful hands he led them.

HE CHOSE DAVID. This psalm ends on a high note. It tells how, despite Israel's disobedience, God built his temple (verses 68–69) and chose a leader, David, to be the shepherd-king (verses 70–71). But we know that, contrary to the hopes of the psalmist, history *did* repeat itself, and the line of Davidic kings failed to obey God as well. The human race required a greater King, the descendant of David who was prophesied (1 Samuel 7:11–18), the Savior who was the final temple and sacrifice for sin (John 2:19–21; Hebrews 9:11–14). Jesus is our true Shepherd-King. Only he is wise and skillful enough to direct your life. Don't entrust yourself to the hands of any other, not even your own. Trust yourself to him and you shall not want.

Prayer: Lord, I confess my overconfidence. I don't feel like a sheep that needs a shepherd to do absolutely *everything* for it, but I am. I rely on my own wisdom, my career and bank account, my well-connected friends instead of on you. You, my great shepherd, are my only security. I put myself in your hands. Amen.

July 12

READ Psalm 79:1–8. **1** O God, the nations have invaded your inheritance; they have defiled your holy temple, they have reduced Jerusalem to rubble. **2** They have left the dead bodies of your servants as food for the birds of the sky, the flesh of your own people for the animals of the wild. **3** They have poured out blood like water all around Jerusalem, and there is no one to bury the dead. **4** We are objects of contempt to our neighbors, of scorn and derision to those around us. **5** How long, LORD? Will you be angry forever? How long will your jealousy burn like fire? **6** Pour out your wrath on the nations that do not acknowledge you, on the kingdoms that do not call on your name; **7** for they have devoured Jacob and destroyed his homeland. **8** Do not hold against us the sins of past generations; may your mercy come quickly to meet us, for we are in desperate need.

THE JEALOUSY OF GOD. God allowed the destruction of Jerusalem by the Babylonian army because of his "jealousy" (verse 5). Paul speaks of having a "godly jealousy" for his friends (2 Corinthians 11:2). It is love angered by anything that is defacing or destroying the loved one. A parent's love, for example, is "jealous" for a child's success and happiness and is zealous to remove any sins that are barriers to these things. If God had allowed Israel to go its idol-worshipping way, its people would have been totally lost to him. Christians know that in Christ their sins can't bring them into condemnation (Romans 8:1), but it is *because* we are so loved that God will also discipline us if we go astray (Hebrews 12:4–11).

Prayer: Lord, you love me like a father, and when I am in pain you are grieved. And yet, like a father, you love me too much to let me alone when I am living foolishly. When troubles happen, instead of crying, "Unfair!" help me to ask, "Is there anything you are trying to show me?" Then show me. Amen.

July 13

READ Psalm 79:9–13. **9** Help us, God our Savior, for the glory of your name; deliver us and forgive our sins for your name's sake. **10** Why should the nations say, "Where is their God?" Before our eyes, make known among the nations that you avenge the outpoured blood of your servants. **11** May the groans of the prisoners come before you; with your strong arm preserve those condemned to die. **12** Pay back into the laps of our neighbors seven times the contempt they have hurled at you, Lord. **13** Then we your people, the sheep of your pasture, will praise you forever; from generation to generation we will proclaim your praise.

BLOOD CRIES OUT. The psalmist hears the victims' blood crying out to be avenged (verse 10). The Bible often speaks of injustice "crying out" to God, as did the shed blood of Abel against Cain (Genesis 4:10–11). The psalmist calls for God to pay back the invaders (verse 12). What he did not know was that Christ's blood would someday be poured out in Jerusalem too, blood that "speaks a better word than the blood of Abel" (Hebrews 12:24). It demands forgiveness rather than retribution for those who believe. Christians too can praise God in the face of mistreatment (verse 13). But in addition they love their enemies and pray for their salvation (Matthew 5:43–48).

Prayer: Lord, how can I, who live only by your mercy and grace, withhold the same from anyone else? Thank you for lifting from me the impossible burden of thinking that I know what others deserve who have wronged me. Help me to leave that to you. Amen.

July 14

READ Psalm 80:1–7. **1** Hear us, Shepherd of Israel, you who lead Joseph like a flock. You who sit enthroned between the cherubim, shine forth **2** before Ephraim, Benjamin and Manasseh. Awaken your might; come and save us. **3** Restore us, O God; make your face shine upon us, that we may be saved. **4** How long, LORD God Almighty, will your anger smolder against the prayers of your people? **5** You have fed them with the bread of tears; you have made them drink tears by the bowlful. **6** You have made us an object of derision to our neighbors, and our enemies mock us. **7** Restore us, God Almighty; make your face shine upon us, that we may be saved.

BACKSLIDING. To have light from God's face (verses 3 and 7) is not just to believe in God but to experience his presence. It is also to have a life conformed to his, not merely by compulsion out of a sense of duty but by inner desire out of a sense of his beauty. Most believers live in the gray area between these two poles. When we begin to slide toward the one pole, into mechanical religion, we need spiritual renewal from our "backslidings" (Ezekiel 37:23). How? The one constant element in all spiritual revivals is prevailing, extraordinary prayer. Three times (verses 3, 7, and 19) the psalmist calls out to be renewed and restored to spiritual reality.

Prayer: Lord, you said to the Ephesian church that they had "forsaken the love [they] had at first" (Revelation 2:4–5), and I sometimes feel the same is happening to me. How can I lose my attraction to the most beautiful face in the universe? Revive my soul and reopen my eyes to your glory and grace. Amen.

July 15

READ Psalm 80:8–13. **8** You transplanted a vine from Egypt; you drove out the nations and planted it. **9** You cleared the ground for it, and it took root and filled the land. **10** The mountains were covered with its shade, the mighty cedars with its branches. **11** Its branches reached as far as the Sea, its shoots as far as the River. **12** Why have you broken down its walls so that all who pass by pick its grapes? **13** Boars from the forest ravage it, and insects from the fields feed on it.

THE VINE OF GOD. The people of God are like a vine. A vine is not pieced together by human ingenuity but is a living thing (verses 8–9). So Christians are creations of God's Spirit, whose life is implanted within them (Romans 8:9–10), bearing the spiritual fruit of love and joy, peace and humility (Galatians 5:22–25). Vines do not naturally grow towering and tall, and it is incongruous that this vine overshadows mountains and the tallest trees (verse 10). So Christians are creations of God's supernatural grace. In themselves they are foolish, weak, and lowly (1 Corinthians 1:26–31), but through Christ they can change the world (Acts 17:6). Are you just a nice person or a new spiritually new person? Is your character changing, growing in spiritual fruit?

Prayer: Lord, I should be growing more loving, more courageous, more self-forgetful every year. But I confess to you that I am not. Help me see where I am not bearing fruit. Thank you for being a God of life! Help me put my roots deeper into you so I can honor you by growing into your likeness. Amen.

July 16

READ Psalm 80:14–19. **14** Return to us, God Almighty! Look down from heaven and see! Watch over this vine, **15** the root your right hand has planted, the son you have raised up for yourself. **16** Your vine is cut down, it is burned with fire; at your rebuke your people perish. **17** Let your hand rest on the man at your right hand, the son of man you have raised up for yourself. **18** Then we will not turn away from you; revive us, and we will call on your name. **19** Restore us, LORD God Almighty; make your face shine upon us, that we may be saved.

REVIVAL. How does spiritual renewal take place? Each time God is called upon (verses 3, 7, and 19) the divine name is fuller, showing a constantly growing crescendo of prayer. Renewal also requires repentance, a turning back to God (verses 18–19). Finally spiritual revival requires "the man at your right hand" (literally, the *Benjamin*, verse 17). In the history of the revivals of the church, God often chose to work through a dynamic, anointed leader. But Jesus is the true Benjamin, the one who gives full access to the presence of God (Ephesians 2:18). And Jesus is the true vine (John 15:1–6). Only through uniting with him by faith can we become branches and have God's life flow into us. Through him we can be revived.

Prayer: "O Jesus, make thyself to me, a living, bright reality. More present to Faith's vision keen than any outward object see. More near, more intimately nigh, than e'en the sweetest earthly tie."[77] Amen.

July 17

READ Psalm 81:1–4. **1** Sing for joy to God our strength; shout aloud to the God of Jacob! **2** Begin the music, strike the timbrel, play the melodious harp and lyre. **3** Sound the ram's horn at the New Moon, and when the moon is full, on the day of our festival; **4** this is a decree for Israel, an ordinance of the God of Jacob.

THE COMMAND TO REJOICE. The very strength of this call to worship raises questions. We are not merely invited but commanded as a *decree* and *statute* to worship God with joy (verses 4). How can we "rejoice to order"? There are many ways we can do so. Since there are solid reasons why Christians ought to have joy, there are "valid means of awakening and ensnaring it."[78] Ephesians 5:19 tells us to use skillful music, to immerse ourselves in the psalms themselves, and to learn how to turn our hearts to God in gratitude moment by moment during the day. Also, we are commanded to meet regularly with one another for public worship (Hebrews 10:25), and we should not neglect this. Are you rejoicing in God?

Prayer: Lord, my mind has no inclination to fix itself on you and your worthiness, purity, and beauty. My thoughts attach to useless things. Help me turn them toward you and your grace habitually, all day, so that I can "make music in my heart" (Ephesians 5:19) to you. Amen.

July 18

READ Psalm 81:5–10. **5** When God went out against Egypt, he established it as a statute for Joseph. I heard an unknown voice say: **6** "I removed the burden from their shoulders; their hands were set free from the basket. **7** In your distress you called and I rescued you, I answered you out of a thundercloud; I tested you at the waters of Meribah. **8** "Hear me, my people, and I will warn you—if you would only listen to me, Israel! **9** You shall have no foreign god among you; you shall not worship any god other than me. **10** I am the LORD your God, who brought you up out of Egypt. Open wide your mouth and I will fill it.

THE JOY OF OBEDIENCE. Verses 8–10 echo Exodus 20:2: "I am the Lord your God, who brought you out of Egypt." Immediately after saying these words in Exodus 20:2, God gives the Ten Commandments—do not worship other Gods, do not kill, do not bear false witness (Exodus 20:2–17). Yet here, just where we expect him to list his commands, God makes a sheer promise: "Open wide your mouth and I will fill it" (verse 10). God's laws are not merely onerous busywork. They are for our good, that we may prosper (Deuteronomy 6:24); they reflect consummate wisdom; they help us live in such a way that fulfills our designed nature. This text means that the ultimate purpose of obedience is joy, the fulfillment of knowing the God you were built to love.

Prayer: Lord, I praise you for your holy law. Because I am saved by Jesus's work, it is no way of salvation for me, but it is a rule of *life.* Indeed, the more I obey it, the more spiritually alive I become, the more I become the self you made me to be. Help me obey you more and more. Amen.

July 19

READ Psalm 81:11–16. **11** "But my people would not listen to me; Israel would not submit to me. **12** So I gave them over to their stubborn hearts to follow their own devices. **13** "If my people would only listen to me, if Israel would only follow my ways, **14** how quickly would I subdue their enemies and turn my hand against their foes! **15** Those who hate the LORD would cringe before him, and their punishment would last forever. **16** But you would be fed with the finest of wheat; with honey from the rock I would satisfy you."

HONEY FROM THE ROCK. If you rejoice in God (verses 1–5) and obey him (verses 6–10), then a remarkable promise becomes yours. Even hard times and suffering ("the rock") will produce spiritual growth and the sweetness of fellowship with him ("honey") (verse 16). This is a principle that shows up in various ways throughout the Bible. "Out of the eater, something to eat. Out of the strong, something sweet" (Judges 14:14). "When I am weak, then I am strong" (2 Corinthians 12:10). God uses troubles to show us where true joys are to be found. "He gives the best, and brings sweetness out of what is harsh, forbidding and wholly unpromising."[79] In the cross we have the ultimate example of triumph coming out of defeat, honey from the hardness.

Prayer: Dearest Lord, you have been with me long enough to prove yourself. Out of one rock after another you have brought a sweetness that overwhelms the bitter. Yet here I am in another hard place where I am doubting you. Forgive me. I will trust you in this. Amen.

July 20

READ Psalm 82. **1** God presides in the great assembly; he renders judgment among the "gods": **2** "How long will you defend the unjust and show partiality to the wicked? **3** Defend the cause of the weak and fatherless; uphold the cause of the poor and the oppressed. **4** Rescue the weak and the needy; deliver them from the hand of the wicked. **5** "The 'gods' know nothing, they understand nothing. They walk about in darkness; all the foundations of the earth are shaken. **6** "I said, 'You are "gods"; you are all sons of the Most High.' **7** But you will die like mere mortals; you will fall like every other ruler." **8** Rise up, O God, judge the earth, for all the nations are your inheritance.

THE GOD OVER THE GODS. The "gods" could be world rulers (verses 6–7), though this might also refer to the evil spiritual forces behind them (Ephesians 6:12). God is intensely concerned for the weak, the orphaned, the poor, and the powerless (verses 3–4). Christians will be moved to help the needy and the poor if their faith is genuine (James 2:14–17; 1 John 3:16–18). God is committed to justice because, remarkably, he identifies with the poor. To oppress the poor is to disdain him (Proverbs 14:31). Only in Jesus Christ do we learn just how far God would go to identify with the poor and oppressed. He became a poor human being who died on the cross, a victim of human injustice.

Prayer: Lord, because I live in a relatively comfortable and safe part of the world and society, I am not as sensitive to the needs of the weak as you are. Help me to hate the injustice you hate and love the poor and needy whom you love. Amen.

July 21

RETHINKING YOUR ENEMIES. This is a psalm about enemies. How should we respond to them? The first verses say to God, "See how *your* enemies growl, how *your* foes rear their heads" (verse 2.) This perspective is crucial. All sin is fighting God, usurping his authority, taking his place. Even believers must acknowledge that in every wrongdoing they are making themselves God's enemies. ("Against you, you *only*, have I sinned," Psalm 51:4.) So if someone is wronging you, look at them primarily as someone who is at war with God. That will keep you from feeling alone against them. It will also comfort you to know that ultimately it is God's business to deal with them.

Prayer: Lord Jesus, there are indeed people who mistreat me, but none of them have crucified me as your enemies did to you. Yet you prayed for their forgiveness and put your Spirit in God's hands. Help me to do the same. Amen.

July 22

READ Psalm 83:9–13. **9** Do to them as you did to Midian, as you did to Sisera and Jabin at the river Kishon, **10** who perished at Endor and became like dung on the ground. **11** Make their nobles like Oreb and Zeeb, all their princes like Zebah and Zalmunna, **12** who said, "Let us take possession of the pasturelands of God." **13** Make them like tumbleweed, my God, like chaff before the wind.

RELOCATING YOUR ENEMIES. How do we respond to these "imprecatory" psalms that ask God to destroy enemies instead of forgiving them? We should recognize something important here, namely that even in the Old Testament the psalmist is not trying to take revenge himself. These psalms, then, "allow us to turn our anger over to God for him to act as he sees fit" and align us with Paul's advice to "not take revenge, my dear friends, but leave room for God's wrath" (Romans 12:19).[80] Once you relocate your enemies—taking them out of your hands and putting them into God's—you may find yourself developing sympathy for them. Ultimately, no one will get away with anything (verses 9–13).

Prayer: Lord, teach me not to resent those who mistreat me but rather to pity them. They have taken *you* on, and you are the judge who will not overlook anything. I leave them, and myself, in your hands. Amen.

July 23

READ Psalm 83:14–18. **14** As fire consumes the forest or a flame sets the mountains ablaze, **15** so pursue them with your tempest and terrify them with your storm. **16** Cover their faces with shame, LORD, so that they will seek your name. **17** May they ever be ashamed and dismayed; may they perish in disgrace. **18** Let them know that you, whose name is the LORD—that you alone are the Most High over all the earth.

CONVERTING YOUR ENEMIES. The psalmist seems to want only death for his enemies, but the surprise in verses 14–16 is his prayer that wrongdoers be brought to see the truth and come to know God's name (verse 18). In biblical times that would have been a remote possibility for the pagan nations surrounding Israel. And the psalmist is more interested in God's vindication than his enemies' salvation. But in the light of Christ and the cross, we see that this is the main way we are to defeat evil. Christ gives us great resources for turning enemies into God's friends. He died for us while we were yet God's enemies (Romans 5:10), which motivates us to overcome evil with good (Romans 12:14–21).

Prayer: Lord, I praise you because when I was your enemy, you lovingly drew me to yourself. How can I respond any differently to those who are making my life difficult? Help me to forgive those who mistreat me from the heart, and then seek their good, even if and when I tell them things they don't want to hear. Amen.

July 24

READ Psalm 84:1–4. **1** How lovely is your dwelling place, LORD Almighty! **2** My soul yearns, even faints, for the courts of the LORD; my heart and my flesh cry out for the living God. **3** Even the sparrow has found a home, and the swallow a nest for herself, where she may have her young—a place near your altar, LORD Almighty, my King and my God. **4** Blessed are those who dwell in your house; they are ever praising you.

LOVE SONG. This is the intense language of love poetry. The psalmist finds the very courts of the temple to be beautiful (verses 1–2), not for their architectural virtues but because God is there (verse 2). He is fully aware that all of his heart's deepest longings will be satisfied not by belief in some remote, impersonal divine force but only by a *living* God—one who is encountered as a personal, living presence (verse 2). Make constant, immediate fellowship with God a priority. Stop flitting around like a bird and learn to live a life near God (verse 3).

Prayer: Lord, my fellowship with you comes and goes. My nearness to you waxes and wanes. But today I resolve to live my whole life near you, to build my home near your altar. Show me what that will entail, and give me enough love and grace to do it. Amen.

July 25

READ Psalm 84:5–8. **5** Blessed are those whose strength is in you, whose hearts are set on pilgrimage. **6** As they pass through the Valley of Baka, they make it a place of springs; the autumn rains also cover it with pools. **7** They go from strength to strength, till each appears before God in Zion. **8** Hear my prayer, LORD God Almighty; listen to me, God of Jacob.

SPIRITUAL PILGRIMAGE. The longing for nearness to God (see verses 1–4) will not be fulfilled in a stroke. Anyone who wants God must also go on a journey (verse 5). We go from one degree of strength to another (verse 7). As Paul puts it, when we encounter the Lord in his Word, seeing more and more who he really is by faith, we are transformed from one degree of glory to the next (2 Corinthians 3:18). Verses 5–8 tell us to expect the "Valley of Baka" (a place without water), times of dryness and difficulty. But those times are crucial for progress (verses 6–7). God helps you find new growth *through* suffering. It is again "honey from the rock" (Psalm 81:16).

Prayer: Lord, I already have enough history with you to see that my driest and poorest times have been my richest. I still dread such periods, and that is right, but help me not to give up in them or forget that you are working out great things. Amen.

July 26

READ Psalm 84:9–12. **9** Look upon our shield, O God; look with favor on your anointed one. **10** Better is one day in your courts than a thousand elsewhere; I would rather be a doorkeeper in the house of my God than dwell in the tents of the wicked. **11** For the LORD God is a sun and shield; the LORD bestows favor and honor; no good thing does he withhold from those whose walk is blameless. **12** LORD Almighty, blessed is the one who trusts in you.

BETTER IS ONE DAY. A day near God is better than a thousand days experiencing anything else (verse 10). To know God and have even the lowest position in life ("a doorkeeper in the house of my God") is infinitely better than living in luxury without God (verse 10). This is not hyperbole, for "no good thing does he withhold" (verse 11) from those who trust in him (verse 12). The New Testament will reveal the unimaginable scope of this. If he did not begrudge us his own Son, "how will he not also, along with him, graciously give us all things?" (Romans 8:32). He does this for the sake of his anointed one (verse 9). For Christians this can only be Jesus.

Prayer: Lord, fellowship with you is the "pearl of great price" (Matthew 13:45–46). It is the one treasure that makes everything else look like baubles. Help me see this and incline my heart to desire you, or I won't endure on this spiritual pilgrimage into your presence. Amen.

July 27

READ Psalm 85:1–8. **1** You, LORD, showed favor to your land; you restored the fortunes of Jacob. **2** You forgave the iniquity of your people and covered all their sins. **3** You set aside all your wrath and turned from your fierce anger. **4** Restore us again, God our Savior, and put away your displeasure toward us. **5** Will you be angry with us forever? Will you prolong your anger through all generations? **6** Will you not revive us again, that your people may rejoice in you? **7** Show us your unfailing love, LORD, and grant us your salvation. **8** I will listen to what God the LORD says; he promises peace to his people, his faithful servants—but let them not turn to folly.

BLUEPRINT FOR REVIVAL. This psalm is a blueprint for how to respond when your church community declines. Study past seasons of revival and reformation (verse 1). Church history is convicting and encouraging, showing how far we have fallen yet also what God can do. Next must come repentance, acknowledgment that our hard hearts and sin have put a barrier between God and us (verses 4–5). We must also cry out to God in prayer that he "show us" his unfailing love (verse 7). Revivals always involve a fresh "seeing" of the Gospel of grace—grasping it theologically and knowing it experientially. Finally we must wait on him, listening faithfully to his Word (verse 7–9).

Prayer: Lord, I'm spiritually dry; send me the water of your Spirit. I was created and destined to "enjoy you forever,"[81] and yet I am not doing that even now. "Will you not revive us again, that your people may rejoice in you?" Amen.

July 28

READ Psalm 85:9–13. **9** Surely his salvation is near those who fear him, that his glory may dwell in our land. **10** Love and faithfulness meet together; righteousness and peace kiss each other. **11** Faithfulness springs forth from the earth, and righteousness looks down from heaven. **12** The LORD will indeed give what is good, and our land will yield its harvest. **13** Righteousness goes before him and prepares the way for his steps.

TRUE CONCORD. Love and truth (the meaning of "faithfulness") must meet in harmony (verse 10). But how can God in faithfulness punish sin yet also in love embrace sinners? Christ reconciles all things in heaven and earth by making peace through his blood (Colossians 1:20). When Jesus bore our punishment on the cross, love and holiness "kissed"—they were both fulfilled at once. Love without holiness is mere sentiment; righteousness and law without a grasp of grace is Pharisaism. Our natural temperaments incline us to one or the other, but the Gospel keeps truth and love together in our lives. And the more they are unified within us, the more we are brought into the deepest relationship with those who believe the Gospel too.

Prayer: Lord, your salvation brings all things together, yet I do not give myself to people in friendship and community. I am too wary of opening myself to others. Let your love heal me of my fears. Draw me closer to your other children, so I can have all you want to give me. Amen.

July 29

READ Psalm 86:1–7. **1** Hear me, LORD, and answer me, for I am poor and needy. **2** Guard my life, for I am faithful to you. You are my God; save your servant who trusts in you. You are my God; **3** have mercy on me, Lord, for I call to you all day long. **4** Bring joy to your servant, Lord, for I put my trust in you. **5** You, Lord, are forgiving and good, abounding in love to all who call to you. **6** Hear my prayer, LORD; listen to my cry for mercy. **7** When I am in distress, I call to you, because you answer me.

GOD IN CONTROL. This is a psalm of King David, and he is surrounded by enemies attacking him (verse 14). Again the psalms provide a clinic on how to face life when it seems out of control. David feels solitary, defenseless. He responds by reminding himself over and over who God is. He most often calls God "Lord," the Hebrew word *adonai*, meaning "sovereign." David is drilling his own heart to remember that God is in control. Discern how many of your most difficult emotions, bad attitudes, and foolish actions come from losing your grip, at that moment, on who God is.

Prayer: Lord, I am constantly asking you to give me your strength, to change me and heal me. But nothing is more empowering and life transforming than simply adoring you. Inject the truth of your wisdom, love, holiness, and sovereignty down deep into my heart until it catches fire there and makes me new. Amen.

July 30

READ **Psalm 86:8–13. 8** Among the gods there is none like you, Lord; no deeds can compare with yours. **9** All the nations you have made will come and worship before you, Lord; they will bring glory to your name. **10** For you are great and do marvelous deeds; you alone are God. **11** Teach me your way, LORD, that I may rely on your faithfulness; give me an undivided heart, that I may fear your name. **12** I will praise you, Lord my God, with all my heart; I will glorify your name forever. **13** For great is your love toward me; you have delivered me from the depths, from the realm of the dead.

AN UNDIVIDED HEART. David asks for an "undivided heart" (verse 11). A divided heart can have many forms. There is the insincere heart, in which what is said out loud is not matched by the inner attitude (Psalm 12:1). There is the irresolute heart, which cannot fully commit itself (James 1:6–8). Even hearts regenerated by the Spirit and loving God retain much of their older willful resentment of his authority (Romans 7:15–25).[82] David's goal is not psychological healing for its own sake but to "fear" God—to give him joyful, awe-filled love with his entire being. The way to this new heart is not introspection but deliberate worship (verse 12). "I *will* praise you," he says.

Prayer: Lord, I praise you that your praise also is my greatest good. Now, with all the sincerity I can muster, I give myself to you, *"for my heart's desire unto thine is bent: I aspire to a full consent."*[83] Amen.

July 31

READ Psalm 86:14–17. **14** Arrogant foes are attacking me, O God; ruthless people are trying to kill me—they have no regard for you. **15** But you, Lord, are a compassionate and gracious God, slow to anger, abounding in love and faithfulness. **16** Turn to me and have mercy on me; show your strength in behalf of your servant; save me, because I serve you just as my mother did. **17** Give me a sign of your goodness, that my enemies may see it and be put to shame, for you, LORD, have helped me and comforted me.

LEARN FROM YOUR CRITICS. Proud men are attacking David, men who "have no regard" for God (verse 14). Considering their character, verses 15–16 are remarkable. Instead of invoking God's justice and calling for his enemies' destruction, he turns the spotlight on himself. He appeals to God's mercy, grateful for his patience with him. David is open to correction, willing to examine himself to see if, despite his enemies' evil motivations, there might be something in him that warrants rebuke and needs to change. If someone is criticizing you and the criticism is mostly mistaken, identify the 20 percent of the indictment that *is* fair. Without excuse be willing to take it to heart. The strongest Christians are the ones most willing to repent.

Prayer: Lord, you not only show us ourselves through your Word and through our friends. You also have messages for us that are carried by our critics and opponents. Give me the security in your love that I will need to profit from them. Amen.

August 1

READ Psalm 87. **1** He has founded his city on the holy mountain. **2** The LORD loves the gates of Zion more than all the other dwellings of Jacob. **3** Glorious things are said of you, city of God: **4** "I will record Rahab and Babylon among those who acknowledge me—Philistia too, and Tyre, along with Cush—and will say, 'This one was born in Zion.'" **5** Indeed, of Zion it will be said, "This one and that one were born in her, and the Most High himself will establish her." **6** The LORD will write in the register of the peoples: "This one was born in Zion." **7** As they make music they will sing, "All my fountains are in you."

ALL MY JOY. Here is a vision of the new world city of the future, its citizens coming from every tongue, tribe, people, and nation. Even former enemies are reconciled (verses 4–6). Through faith in Christ we, his former enemies, are recorded in the book of life (Philippians 4:3). We are already citizens of that future city which is filled with fountains of endless joy (verse 6; Philippians 3:20). Can any fountain be ugly? The music of running water and the beauty of water leaping and falling are always joyful in a special way. Those whom God numbers among his people know that all their joy comes from God, springing, dancing, descending, and ascending like a fountain.

Prayer: Lord Jesus, you alone have the "water of life" that brings satisfaction and joy—your grace and eternal life. Prevent me from looking to anything else for my happiness. *"Who can faint while such a river, ever flows, our thirst to assuage? Grace which like the Lord the Giver, never fails from age to age?"*[84] Amen.

August 2

READ Psalm 88:1–9. **1** LORD, the God who saves me; day and night I cry out to you. **2** May my prayer come before you; turn your ear to my cry. **3** I am overwhelmed with troubles and my life draws near to death. **4** I am counted among those who go down to the pit; I am like one without strength. **5** I am set apart with the dead, like the slain who lie in the grave, whom you remember no more, who are cut off from your care. **6** You have put me in the lowest pit, in the darkest depths. **7** Your wrath lies heavily on me; you have overwhelmed me with all your waves. **8** You have taken from me my closest friends and have made me repulsive to them. I am confined and cannot escape; **9** my eyes are dim with grief. I call to you, LORD, every day; I spread out my hands to you.

THE DARKEST DEPTHS. The psalmist feels overwhelmed and forgotten. This prayer will end in darkness, without a note of hope. But the psalm title tells us the author was Heman, a leader of the Kohathite guild of musicians who wrote many of the psalms, some of the greatest literature in world history. His experiences of darkness turned him into an artist who has helped millions of people. In his despair he thought God had abandoned him, but he hadn't. Christians know that Jesus took the ultimate darkness of God's wrath (Matthew 27:45). Since he took the abandonment we deserve, we know that God will not abandon us (Hebrews 13:5). He is there with us, even when we can't feel him at all.

Prayer: Lord, these psalms teach that we can bring you our anger, fear, and despair and lay them before you unfiltered. You understand. Yet as I do so I pray you will make yourself real to my heart so that, like a morning fog, these things can be burned away by the light of your presence. Amen.

August 3

READ Psalm 88:10–18. **10** Do you show your wonders to the dead? Do the spirits rise up and praise you? **11** Is your love declared in the grave, your faithfulness in Destruction? **12** Are your wonders known in the place of darkness, or your righteous deeds in the land of oblivion? **13** But I cry to you for help, LORD; in the morning my prayer comes before you. **14** Why, LORD, do you reject me and hide your face from me? **15** From my youth I have suffered and been close to death; I have borne your terrors and am in despair. **16** Your wrath has swept over me; your terrors have destroyed me. **17** All day long they surround me like a flood; they have completely engulfed me. **18** You have taken from me my friend and neighbor—darkness is my closest friend.

SATAN DEFEATED. This is one of the few psalms that end without some light, without an expression of hope and trust. Why did God include this psalm in his Scripture, where it would be recited and sung for thousands of years? First, it teaches us that sometimes periods of spiritual darkness can last a long time. Also, it shows us what to do in such periods: tell God about our hopelessness. We can worship God even with our despair. And such prayers in the dark are more victorious than they look. Satan told God that no one serves him unless they are getting something out of it, but here we see a man praying and serving God for nothing (Job 1:9). So Satan is defeated.

Prayer: Lord, I praise you that you are a God who understands what it is like to be human! That you understand what it is to be hopeless in the dark. That you have been tried and tempted in every way, as we have. So when I struggle I can go to you, my wonderful counselor, in my need. Amen.

August 4

READ Psalm 89:1–8. **1** I will sing of the LORD's great love forever; with my mouth I will make your faithfulness known through all generations. **2** I will declare that your love stands firm forever, that you established your faithfulness in heaven itself. **3** You said, "I have made a covenant with my chosen one, I have sworn to David my servant, **4** 'I will establish your line forever and make your throne firm through all generations.'" **5** The heavens praise your wonders, LORD, your faithfulness too, in the assembly of the holy ones. **6** For who in the skies above can compare with the LORD? Who is like the LORD among the heavenly beings? **7** In the council of the holy ones God is greatly feared; he is more awesome than all who surround him. **8** Who is like you, LORD God Almighty? You, LORD, are mighty, and your faithfulness surrounds you.

MAKING YOUR CASE. God invites us through this psalm to argue with him, the way a lawyer argues a case. The psalmist tells God not merely what he wants but why it fits with God's own character and purposes. He begins his case by pointing to God's covenant faithfulness (verses 1–2) and his promise to establish the line of David *forever* (verses 2 and 4). This is a model for our prayers. We should give theological reasons for what we ask, explaining how they fit in with God's character, salvation, and goals for the world. If we make our petitions this way, we will both deepen our own understanding of his ways and come away with a sense that we have really cast our burdens on him.

Prayer: Lord, my prayer life is so thin and cursory. Move me and teach me to lay my needs and concerns before you, grounding my requests in your own promises and Word. Such prayers honor you and deepen me and lift my heart and change the world. Amen.

August 5

READ Psalm 89:9–18. **9** You rule over the surging sea; when its waves mount up, you still them. **10** You crushed Rahab like one of the slain; with your strong arm you scattered your enemies. **11** The heavens are yours, and yours also the earth; you founded the world and all that is in it. **12** You created the north and the south; Tabor and Hermon sing for joy at your name. **13** Your arm is endowed with power; your hand is strong, your right hand exalted. **14** Righteousness and justice are the foundation of your throne; love and faithfulness go before you. **15** Blessed are those who have learned to acclaim you, who walk in the light of your presence, LORD. **16** They rejoice in your name all day long; they celebrate your righteousness. **17** For you are their glory and strength, and by your favor you exalt our horn. **18** Indeed, our shield belongs to the LORD, our king to the Holy One of Israel.

MIGHT AND RIGHT. Here are two attributes of God. He is all-powerful (verses 9–13) and he is perfectly righteous (verses 14–18). To those confident of their own insight, suffering disproves the existence of such a God. They reason that he would want to end suffering if he were good, and he would do so if he were omnipotent. Since evil continues, they conclude, God can't be both. But we should admit that an infinite God could have good reasons for allowing suffering that our finite minds can't fathom. Once we take the more humble stance, God's attributes are of deep comfort. Because he is all-powerful, nothing is out of his control. Because he is perfectly righteous, everything will eventually work together for good in the end (Genesis 50:20).

Prayer: Lord, my heart often resents your power and questions your righteousness. But when I think I know better than you, I sink under anxiety. How truly "blessed are those who have learned to acclaim you" (verse 15)! The more I accept your goodness and control of things, the more I can relax. Amen.

August 6

LOOK ON THE HEART. The psalmist recounts how David became king (1 Samuel 16–17). While Saul and David's brother Eliab were kingly in height and stature, God chose young David. Even the prophet Samuel was fooled, but God warned him, "People look at the outward appearance, but the LORD looks at the heart" (1 Samuel 16:7). Only God sees things truly, and true beauty and greatness are a matter of character (1 Peter 3:3–4). Contrary to our culture's idolization of sleekness, heart character is infinitely more important than physical beauty. It is also more important than talent or brilliance, neither of which can prevent life shipwrecks. Are you growing less selfish, more loving, less self-pitying, less vain, more joyful, wiser, less sensitive to criticism? That's what matters.

Prayer: Father, David was not driven but called. He was not a career-oriented empire builder; he simply wanted to do your will, and you used him. Make me like David by your grace, which I have received only through faith in David's greater Son, Jesus. Amen.

August 7

READ Psalm 89:27–37. **27** And I will also appoint him to be my firstborn, the most exalted of the kings of the earth. **28** I will maintain my love to him forever, and my covenant with him will never fail. **29** I will establish his line forever, his throne as long as the heavens endure. **30** "If his sons forsake my law and do not follow my statutes, **31** if they violate my decrees and fail to keep my commands, **32** I will punish their sin with the rod, their iniquity with flogging; **33** but I will not take my love from him, nor will I ever betray my faithfulness. **34** I will not violate my covenant or alter what my lips have uttered. **35** Once for all, I have sworn by my holiness—and I will not lie to David— **36** that his line will continue forever and his throne endure before me like the sun; **37** it will be established forever like the moon, the faithful witness in the sky."

EXPECTATION RAISED. If before you walk into a room you are told, "This is a prison cell," you may think, "This is pretty nice." But if before you walk into that same room you are told, "This is a honeymoon suite," you may respond, "What a dump!" Expectations control how we interpret experience. God said David's kingdom would last forever (verse 29; 2 Samuel 7:4–17) and would grow to encompass the other nations on the earth (verse 27). The psalmist, as we will see, thought this language meant that the political nation of Israel could never fail. We too listen to God's promises and read our own expectations into them. Then we find ourselves disappointed with God. But it is really our fault.

Prayer: Lord, I read into your promises—to bless me, care for me, and keep me—my own agenda and then hold you responsible if you don't serve it. Thus I turn you into my servant instead of turning myself into your servant. Forgive me for wronging you in this way! Amen.

August 8

READ Psalm 89:38–45. **38** But you have rejected, you have spurned, you have been very angry with your anointed one. **39** You have renounced the covenant with your servant and have defiled his crown in the dust. **40** You have broken through all his walls and reduced his strongholds to ruins. **41** All who pass by have plundered him; he has become the scorn of his neighbors. **42** You have exalted the right hand of his foes; you have made all his enemies rejoice. **43** Indeed, you have turned back the edge of his sword and have not supported him in battle. **44** You have put an end to his splendor and cast his throne to the ground. **45** You have cut short the days of his youth; you have covered him with a mantle of shame.

EXPECTATION DISAPPOINTED. The psalmist complains that God has renounced his covenant with David (verse 39). Israel has been plundered, conquered, and led into exile (verses 40–45). How could the promises given to David for an endless kingdom fit with such a disaster? Many who welcomed Jesus as Messiah also had their expectations disappointed when he failed to take power. When he died on the cross, they could not imagine how God could be honoring his promises to save us by letting such tragedy happen. But the exile to Babylon and the horror of the cross were events that moved the history of our salvation forward. Learn that God always fulfills his promises but does so at a level of greater complexity than we can easily discern.

Prayer: Lord, you hide yourself in history, but you don't hide yourself in your Word. Often I can't discern you working in my life, but when I read about your saving purposes in the lives of Joseph, Job, David, and Jesus himself, it becomes clear that you never fail to help and save. Thank you for your Word; help me trust in it. Amen.

August 9

READ Psalm 89:46–52. **46** How long, LORD? Will you hide yourself forever? How long will your wrath burn like fire? **47** Remember how fleeting is my life. For what futility you have created all humanity! **48** Who can live and not see death, or who can escape the power of the grave? **49** Lord, where is your former great love, which in your faithfulness you swore to David? **50** Remember, Lord, how your servant has been mocked, how I bear in my heart the taunts of all the nations, **51** the taunts with which your enemies, LORD, have mocked, with which they have mocked every step of your anointed one. **52** Praise be to the LORD forever! Amen and Amen.

EXPECTATION FULFILLED. The psalmist faces the conflict between God's apparent offer and its lack of fulfillment. He does not shy away from expressing disappointment, yet there is more perplexity than bitterness. We now know that, contrary to appearances, God's promises to David did not fall short of expectations. Indeed their fulfillment in Jesus Christ exceeded all expectations in undreamed-of ways. Jesus was the descendant of David who was literally God's firstborn Son, who is drawing all nations to himself and who will literally rule the world forever (verse 26–29). So this psalm is a model. Pray your disappointments but leave them with God. Remember, you just can't see. And when he answers us, it will be far better and more astonishing than anything we could have asked for.

Prayer: Lord, I praise you that your promises will always give us *more* than we dare think they promise us, not less. I've had a small taste of this over the years. You have helped me in deeper, wiser, and better ways than I originally imagined as a new believer. Let me live in joyful anticipation of my unimaginably great future with you. Amen.

August 10

READ Psalm 90:1–4. **1** Lord, you have been our dwelling place throughout all generations. **2** Before the mountains were born or you brought forth the whole world, from everlasting to everlasting you are God. **3** You turn people back to dust, saying, "Return to dust, you mortals." **4** A thousand years in your sight are like a day that has just gone by, or like a watch in the night.

THIS SHORT LIFE. Verse 4 is one the most widely quoted verses in the psalms because it comforts us when we are frustrated with God's timing. Time moves slowly for us, as we crawl from moment to moment. God, who inhabits eternity, sees all of history in a single moment, so his timetable is unlikely to match our own. The psalm's author, Moses, seems to look at life from the vantage point of old age, from where we can finally see, as God does, that our time here is short. Let this psalm make you wise before your time (see verse 12), when you still can determine to not waste your life on trifles. Soon it will be too late.

Prayer: Lord, life is going by so fast! It frightens me unless I remember your eternity. We are as rootless as tumbleweeds and will be blown about all our lives unless you are our dwelling place. In you we are *home.* What I have in you I can never lose and will have forever. I praise you for this unfathomable comfort. Amen.

August 11

READ Psalm 90:5–12. **5** Yet you sweep people away in the sleep of death—they are like the new grass of the morning: **6** In the morning it springs up new, but by evening it is dry and withered. **7** We are consumed by your anger and terrified by your indignation. **8** You have set our iniquities before you, our secret sins in the light of your presence. **9** All our days pass away under your wrath; we finish our years with a moan. **10** Our days may come to seventy years, or eighty, if our strength endures; yet the best of them are but trouble and sorrow, for they quickly pass, and we fly away. **11** If only we knew the power of your anger! Your wrath is as great as the fear that is your due. **12** Teach us to number our days, that we may gain a heart of wisdom.

WE FLY AWAY. We are painfully reminded that our lives are exercises in disintegration—we are wearing down and wearing out until we are dust again (verse 3; cf. Genesis 2:7). Verses 7–11 remind us that death is not the natural order of things but the effect of our turning from God and the curse on all creation (Genesis 3:1–19). Without this robust doctrine of sin, we will not be wise (verse 12). We will be constantly shocked by what people (and we) are capable of, by how life swiftly takes away everything we love. We will trust in our own abilities too much and seek satisfaction in things that we will inevitably lose. Face sin and death or be out of touch with reality.

Prayer: Lord, I have not done the profound soul work necessary to be ready to die. Give me the strength to ask the big question: Would I be ready to die tomorrow? Be such a "living, bright reality"[85] to me that I can answer that question wisely and then do what is necessary. Amen.

August 12

READ Psalm 90:13–17. **13** Relent, LORD! How long will it be? Have compassion on your servants. **14** Satisfy us in the morning with your unfailing love, that we may sing for joy and be glad all our days. **15** Make us glad for as many days as you have afflicted us, for as many years as we have seen trouble. **16** May your deeds be shown to your servants, your splendor to their children. **17** May the favor of the Lord our God rest upon us; establish the work of our hands for us—yes, establish the work of our hands.

UNFAILING LOVE. We never want to lose those we really love. We finite beings cannot realize that goal. But if we connect ourselves to God's "unfailing," unending love (verse 14), that love overcomes our mortality, and then we never end. This is Moses's intuition, but Christians know that those who believe in Jesus, the Resurrection and the Life, "shall live, even though they die" (John 11:25). So let nothing trouble you, but get satisfaction in his love every morning (verse 14). And let nothing dazzle you, but see God's splendor as the only enduring kind (verse 16). And let nothing move you, for God will establish the work of your hands (verse 17).

Prayer: Lord, once your love takes hold of me, even death can only bring me closer to you. *"The sinner, sleeping in his grave, shall at my voice awake; For when I once begin to save, my work I ne'er forsake."*[86] I love you for loving me like that! Amen.

August 13

READ Psalm 91:1–4. **1** He who dwells in the shelter of the Most High will rest in the shadow of the Almighty. **2** I will say of the Lord, "He is my refuge and my fortress, my God, in whom I trust." **3** Surely he will save you from the fowler's snare and from the deadly pestilence. **4** He will cover you with his feathers, and under his wings you will find refuge; his faithfulness will be your shield and rampart.

TWO WAYS GOD PROTECTS. Two contrasting metaphors are used for God's protection: a fortress filled with shields and ramparts; and a mother bird gathering her brood underneath her wings. The fortress has walls of impregnable strength. Spears and arrows make not a dent. The mother bird, however, shelters with wings that are essentially fragile. She shelters her young from burning heat or rain and cold only by bearing them herself. The Old Testament does not explain how this impervious strength and sacrificial, loving weakness could be combined in God. It is on the cross where we see the absolute righteous power and the tender, sacrificial love of God combine and shine forth brilliantly, both equally fulfilled.

Prayer: Lord, I praise you for both your majesty and your meekness in Jesus Christ. *"Let us wonder! Grace and justice join and point to mercy's store; When through grace in Christ our trust is, justice smiles and asks no more: He Who washed us with His blood has secured our way to God."*[87] Amen.

August 14

READ Psalm 91:5–13. **5** You will not fear the terror of night, nor the arrow that flies by day, **6** nor the pestilence that stalks in the darkness, nor the plague that destroys at midday. **7** A thousand may fall at your side, ten thousand at your right hand, but it will not come near you. **8** You will only observe with your eyes and see the punishment of the wicked. **9** If you say, "The LORD, is my refuge," and you make the Most High your dwelling, **10** no harm will overtake you, no disaster will come near your tent. **11** For he will command his angels concerning you to guard you in all your ways; **12** they will lift you up in their hands, so that you will not strike your foot against a stone. **13** You will tread on the lion and the cobra; you will trample the great lion and the serpent.

NO HARM WILL BEFALL YOU. These verses seem to promise that nothing bad will ever happen to believers. And when Satan quotes verse 11 to Jesus in the wilderness, that is what he suggests (Luke 4:9–12). The devil wants us to think that God's promises have failed if he lets us suffer. But the psalm later clarifies that God will save us *"in* trouble" not *from* it (see verse 15). Luke 21:16–18 says paradoxically that under God's care "not a hair of your head will perish" and yet "they will put some of you to death." The only things faithful people can lose in suffering are things that are finally expendable. The real you, the one God is creating (Philippians 1:6; 2 Corinthians 3:18, 4:16–17), cannot be harmed.

Prayer: Lord, I value worldly things over grace, love, and holiness, so I am too discouraged by trials and troubles. They can harm my false self—the one built on appearance, social status, and human approval. But they can't harm my true identity as your child. They can only make it stronger! Teach me how to grow into your likeness in my afflictions. Amen.

August 15

READ Psalm 91:14–16. **14** "Because he loves me," says the LORD, "I will rescue him; I will protect him, for he acknowledges my name. **15** He will call on me, and I will answer him; I will be with him in trouble, I will deliver him and honor him. **16** With long life will I satisfy him and show him my salvation."

SWEETS COMPACTED. In short compass God makes seven promises to those who set their love on him (verse 14). The first four are practical. He will rescue and protect us, answer our prayers, and be by our side in trouble (verses 14–15). The last three, however, take us to a horizon just beyond our sight. He gives us "honor," or literally *glory* (verse 15). The esteem and worth we strive so hard to achieve and to get from others he bestows on us. It is beyond imagining: *his* high regard, his "Well done"—a gift of his grace. He also gives us endless, eternal life and a salvation of body and soul no longer waited for but known fully (Romans 8:11, 23–25). Here is truly "a box where sweets compacted lie."[88]

Prayer: Father, I want applause, approval, and praise from others. But that enslaves me. At night I toss in bed at snubs, at being ignored. Criticism feels like death. Help me live out of the joy and stability of knowing that I am your child and heir and that in Christ you delight in me. Amen.

August 16

READ Psalm 92:1–4. **1** It is good to praise the LORD and make music to your name, O Most High, **2** proclaiming your love in the morning and your faithfulness at night, **3** to the music of the ten-stringed lyre and the melody of the harp. **4** For you make me glad by your deeds, LORD; I sing for joy at what your hands have done.

SONG FOR THE SABBATH. This psalm's title is "A Song for the Sabbath Day." To us the word "rest" conveys mainly inactivity, but the main way the Biblical Sabbath day renews strength and joy is through worship. Praise is "good" (verse 1). Anything that we love or serve more than God becomes an idol that saps our strength. Idols of career or money or relationship are never satisfied. So the worship of the true God of perfect love restores and invigorates us. Verse 4 says we should find our joy in "what [God's] hands have done" (verse 4). Christians know more about his work of salvation than did former generations. We have far more reason to sing for joy than anyone, because we are loved with the costly love of the cross.

Prayer: Lord, let me know the rest and restoration that come from real worship. Only there can I get relief from the drain of worry, of self-consciousness, and of resentment. Send your Spirit to "make me glad by your deeds" and "sing for joy at what your hands have done." Amen.

August 17

READ Psalm 92:5–9. **5** How great are your works, LORD, how profound your thoughts! **6** Senseless people do not know, fools do not understand, **7** that though the wicked spring up like grass and all evildoers flourish, they will be forever destroyed. **8** But you, LORD, are forever exalted. **9** For surely your enemies, LORD, surely your enemies will perish; all evildoers will be scattered.

OPEN OUR EYES. The worship of God does not only make us rejoice; it also opens our minds and makes us think. We are all naturally as blind to spiritual realities as a physically blind person is to his or her surrounding environment. We look at nature and can't discern an author. We look at history and can't see God's hand, so we take credit for things that are his gifts. We read the Gospel and find it a foolish story. Even believers find that there is a dullness to their vision, that they don't see things clearly. They see men who "look like trees walking" (Mark 8:24) and need continual sight improvement through the healing touch of Jesus.

Prayer: Lord, through your Spirit's work in my life I see things now in my heart I used to be blind to. I see wondrous, moving, captivating things in your Word that I used to find uninteresting. Keep touching my eyes, my healer, until I see clearly. Amen.

August 18

READ Psalm 92:10–15. **10** You have exalted my horn like that of a wild ox; fine oils have been poured on me. **11** My eyes have seen the defeat of my adversaries; my ears have heard the rout of my wicked foes. **12** The righteous will flourish like a palm tree, they will grow like a cedar of Lebanon; **13** planted in the house of the LORD, they will flourish in the courts of our God. **14** They will still bear fruit in old age, they will stay fresh and green, **15** proclaiming, "The LORD is upright; he is my Rock, and there is no wickedness in him."

FRESHNESS WITH AGE. Verse 10 speaks of a "horn," a symbol of strength, being anointed, a symbol of refreshment. Only through worship are we restored to vigor from the exhaustion and burnout of seeking our own glory. And if we maintain fellowship with God over the years (verse 13), there is a kind of "freshness" that can come with increasing age. It is not the naïveté of perpetual spiritual adolescence. It is the spiritual vigor that grows only out of years of trusting God in prayer, coupled with the wisdom that comes from a treasure chest of rich memories, both sorrowful and sweet. "Though outwardly we are wasting away, yet inwardly we are being renewed day by day" (2 Corinthians 4:16).

Prayer: Lord, as I age let there be a flourishing of my faith and a liveliness to my worship that I didn't have in earlier years. Make me stronger in spirit the weaker I become in the flesh. Amen.

August 19

READ Psalm 93. **1** The LORD reigns, he is robed in majesty; the LORD is robed in majesty and armed with strength. Indeed, the world is established, firm and secure. **2** Your throne was established long ago; you are from all eternity. **3** The seas have lifted up, LORD, the seas have lifted up their voice; the seas have lifted up their pounding waves. **4** Mightier than the thunder of the great waters, mightier than the breakers of the sea—the LORD on high is mighty. **5** Your statutes, LORD, stand firm; holiness adorns your house for endless days.

MIGHTIER THAN THE SEA. The sea was feared as the source of chaos and the habitat of monsters, but God's rule is absolute over all such forces (verses 3–4). It is for this reason that we should obey his word ("your statutes," verse 5) and put on holiness in his presence. But God's holiness is more threatening than the stormy sea. How can we stand before a holy God? Jesus's stilling of the storm (Mark 4:35–41) is a sign of his triumph over the ultimate chaos of sin and death on the cross. Because of God's power, both in creation and salvation, the world is safe for you. When you stand on the seashore, do you let it move you to praise our Creator and Redeemer?

Prayer: Lord, when I see a ray of brilliant light, my eye naturally runs up the shaft to see its source. Why don't I do that with the mountains and the sea and the other wonders of your natural world? Give me the habit of mind that uses all good things as ways to understand and enjoy you better. Amen.

August 20

READ Psalm 94:1–10. **1** The LORD is a God who avenges. O God who avenges, shine forth. **2** Rise up, Judge of the earth; pay back to the proud what they deserve. **3** How long, LORD, will the wicked, how long will the wicked be jubilant? **4** They pour out arrogant words; all the evildoers are full of boasting. **5** They crush your people, LORD; they oppress your inheritance. **6** They slay the widow and the foreigner; they murder the fatherless. **7** They say, "The LORD does not see; the God of Jacob takes no notice." **8** Take notice, you senseless ones among the people; you fools, when will you become wise? **9** Does he who fashioned the ear not hear? Does he who formed the eye not see? **10** Does he who disciplines nations not punish? Does he who teaches mankind lack knowledge?

OPPRESSORS. There is much anger today against the greedy and heartless wealthy. God is the avenger of those who have been oppressed in every age, and he will judge those who use the power of their money to enhance their lives at the expense of others. Riches are not an evil in themselves, as Abraham and Job demonstrate, but they are an enormous temptation to self-sufficiency (1 Timothy 6:9–10). George Herbert's stinging poem "Avarice" describes how, by overloving money, we give it a power over us that dehumanizes us. He says to money: "Man calleth thee his wealth, who made thee rich; And while he digs out thee, falls in the ditch."[89] God's judgment on oppressors takes many forms.

Prayer: Lord, I praise you for being a God who avenges the weak and marginalized. But this truth is a two-edged sword. It comforts me when I see the horrendous inequities in the world. Yet it also confronts me with my own complacency in my comfortable life and my indifference to those in need. Go on dealing with my heart until I change my life. Amen.

August 21

READ Psalm 94:11–15. **11** The LORD knows all human plans; he knows that they are futile. **12** Blessed is the one you discipline, LORD, the one you teach from your law; **13** you grant them relief from days of trouble, till a pit is dug for the wicked. **14** For the LORD will not reject his people; he will never forsake his inheritance. **15** Judgment will again be founded on righteousness, and all the upright in heart will follow it.

BLESSED DISCIPLINE. If all our inward thoughts on Monday were somehow put out on the Internet on Tuesday, we would lose all our friends. We think we can hide our self-indulgent, cruel, envious, lustful thoughts, but God sees (verse 11). That is why wise believers actually rejoice in discipline, the kind of trouble that drives them to God's law and Word (verse 12). Through this they get "relief" (verse 13), a word that means "inward quietness in face of outward troubles."[90] While God may test and refine us, he won't abandon us (verse 14) despite our sin. Why not? It is because God passed sentence on evil and then suffered the punishment himself in Jesus. Thus we can know "he will never forsake his inheritance" (verse 14).

Prayer: Lord, help me to remember that you know all my thoughts. During the day let me live—and think—before your face. Let me practice your presence all day. Then I will not give in to foolish lines of inner self-talk that only darken my heart. Change my futile thoughts, O Lord. Amen.

August 22

YOUR CONSOLATION. The psalmist confesses that he experienced great anxiety and was saved from it only by God's consolations (verse 19). What are those consolations? Chief among them is the theme of the psalm, namely, that God will not get history—yours, mine, the world's—wrong. He will right all wrongs in the world. He will allow into our lives only the troubles that refine us. But the deeper comfort beneath even these comforts is that in Jesus we have a champion. When the psalmist asks for someone to fight on his behalf (verse 16), he is asking for a champion like David, who fought Goliath so the Israelites didn't have to. Jesus is our champion, who took our punishment so we don't have to.

Prayer: Father, your servant David risked his life to fight the giant on his people's behalf. But your Son *lost* his life to fight sin and death on my behalf. Help me to gaze on and contemplate the courage of Jesus on my behalf, until it creates self-forgetful courage in me. Amen.

August 23

READ Psalm 95.1–4. 1 Come, let us sing for joy to the LORD; let us shout aloud to the Rock of our salvation. 2 Let us come before him with thanksgiving and extol him with music and song. 3 For the LORD is the great God, the great King above all gods. 4 In his hand are the depths of the earth, and the mountain peaks belong to him.

RISE UP. This psalm and the next give us almost a liturgy for a service of gathered worship. The first stage is adoration. Let us *rise up in joy to God the Creator* (verses 1–5). Let us praise him for being the maker and sustainer of the world. Worshipping is not always quiet and decorous. It can entail shouting, praising, leaping to our feet, singing our hearts out. When the love of the immeasurably great and transcendent God of the universe becomes real to us, the joy should be uncontainable.

Prayer: Lord, you are eternal, ever present, perfect in knowledge and wisdom, absolute in power, spotless in your purity, completely just and righteous, beautiful in your glory. You are all this, yet my praise falls so short of your reality that I am ashamed. Accept my praise through the merits of Jesus, my Savior. Amen.

August 24

READ Psalm 95:5–7. **5** The sea is his, for he made it, and his hands formed the dry land. **6** Come, let us bow down in worship, let us kneel before the LORD our Maker; **7** for he is our God and we are the people of his pasture, the flock under his care.

KNEEL DOWN. The next element of worship is confession of our sin and need. Let us *bow down in humility to God the Redeemer* (verses 6–7). In contrast to the exuberance of the first five verses, which fits with the postures of standing or even dancing, each of the three verbs in verse 6 have to do with getting low before God, since the Hebrew word for "worship" here literally means to prostrate oneself. We are to bow reverently, to kneel humbly before God, admitting our sinfulness and dependence. While adoration comes from seeing a God of glory, submission comes from seeing a God of grace, one who is *our* covenant God, who redeemed us and brought us as sheep into his fold (verse 7).

Prayer: Lord, I confess the blindness of my understanding, the stubbornness of my will, the foolishness of my thought life, and the addiction of my heart to things of this world. *"False and full of sin I am; Thou art full of truth and grace."*[91] Without that grace I am lost. I praise you that in Christ your grace abounds to me. Amen.

August 25

READ Psalm 95:8–11. Today, if only you would hear his voice, **8** "Do not harden your hearts as you did at Meribah, as you did that day at Massah in the wilderness, **9** where your ancestors tested me; they tried me, though they had seen what I did. **10** For forty years I was angry with that generation; I said, 'They are a people whose hearts go astray, and they have not known my ways.' **11** So I declared on oath in my anger, 'They shall never enter my rest.'"

LISTEN WELL. Let us *listen now to the rest giver* (verses 7–11). The third element in corporate worship is to soften our hearts and listen to God's Word read, studied, and taught. Israel failed to do this (Numbers 14:1–44), but Hebrews 4:1–13 says that we too can fail. In Christ we are offered not a physical promised land but the ultimate rest—rest from the crushing burden of self-salvation through effort and performance (Hebrews 4:10). Why wouldn't everyone want to enter such rest? Because it is a freedom unknown to modern people—one that is on the far side of trusting God rather than ourselves.

Prayer: Father, how I need rest! I am weary with obeying the dictates of my fears, my drives, my need for approval and control. I need the deep peace of soul that comes when I stop trying to earn my salvation through my works and rest in your Son's finished work of salvation for me. Amen.

August 26

READ Psalm 96:1–9. **1** Sing to the LORD a new song; sing to the LORD, all the earth. **2** Sing to the LORD, praise his name; proclaim his salvation day after day. **3** Declare his glory among the nations, his marvelous deeds among all peoples. **4** For great is the LORD and most worthy of praise; he is to be feared above all gods. **5** For all the gods of the nations are idols, but the LORD made the heavens. **6** Splendor and majesty are before him; strength and glory are in his sanctuary. **7** Ascribe to the LORD, all you families of nations, ascribe to the LORD glory and strength. **8** Ascribe to the LORD the glory due his name; bring an offering and come into his courts. **9** Worship the LORD in the splendor of his holiness; tremble before him, all the earth.

SPEAK OUT. Worship is to be done "among the nations" (verse 3). Verse 2 says that as we worship we are "proclaim[ing] his salvation"—literally bearing tidings of good news. There is no better way to show skeptics the greatness of God and the beauty of his truth than through worship (verses 4–10). Our worship is to be compelling to nonbelievers; that is "a corrective to static worship and shallow preaching alike."[92] And dynamic worship is not just a means to winning the world but it also provides our motivation to do so. Only a heart filled with overflowing joy will want to share the source of that joy with everyone they meet. If you had the cure for cancer, would you keep it a secret? Worship propels us into the world to serve and love.

Prayer: Lord, grow my understanding of your grace until it rids me of the self-consciousness, lethargy, and pessimism that keep me from opening my mouth and identifying as a Christian in public. Forgive me for being silent about all you've done for me. Amen.

August 27

READ Psalm 96:10–13. **10** Say among the nations, "The LORD reigns." The world is firmly established, it cannot be moved; he will judge the peoples with equity. **11** Let the heavens rejoice, let the earth be glad; let the sea resound, and all that is in it. **12** Let the fields be jubilant, and everything in them; let all the trees of the forest sing for joy. **13** Let all creation rejoice before the LORD, for he comes, he comes to judge the earth. He will judge the world in righteousness and the peoples in his faithfulness.

LOOK FORWARD. All creation will rejoice at God's final coming to earth, when the long night of oppression, evil, and sin will be ended. The trees will sing praise when the world healer finally returns to judge and renew the earth (verses 11–13). "Where God rules . . . His humblest creatures can be themselves; where God is there is singing. At the creation 'the morning stars sang together'; at His coming, the earth will at last join in again; meanwhile the Psalter itself shows what effect His presence has on those who, even through a glass, darkly, already see his face."[93] Will you rejoice to see that day, knowing that in Christ there is no condemnation of you, only loving acceptance into God's family? Or are you still unsure?

Prayer: Lord, fill me with the daily joy and hope that come from my desire to see you face to face on that final day. *"Weak is the effort of my heart, and cold my warmest thought; But when I see Thee as Thou art, I'll praise Thee as I ought."*[94] Amen.

August 28

READ Psalm 97:1–5. **1** The LORD reigns, let the earth be glad; let the distant shores rejoice. **2** Clouds and thick darkness surround him; righteousness and justice are the foundation of his throne. **3** Fire goes before him and consumes his foes on every side. **4** His lightning lights up the world; the earth sees and trembles. **5** The mountains melt like wax before the LORD, before the Lord of all the earth.

THE FIRE OF GOD. God's return to renew the world will bring worldwide joy (verse 1). But the psalm then describes an intimidating scenario. God's presence burns and consumes all that is unwell and twisted in his world. There will be those who refuse his kingship, and for them his coming will bring dismay (verses 1–5). What is this fire? It is the fire of God's holy love, which must remove the impurities that ruin the creation he loves (verse 3; Deuteronomy 4:24; Hebrews 12:29). We should not find this strange. If we love someone, we must hate whatever is ruining their lives, even if it is their own choices. Because God is perfect love, he cannot abide evil and sin.

Prayer: Lord, I praise you that you are perfect in your holiness and moral beauty. There is no evil in you, nor can it exist in your presence. This is all my hope for change. Draw me nearer to you so the remaining sin in me can be exposed and consumed by your grace. Amen.

August 29

READ Psalm 97:6–9. **6** The heavens proclaim his righteousness, and all peoples see his glory. **7** All who worship images are put to shame, those who boast in idols—worship him, all you gods! **8** Zion hears and rejoices and the villages of Judah are glad because of your judgments, LORD. **9** For you, LORD, are the Most High over all the earth; you are exalted far above all gods.

WORSHIP HIM, ALL YOU GODS! We must forsake our idols (verse 7). Idols are often good things that have become ultimate sources of meaning. Good things need not be removed from our lives, but their place within our hearts must be transformed. In an interesting phrase, these gods are called to "worship him!" (verse 7). When we make our career into a god, it demands, as it were, to be considered an end in itself. It whispers, "Only if you have me, only if you are successful, will your life be valid." Instead you must let God's love and regard for you be the new ground of your identity. Then your career can be made to say, "I'm important, but not all-important. I'm just a way to serve God."

Prayer: Lord, your grace has cut down the tree of sin in my life, but the stump and its roots are still there and go deep. *"Lord! Must I always guilty prove, and idols in my heart have room? Oh! Let the fire of heavenly love the very stump of Self consume."*[95] Amen.

August 30

READ Psalm 97:10–12. **10** Let those who love the LORD hate evil, for he guards the lives of his faithful ones and delivers them from the hand of the wicked. **11** Light shines on the righteous and joy on the upright in heart. **12** Rejoice in the LORD, you who are righteous, and praise his holy name.

LIGHT IS SOWN ON THE RIGHTEOUS. If we remove our idols (verse 7), light shines on us (verse 11). Some older translations say light is "sown" in us. Light refers both to truth and the clarity it brings as well as to holiness and the beauty it brings. God's light is perfect knowledge and infinite glory. When we believe in Christ, God's Spirit indwells us (1 Corinthians 3:16; 2 Timothy 1:14; Romans 8:9–11). God then indeed "sows" light in us, and like a seed that grows it will spread wisdom and beauty in our lives. Christians find what they see in the world and in their own hearts making more sense. And people around Christians see them slowly but surely turning into something loving and beautiful.

Prayer: Lord, I praise you that you are a God of light, that in you is no darkness at all. There is still, however, plenty of darkness in me. I am blind to my faults; I find it hard to "see" your glory and love during the day. Fill my inner being with your light, whatever the cost. Amen.

August 31

READ Psalm 98.1-6. **1** Sing to the LORD a new song, for he has done marvelous things; his right hand and his holy arm have worked salvation for him. **2** The LORD has made his salvation known and revealed his righteousness to the nations. **3** He has remembered his love and his faithfulness to Israel; all the ends of the earth have seen the salvation of our God. **4** Shout for joy to the LORD, all the earth, burst into jubilant song with music; **5** make music to the LORD with the harp, with the harp and the sound of singing, **6** with trumpets and the blast of the ram's horn—shout for joy before the LORD, the King.

SHOUT! This psalm praises God for the exodus (verses 1–3). We know, however, that from the cross Jesus Christ accomplished a greater liberation and reached the nations on a scale beyond anything the exodus did. And Jesus's victory on the cross explains how Psalm 97, with its intimidating depiction of God's holiness and wrath, can be followed up by the exuberant praise and joy of Psalm 98. Christ paid for our sins. God sees us as beautifully perfect and righteous "in him" (Philippians 3:9). This means the righteousness of God is not against us but *for* us. So how do we live? Always live your daily life against the background music of joy (verses 4–6).

Prayer: "Jesus! my Shepherd, Husband, Friend, O Prophet, Priest and King. My Lord, my Life, my Way, my End, accept the praise I bring."[96] Amen.

September 1

READ Psalm 98:7–9. 7 Let the sea resound, and everything in it, the world, and all who live in it. **8** Let the rivers clap their hands, let the mountains sing together for joy; **9** let them sing before the LORD, for he comes to judge the earth. He will judge the world in righteousness and the peoples with equity.

THE RIVERS CLAP THEIR HANDS. The imagery of the trees and fish praising God (Psalm 96:11–12), with the rivers and the mountains clapping and singing (verse 8), is more than just poetry. Romans 8:18–25 says that nature was made to be far more alive and glorious than it is in its current state. Modern philosophies cannot fathom that the natural world will not come into its own until the human race is made righteous again. Jesus will come to restore this ancient harmony (verse 9). So our future hope is powerful. If rivers and mountains will be like this when he returns, what will we be like (1 John 3:2–3)?

Prayer: Lord, I once thrilled to hear tales in which trees and animals could talk, magic helped people escape death and the ravages of time, and love triumphed over evil. Because Jesus was raised from the dead, we will be too, and all these things will be ours. Let me live all day in the joyful hope of my final rising. Amen.

September 2

READ Psalm 99:1–5. **1** The LORD reigns, let the nations tremble; he sits enthroned between the cherubim, let the earth shake. **2** Great is the LORD in Zion; he is exalted over all the nations. **3** Let them praise your great and awesome name—he is holy. **4** The King is mighty, he loves justice—you have established equity; in Jacob you have done what is just and right. **5** Exalt the LORD our God and worship at his footstool; he is holy.

HE IS HOLY. What does it mean to say God is holy? The Hebrew word means literally to be completely "set apart." When applied to God, the word means there is none like him, that he is infinitely above us and all things in power, perfection, and righteousness. When people are holy (Leviticus 11:44; 1 Peter 1:16), it means they belong wholly to God. They serve not with divided loyalties but with their whole heart. For the Christian church to be holy means it should be radically *different.* The early Christians stuck out in the Greco-Roman pagan society because of their integrity and honesty, their sympathy and forgiveness, their sexual chastity, and their astonishing financial generosity. They were holy. Are we?

Prayer: Lord, when I first became a Christian I tried to live morally. To be holy is not less than that, but it is more. I want to belong completely to you, reserve myself only for you. I want you to take title to my heart and not let it invest itself more in other things. Make me holy, because you are holy. Amen.

September 3

READ Psalm 99:6–9. **6** Moses and Aaron were among his priests, Samuel was among those who called on his name; they called on the LORD and he answered them. **7** He spoke to them from the pillar of cloud; they kept his statutes and the decrees he gave them. **8** LORD our God, you answered them; you were to Israel a forgiving God, though you punished their misdeeds. **9** Exalt the LORD our God and worship at his holy mountain, for the LORD our God is holy.

THE GIFT OF PRAYER. One of God's greatest gifts is access to him in prayer (verse 6). Samuel had a high theology of prayer, as seen when he said, "Far be it from me that I should sin against the LORD by failing to pray for you" (1 Samuel 12:23). But how can a holy God (verses 1–5) hear the prayers of sinful humans? Verse 8 connects prayer access to God's forgiveness. The reference to cherubim (verse 1) reminds us of the Ark of the Covenant and the tabernacle where blood was sprinkled to atone for sin (Exodus 25:17). That was just a symbol. Jesus's blood brings us with full assurance into the presence of a holy God (Hebrews 9:5, 11–14, 10:19–25).

Prayer: Lord, prayerlessness is a sin against you. It comes from a self-sufficiency that is wrong and that dishonors you. Prayerlessness is also a sin against those around me. I should be engaging my heart and your power in their needs. Lord, I pray with all my heart that you would give me a heart for prayer. Amen.

September 4

READ PSALM 100. **1** Shout for joy to the Lord, all the earth. **2** Worship the Lord with gladness; come before him with joyful songs. **3** Know that the Lord is God. It is he who made us, and we are his; we are his people, the sheep of his pasture. **4** Enter his gates with thanksgiving and his courts with praise; give thanks to him and praise his name. **5** For the Lord is good and his love endures forever; his faithfulness continues through all generations.

THE MORE HIS, THE MORE FREE. The psalm summons us to offer ourselves to God, acknowledging that we are not our own (verse 3). This self-offering is to be conducted with delight and joy (verses 1–2). Neither moralistic religion (which sees obedience as necessary drudgery in order to put God in our debt) nor modern self-determination (which sees the loss of independence as a kind of death) can grasp this. Christians have an enhanced motivation for joyful self-giving. "You are not your own; you were bought at a price" (1 Corinthians 6:19–20). This indeed makes obedience a delight, a way to know, serve, please, and come to resemble the one whose sacrificial love for us endures forever (verse 5).

Prayer: "Let all the world in every corner sing, my God and King! The heavens are not too high, his praise may thither fly, the earth is not too low, his praises there may grow. Let all the world in every corner sing, my God and King!"[97] *Amen.*

September 5

READ Psalm 101. **1** I will sing of your love and justice; to you, LORD, I will sing praise. **2** I will be careful to lead a blameless life—when will you come to me? I will conduct the affairs of my house with a blameless heart. **3** I will not look with approval on anything that is vile. I hate what faithless people do; I will have no part in it. **4** The perverse of heart shall be far from me; I will have nothing to do with what is evil. **5** Whoever slanders their neighbor in secret, I will put to silence; whoever has haughty eyes and a proud heart, I will not tolerate. **6** My eyes will be on the faithful in the land, that they may dwell with me; the one whose walk is blameless will minister to me. **7** No one who practices deceit will dwell in my house; no one who speaks falsely will stand in my presence. **8** Every morning I will put to silence all the wicked in the land; I will cut off every evildoer from the city of the LORD.

A BLAMELESS LIFE. This is a psalm of David. The claims to be "blameless" (verses 2–3) and to have "nothing to do with what is evil" (verse 4) are not pharisaical delusions of moral purity but a king's desire for an uncorrupt administration ("house," verse 2). He won't allow slander (verse 5) or dishonesty in his politics (verse 7). He seeks justice in the land (verse 8). This is a great set of ideals for all in government. But it also chastens, exposing how far human societies fall short of the vision. Most tragically, we know David and his son Solomon, the greatest of Israel's kings, themselves violated this standard. "Happily the last word is not with David . . . but with his Son. There, there is no shadow."[98]

Prayer: Lord, I pray for the leaders of states and nations, of business and commerce, of the arts and cultural institutions. I pray that honesty, wisdom, skillfulness, justice, and virtue characterize all their duties, and that their work be a public blessing. Amen.

September 6

READ Psalm 102:1–11.] Hear my prayer, LORD; let my cry for help come to you. L Do not hide your face from me when I am in distress. Turn your ear to me; when I call, answer me quickly. **3** For my days vanish like smoke; my bones burn like glowing embers. **4** My heart is blighted and withered like grass; I forget to eat my food. **5** In my distress I groan aloud and am reduced to skin and bones. **6** I am like a desert owl, like an owl among the ruins. 7 I lie awake; I have become like a bird alone on a roof. **8** All day long my enemies taunt me; those who rail against me use my name as a curse. **9** For I eat ashes as my food and mingle my drink with tears **10** because of your great wrath, for you have taken me up and thrown me aside. **11** My days are like the evening shadow; I wither away like grass.

YOU ARE NOT ALONE. Suffering in all its aspects is depicted. There is burning with fever (verse 3) and physical wasting (verse 4). There are the signs of depression, including sleeplessness (verse 7), lack of appetite (verse 4), and uncontrollable weeping (verse 9). The psalmist feels so rejected and isolated he likens himself to a solitary owl in a ruined house (verse 6). We all need this psalm. It helps those in comfortable circumstances to enter into the pain of the troubled and share their burdens (Galatians 6:2). But most of all it helps anyone feeling like this to see they are *not* alone, that others including Jesus himself (verses 23–27) have been there and came through.

Prayer: Lord, the realism of your Word scares me. I don't want to believe that *I* might go through pain like this. And I avoid people who are. That is wicked of me. Lord, you suffered infinitely, voluntarily for me. So I can face affliction—and help others face it—with you. Amen.

September 7

READ Psalm 102:12–17. **12** But you, LORD, sit enthroned forever; your renown endures through all generations. **13** You will arise and have compassion on Zion, for it is time to show favor to her; the appointed time has come. **14** For her stones are dear to your servants; her very dust moves them to pity. **15** The nations will fear the name of the LORD, all the kings of the earth will revere your glory. **16** For the LORD will rebuild Zion and appear in his glory. **17** He will respond to the prayer of the destitute; he will not despise their plea.

NO UNANSWERED PRAYER. A disaster has left Jerusalem in ruins and many imprisoned (verses 16 and 20). The psalmist prays for God to restore Zion to a glory the whole world can see (verse 16)—*now* (verse 13). That did not happen. Unanswered prayer? Not really. God's answer was "Not now, and not the way you think." The answer, through Jesus, was far greater than he could have imagined (Hebrews 12:12–28). Likewise, when Elijah prayed to die (1 Kings 19:4), the answer was "Don't be silly, you are not going to die at all!"[99] There is ultimately no such thing as unanswered prayer. If the answer at first is "no" or "not yet," it is because he gives us what we want in ways better than we asked.

Prayer: Lord, I confess that your promise to always hear prayer (verse 17) is of little comfort to me, and it's my fault. I am so sure of exactly what a good and happy life must look like. Remind me that sometime your wise love *"feeds us with hunger. . . . Lord, spoil my fool's heaven on earth, that I may be saved forever."*[100] Amen.

September 8

READ Psalm 102:18–22. **18** Let this be written for a future generation, that a people not yet created may praise the LORD: **19** "The LORD looked down from his sanctuary on high, from heaven he viewed the earth, **20** to hear the groans of the prisoners and release those condemned to death." **21** So the name of the LORD will be declared in Zion and his praise in Jerusalem **22** when the peoples and the kingdoms assemble to worship the LORD.

THE GATES OF HELL WILL NOT PREVAIL. In every era God will be creating a new generation of his people by his grace (verse 18). We all start as "not a people" but through the new birth are created to be "God's people" (1 Peter 1:3; 2:9–10). There will always be those who are praising God for how he saves them from the death sentence (verse 20). Little could the psalmist realize the infinite breadth and depth of this salvation, that through faith in Jesus there would be "no condemnation" at all for us— eternal freedom from the penalty of sin (Romans 8:1). The church endures, rolling on while competing forms of religion and nonbelief rise, wane, and are forgotten. Christianity faithful to God's Word will last until the end of time and beyond (Matthew 16:18).

Prayer: Lord, so many forces are hostile to our faith. Popular culture disdains it as narrow, many world leaders find it threatening, powerful institutions want it gone or only believed in secret. Remind my heart now that none of this opposition will prevail. I thank you that, because you yourself live within the church, even the gates of hell will not overcome it. Amen.

September 9

READ Psalm 102:23–28. **23** In the course of my life he broke my strength; he cut short my days. **24** So I said: "Do not take me away, my God, in the midst of my days; your years go on through all generations. **25** In the beginning you laid the foundations of the earth, and the heavens are the work of your hands. **26** They will perish, but you remain; they will all wear out like a garment. Like clothing you will change them and they will be discarded. **27** But you remain the same, and your years will never end. **28** The children of your servants will live in your presence; their descendants will be established before you."

PERSPECTIVE. The psalmist faces a short life span and untimely death (verse 23). He did not know it, but his rejection, agony, early death, and wasting under God's wrath (verse 10) foreshadowed the sufferings of Jesus (Hebrews 1:10–12) who bore our sin and brought in the kingdom that the psalmist longed for. But the heavenly Zion, to which all nations would stream, would be one beyond his imagining (Hebrews 12:22–27). Today, in heaven, this psalmist knows all this! So when "at length saw his experience and his words in the light of the Son of God, was he not glad that the Lord refused his request but heard his prayer?"[101]

Prayer: Lord, nothing here *lasts.* But I praise you that while all things perish, even the uttermost foundations of the earth, you are eternal, and if we cling to you and you embrace us with your love, then we will live forever in our true country, where finally our hearts may rest. I praise you for so great a comfort and salvation. Amen.

September 10

READ Psalm 103:1–5. **1** Praise the LORD, my soul; all my inmost being, praise his holy name. **2** Praise the LORD, my soul, and forget not all his benefits— **3** who forgives all your sins and heals all your diseases, **4** who redeems your life from the pit and crowns you with love and compassion, **5** who satisfies your desires with good things so that your youth is renewed like the eagle's.

PRAYING THE GOSPEL. Here is how to work the Gospel into one's own heart until it transforms. It happens through inward dialogue, speaking directly and forcefully to your own heart ("my soul") rather than just listening to it. Biblical meditation, unlike the popular varieties, is not a relaxation technique for emptying the mind but rather one that fills it with truth, using thought and memory to set your heart on fire. Here David dwells on the truth that God forgives sin and eventually will remove all suffering and diseases. When we ask, we get forgiveness now (1 John 1:8–9), but we may not get suffering removed now (2 Corinthians 12:8–9; 2 Samuel 12:13–23). That is because while sin always blocks our relationship with God, suffering can deepen it.

Prayer: Lord, I confess how much of my fear, anger, anxiety, and discouragement is wholly due to my forgetting your benefits, forgetting all you've given me and promised me in Christ. My mind knows but my heart forgets I'm forgiven, delighted in, guaranteed a crown, a feast. Forgive me, and help me speak to my soul until strength is renewed. Amen.

September 11

SLOW ANGER; IMMEASURABLE LOVE. God's anger is different from ours. We are quick to anger, we make people pay who have wronged us, and then, nonetheless, we nurse our grievances. God is slow to anger, provides for our forgiveness, and then remembers our sins no more. Verse 8 is astonishing because it quotes Exodus 34:6, which goes on to say in 34:7 that God "does not leave the guilty unpunished." How can Moses in Exodus be right to say that God will not let sin go unpunished *and* David here also be right in saying he will not punish us as we deserve? Only the cross would reveal what it cost God to punish sin without punishing us. Infinite distances (verses 11–12) are used to convey this infinite love.

Prayer: Lord, my anger is indeed unlike yours. May your Spirit purify me so my anger is not triggered by my hurt ego as much as by real injustice and evil, and so that it does not remain in me to harden and poison my joy but readily gives way to compassion. Amen.

September 12

FATHER LOVE. An adult can see right into the heart of a child who does not have the skills to hide selfishness, impatience, and a lack of wisdom. Parents know their children's besetting sins (verse 14). Yet a good father loves his children anyway (verse 13). Indeed, the more weak and needy a child is, the more the father's heart goes out to him or her. So God knows us to the bottom yet nevertheless loves us to the skies —literally. God does not just pardon our sins. He adopts us into his family, giving us his love, access in prayer, a share in the inheritance of glory, and even his family resemblance—the Holy Spirit, which reproduces God's own character in us (John 1:12–13; Matthew 6:9; Galatians 4:7; 1 John 3:1–3).

Prayer: Lord, I praise you for making yourself not just my King and my shepherd but my Father. To think of the omnipotent God as my Father—infinite power, gentled for me, loving me and working all things for my good! Transform my prayer life through a deeper grasp of your fatherly love to me. Amen.

September 13

READ Psalm 103:19–22. **19** The Lord has established his throne in heaven, and his kingdom rules over all. **20** Praise the Lord, you his angels, you mighty ones who do his bidding, who obey his word. **21** Praise the Lord, all his heavenly hosts, you his servants who do his will. **22** Praise the Lord, all his works everywhere in his dominion. Praise the Lord, my soul.

ALL NATURE SINGS. The psalmist calls on his own soul to praise the Lord (verses 1–2). Then he learns to rejoice inwardly in the unfathomable benefits of gospel salvation. Now, at the end of the psalm, he realizes a oneness with creation that he never imagined possible, for he sees what all nature is doing—rejoicing in God! All his "works" on earth (verse 22) and in heaven (verses 20–21) are already singing to God and to one another, and he has taken up his unique part in the greatest chorus and symphony of all. Faith in the Gospel enables you to hear and join in the music. Jonathan Edwards wrote: "How doth all the world congratulate, embrace, and sing to" a soul given to praising God.[102]

Prayer: Lord, when I am not right with you, I feel alone in the world. But when I praise you the most, I can hear your joy in the birds in the morning and the rain on the water. Lord, I want to be part of this music; I want to sing my part, which both adds to and derives beauty from the whole. Amen.

September 14

READ Psalm 104:1–4. **1** Praise the LORD, my soul. LORD my God, you are very great; you are clothed with splendor and majesty. **2** The LORD wraps himself in light as with a garment; he stretches out the heavens like a tent **3** and lays the beams of his upper chambers on their waters. He makes the clouds his chariot and rides on the wings of the wind. **4** He makes winds his messengers, flames of fire his servants.

THE SPLENDOR OF LIGHT. Psalm 104 is a meditation on the wonders of creation and the wonderful Creator behind it. Unlike in Eastern mysticism, we see here a God who is personal and distinct from his creation yet who is not in any way remote from it. The imagery of garment, palace, and chariot conveys that nature is filled with God's energy and presence, hence the awe and respect that are due the natural world. And as our dazzled eyes cannot take in the brilliance of light, so we must bow before and praise the God is who is more powerful and glorious than our imaginations can comprehend. "All praise we would render, O help us to see, 'tis only the splendor of light hideth thee."[103]

Prayer: Lord, I often find both your words and your ways hard to fathom. My self-justifying heart instinctively tends to put the blame on you. O help me to see that my real problem is the weakness of my spiritual eyes, which cannot take in your great light. Strengthen my spiritual sight, so I can take more in. Amen.

September 15

READ Psalm 104:5–9. **5** He set the earth on its foundations; it can never be moved. **6** You covered it with the watery depths as with a garment; the waters stood above the mountains. **7** But at your rebuke the waters fled, at the sound of your thunder they took to flight; **8** they flowed over the mountains, they went down into the valleys, to the place you assigned for them. **9** You set a boundary they cannot cross; never again will they cover the earth.

YOU SET A BOUNDARY THEY CANNOT CROSS. The psalmist is meditating on creation's third day (Genesis 1:9–10), when God divided the sea from the dry land (verses 7–8). Science is based on the regularity of nature—that if X creates Y under certain conditions, it will do so again under identical conditions. But why should nature be regular? It is because we don't live in a completely random, chaotic world but one with set "boundaries" (verse 9). A personal Creator has filled the world with the principles of physics, mathematics, chemistry, biology, and the like. Because of this we have aerodynamics (making flight possible), electricity, medicine—all harnessing a host of givens and limitations embedded in creation that have made civilization possible. Thank God for them all.

Prayer: Lord, I take for granted so many commonplace things, so many scientific developments that have made my daily life safe and comfortable. I rob you of your glory and myself of satisfaction when I fail to stop, wonder at them, and praise you for them. Teach me that discipline. Amen.

September 16

READ Psalm 104:10–13. **10** He makes springs pour water into the ravines; it flows between the mountains. **11** They give water to all the beasts of the field; the wild donkeys quench their thirst. **12** The birds of the sky nest by the waters; they sing among the branches. **13** He waters the mountains from his upper chambers; the land is satisfied by the fruit of his work.

QUENCHING THEIR THIRST. God also cares for what he has made. Through the waters he created he now quenches the thirst of all creatures (verse 11) and irrigates the earth to make it fertile (verse 13). God's care for all his creation should make believers the protectors, rather than the exploiters, of its goodness. Is the land "satisfied with the fruit of [*our*] work" on it? Or have we failed, through both ignorance and avarice, to properly steward the riches of the world he has given us? We may find it hard not to abuse nature for our profit unless we get the deep inner contentment that comes from the water only Jesus can give, that of eternal life (John 4:13–14).

Prayer: Lord Jesus, I confess I am so concerned for comfort and convenience that I don't want to think about the possible bad effects any of my daily life practices might have on the natural world. But this is *your* world, which you love. So give me the humility and patience to ask these questions for the first time. Amen.

September 17

READ Psalm 104:14–18. **14** He makes grass grow for the cattle, and plants for man to cultivate—bringing forth food from the earth: **15** wine that gladdens human hearts, oil to make their faces shine, and bread that sustains their hearts. **16** The trees of the Lᴏʀᴅ are well watered, the cedars of Lebanon that he planted. **17** There the birds make their nests; the stork has its home in the junipers. **18** The high mountains belong to the wild goats; the crags are a refuge for the hyrax.

THAT GLADDENS THE HEART. God does not simply meet his creatures' physical needs. He wants their joy, he wants our faces to shine, he wants not just our bodies but also our hearts to be sustained (verse 15). Jesus too gave wine to gladden the heart of man (verse 15). He began his ministry by miraculously providing excellent wine to keep a wedding party going (John 2:1–11). Why would he make this his opening, signature miracle? It was to communicate his mission, not just to secure pardon from sin but to restore us to fullness of life, to bring festival joy. You have not received all God wants to give until you have gotten "the oil of joy instead of mourning" (Isaiah 61:3).

Prayer: Lord, I do not honor you merely by obeying you. The way to glorify you the most is to enjoy you. Help me (oh, please) to revel in all you are and have done for me until it awakens joy in my heart. Amen.

September 18

READ Psalm 104:19–24. **19** He made the moon to mark the seasons, and the sun knows when to go down. **20** You bring darkness, it becomes night, and all the beasts of the forest prowl. **21** The lions roar for their prey and seek their food from God. **22** The sun rises, and they steal away; they return and lie down in their dens. **23** Then people go out to his work, to their labor until evening. **24** How many are your works, LORD! In wisdom you made them all; the earth is full of your creatures.

THE EARTH IS FULL OF YOUR CREATURES. Verse 24 stops for reflective worship. There are 5,000 known species of sponges on the ocean floor and over 300,000 species of beetles. There are multitudes of different flowers, trees, birds, and animals, some of them enchantingly beautiful, others enchantingly odd. Why? They reveal the unsearchable wealth of God's creativity, the infinite range of his thought, his love of beauty, even his sense of humor. And because it is all designed by divine "wisdom," this verse invites us not just to marvel at it all but to explore and study it too. It is an invitation to both science and art.

Prayer: Lord, your Word says that your creatures tell us about your existence and greatness, if we don't stop our ears to it. Open my ears! *"In reason's ear they all rejoice, And utter forth a glorious voice. Forever singing as they shine, 'The hand that made us is divine.'"*[104] Amen.

September 19

READ Psalm 104:25–29. 25 There is the sea, vast and spacious, teeming with creatures beyond number—living things both large and small. 26 There the ships go to and fro, and the Leviathan, which you formed to frolic there. 27 All creatures look to you to give them their food at the proper time. 28 When you give it to them, they gather it up; when you open your hand, they are satisfied with good things. 29 When you hide your face, they are terrified; when you take away their breath, they die and return to the dust.

FORMED TO FROLIC. Food comes at proper seasons (verse 27) and is gathered (verse 28). Yet through it all it is God who is giving us food (verse 27). The great sea creatures "frolic" and leap in the air (verse 26), and the swallows perform aerial acrobatics. While those activities may also have practical purposes, in some deeper sense these creatures know the joy and freedom of doing what they were "formed" to do by God. We too can know joy and fulfillment only as we live according to God's design. At this point, nature has us beat. As Elisabeth Elliot has said, "A clam glorifies God better than we do, because the clam is being everything it was created to be, whereas we are not."[105]

Prayer: Lord, disobeying you is easy in the short run but hard in the long run because I am violating my own nature. And so obedience to you can be excruciating to start but is wonderful in time, because by it I become my true self. Oh, help me to remember this when things get hard! Amen.

September 20

READ Psalm 104:30–35. **30** When you send your Spirit, they are created, and you renew the face of the ground. **31** May the glory of the LORD endure forever; may the LORD rejoice in his works— **32** he who looks at the earth, and it trembles, who touches the mountains, and they smoke. **33** I will sing to the LORD all my life; I will sing praise to my God as long as I live. **34** May my meditation be pleasing to him, as I rejoice in the LORD. **35** But may sinners vanish from the earth and the wicked be no more. Praise the LORD, my soul. Praise the LORD.

YOU RENEW THE FACE OF THE EARTH. Those who nurture and cultivate the physical creation are doing something God does. God's Spirit not only regenerates hearts (Titus 3:5–6) but also renews the face of the earth (verse 30), for he is the source of all life, spiritual and biological. God delights in the natural creation. So should we. Yet verse 35 reminds us that the world is fallen and sin must be dealt with. It is not enough simply to care for creation and help people with economic and material needs. So Christians should love their neighbors by caring for both their bodies and the state of their souls.

Prayer: Lord, you made both souls and bodies and you are going to redeem both soul and body on the day of resurrection. Help me, then to serve people not just with words, even Gospel words, but also with practical help and sacrificial generosity. Amen.

September 21

READ **Psalm 105:1–7.** **1** Give praise to the LORD, proclaim his name; make known among the nations what he has done. **2** Sing to him, sing praise to him; tell of all his wonderful acts. **3** Glory in his holy name; let the hearts of those who seek the LORD rejoice. **4** Look to the LORD and his strength; seek his face always. **5** Remember the wonders he has done, his miracles, and the judgments he pronounced, **6** you his servants, the descendants of Abraham, his chosen ones, the children of Jacob. **7** He is the LORD our God; his judgments are in all the earth.

TELL OF HIS WONDERFUL ACTS. This psalm describes God's mighty acts of redemption in history. But before he begins that account, the psalmist calls people to worship and praise him for *all* his wonderful acts (verse 2) and miracles. Believers rightly hear this as a summons to tell others around us what he has done in our own lives. Too often we stay silent about his saving actions in our own histories. We might think that keeping quiet about such things is modesty but its effect is the opposite. It allows others to believe that we have overcome our problems and lived our lives on our own strength.

Prayer: Lord, I praise you that you have broken into my life and brought me up short and opened my eyes and ignited love in my heart for your name. Ah, but you did it in such wise, brilliant, and beautiful ways. Give me the humility and courage I need to begin to testify to others about your goodness toward me. Amen.

September 22

READ Psalm 105:8–11. 8 He remembers his covenant forever, the promise he made, for a thousand generations, **9** the covenant he made with Abraham, the oath he swore to Isaac. **10** He confirmed it to Jacob as a decree, to Israel as an everlasting covenant: **11** "To you I will give the land of Canaan as the portion you will inherit."

THE PROMISE OF HOME. God's promise to give Abraham's descendants a homeland (Genesis 12:1–5) is central to understanding the plan of redemption. We long for home, a place of security, comfort, and love. We were made for a world without death or parting from love, a world in which we walked with God and knew him face to face. The world has been marred by sin and is no longer home, and we are restless exiles since our expulsion from Eden. So when the Son of God came he had no place to lay his head (Luke 9:58) and was crucified outside the city. He took the great exile we deserved so we could be brought into God's household (Ephesians 2:17–19). And someday he will turn the world back into our home indeed (Revelation 21:1–8).

Prayer: Lord, give me the peace that comes from knowing that nothing in this world is truly home. Give me the strength that comes from visiting my future home when I know your love and presence in prayer. I praise you that you will bring us someday to the true country we have been looking for all our lives. Amen.

September 23

READ Psalm 105:12–15. **12** When they were but few in number, few indeed, and strangers in it, **13** they wandered from nation to nation, from one kingdom to another. **14** He allowed no one to oppress them; for their sake he rebuked kings: **15** "Do not touch my anointed ones; do my prophets no harm."

ONLY BY GRACE. This tells of the patriarchs Abraham, Isaac, and Jacob and how God kept them safe during their wanderings. But verse 15 refers to when Abraham told Abimelech that Sarah was his sister, for fear that the king would kill him to take Sarah as a wife. God had to warn Abimelech not to touch Sarah, that Abraham was a prophet (Genesis 20:6). The history of the patriarchs is filled with such missteps and moral failures. How could these be our moral examples? The answer: Biblical faith, unlike other kinds, is not primarily about emulating moral examples. The Bible is a history of God offering his grace to people who do not deserve it nor seek it nor ever fully appreciate it after they have been saved by it.

Prayer: Lord, I praise you that you are a God of grace. I thank you that even more than protecting me from forces around me, you have saved me from myself. Let the knowledge of your grace make me never less but only more intensely devoted to obeying you. Amen.

September 24

READ Psalm 105:16–22. **16** He called down famine on the land and destroyed all their supplies of food; **17** and he sent a man before them— Joseph, sold as a slave. **18** They bruised his feet with shackles, his neck was put in irons, **19** till what he foretold came to pass, till the word of the LORD proved him true. **20** The king sent and released him, the ruler of peoples set him free. **21** He made him master of his household, ruler over all he possessed, **22** to instruct his princes as he pleased and teach his elders wisdom.

SALVATION THROUGH WEAKNESS. Joseph was "sent before" the people in Egypt to save them. But see how he saved them: "as a slave." If Joseph hadn't been betrayed, sold, and imprisoned for years, he never would have escaped his own deadly character flaws, never would have been able to redeem his own family from its generations-deep sins, nor would he have been able to save thousands of people from famine (Genesis 37–50). Joseph reveals the deep pattern of God's salvation. His deliverers, and especially Jesus himself, save through rejection, weakness, and sacrifice. That is also how we connect to this salvation—through the weakness of repentance. After this, God often uses our troubles to rescue us from our own flaws and make us great.

Prayer: Lord, I hate feeling weak and out of control. Yet you told Paul that your "power was made perfect in weakness" (2 Corinthians 12:9). Teach me to go to you, cling to you, repent, and depend on you in my times of weakness, so that through you I can become truly strong. Amen.

September 25

READ **Psalm 105:23–25.** **23** Then Israel entered Egypt; Jacob resided as a foreigner in the land of Ham. **24** The LORD made his people very fruitful; he made them too numerous for their foes, **25** whose hearts he turned to hate his people, to conspire against his servants.

THE PLAN OF GOD. The Egyptians came to hate the Israelites (Exodus 1:1–14), yet it was part of God's plan (verse 25). God used the Assyrians to punish Israel, yet rightly held the Assyrians responsible for their violence (Isaiah 10:5–12). Jesus's death was the result of God's foreordination, but the people who killed him were guilty (Acts 2:23). Here are two crucial biblical truths that must be held together—everything we do is part of God's plan, yet we are never coerced and are completely responsible for our actions. Without the first truth we are stressed by believing it's all up to us how our lives go. Without the second truth we will think our choices don't really matter. Believe this doctrine and escape both complacency and anxiety.

Prayer: Lord, you are sovereign and I am responsible. If I didn't believe the first I'd be frozen by fear that I could ruin your plans for me. If I didn't believe the second I'd be passive and cynical. Let this wonderful, paradoxical doctrine both provoke me to strenuous effort and comfort and reassure me, as it should. Amen.

September 26

READ Psalm 105:26–36. **26** He sent Moses his servant, and Aaron, whom he had chosen. **27** They performed his signs among them, his wonders in the land of Ham. **28** He sent darkness and made the land dark—for had they not rebelled against his words? **29** He turned their waters into blood, causing their fish to die. **30** Their land teemed with frogs, which went up into the bedrooms of their rulers. **31** He spoke, and there came swarms of flies, and gnats throughout their country. **32** He turned their rain into hail, with lightning throughout their land; **33** he struck down their vines and fig trees and shattered the trees of their country. **34** He spoke, and the locusts came, grasshoppers without number; **35** they ate up every green thing in their land, ate up the produce of their soil. **36** Then he struck down all the firstborn in their land, the firstfruits of all their manhood.

THE DARKNESS OF DISOBEDIENCE. The psalmist highlights the ninth Egyptian plague of absolute darkness and says that it came because they had "rebelled against [God's] words" (verse 28). The universal result of disobeying God is darkness of mind, in which our thinking goes around in futile circles, and of heart, in which our emotions are trapped in fear, anger, and despair (Romans 1:21; Ephesians 4:18). The reverse is also true: We must begin to obey before the light dawns and we can fully understand. ("Anyone who chooses to do the will of God will find out," John 7:17.) Don't try to figure everything out before you obey. Remember the one who took the pitch darkness of evil and sin for you (Matthew 27:45–46).

Prayer: Father, I am your child. And like all children, I can't always understand why my father is telling me to do something. But if children waited to obey until they fully understood their parents' minds, it would be a disaster. So I hear and obey, Father, simply because you are my Father. Amen.

September 27

READ Psalm 105:37–42. **37** He brought out Israel, laden with silver and gold, and from among their tribes no one faltered. **38** Egypt was glad when they left, because dread of Israel had fallen on them. **39** He spread out a cloud as a covering, and a fire to give light at night. **40** They asked, and he brought them quail; he fed them well with the bread of heaven. **41** He opened the rock, and water gushed out; like a river it flowed in the desert. **42** For he remembered his holy promise given to his servant Abraham.

THE PROVISION OF GOD. As the people of Israel wandered in the wilderness, God provided finances, protection, and food (verses 37–40). Nevertheless, the Israelites charged Moses and God with bringing them into the desert to die (Exodus 17:1–7). For such slander, God told Moses to take the special rod he used to bring divine judgment on Egypt. But instead of striking the Israelites, Moses was told to bring the rod of judgment down on a rock where God stood. The rock, being struck, brought out life-giving water (verse 41.) Paul said the rock was Christ (1 Corinthians 10:4–6). He was struck and judged in our place, so that the "the sorrow and love flow mingled down" could bring us eternal life.[106]

Prayer: Lord, *"Were the whole the realm of nature mine, that were a present far too small. Love so amazing, so divine, demands my soul, my life, my all."*[107] Amen.

September 28

READ Psalm 105.43–45. **43** He brought out his people with rejoicing, his chosen ones with shouts of joy; **44** he gave them the lands of the nations, and they fell heir to what others had toiled for— **45** that they might keep his precepts and observe his laws. Praise the Lord.

PRAISE THE LORD. As great as Israel's salvation was, it was temporary and incomplete, for Israel did *not* keep his laws and precepts (verse 45). Something more was needed. In Jesus we get a greater Joseph who, taken captive and killed, was raised to the right hand of the throne to forgive and save those who betrayed him. We get a greater Moses who stands in the gap between the people and the Lord and who mediates a new covenant. We get the greater rock of Moses, who, receiving the rod of God's justice, gives us the water of eternal life in a desert of a world. Behind everything God does there is something unimaginably greater. Praise the Lord!

Prayer: Lord, I thank you that your Word reveals that behind everything you do is something "immeasurably more than all we ask or imagine" (Ephesians 3:20). Let me live life confident in the knowledge of this instead of with the vague sense of dread that I usually have. Amen.

September 29

READ Psalm 106:1–5. **1** Praise the LORD. Give thanks to the LORD, for he is good; his love endures forever. **2** Who can proclaim the mighty acts of the LORD or fully declare his praise? **3** Blessed are those who act justly, who always do what is right. **4** Remember me, LORD, when you show favor to your people, come to my aid when you save them, **5** that I may enjoy the prosperity of your chosen ones, that I may share in the joy of your nation and join your inheritance in giving praise.

ALWAYS DO WHAT IS RIGHT. This psalm is all about humankind's constant ingratitude and God's unmerited grace ("chosen ones," verse 5) and patience. The message of grace despite sin is introduced, however, by this beatitude: "Blessed are those. . . who *always* do what is right" (verse 3). The Gospel of grace must never, ever be taken as an even temporary license not to do right. Despite (no, *because* of) God's wonderful patience and mercy, we are always obligated to do right. There is never an excuse for giving in to temptation (1 Corinthians 10:13). Bottomless stores of mercy and unbending demands for righteousness almost never go together in any human being. Our temperament inclines us one way or the other. But these are perfectly combined in God.

Prayer: Lord, your boundless stores of grace are nothing but an incentive for total, uninterrupted righteousness. How can I rebel against the one who did all this for me, and at such cost? Lord, let your grace so dazzle me that I always do what is right. Amen.

September 30

READ Psalm 106:6–12. **6** We have sinned, even as our ancestors did; we have done wrong and acted wickedly. **7** When our ancestors were in Egypt, they gave no thought to your miracles; they did not remember your many kindnesses, and they rebelled by the sea, the Red Sea. **8** Yet he saved them for his name's sake, to make his mighty power known. **9** He rebuked the Red Sea, and it dried up; he led them through the depths as through a desert. **10** He saved them from the hand of the foe; from the hand of the enemy he redeemed them. **11** The waters covered their adversaries; not one of them survived. **12** Then they believed his promises and sang his praise.

THE SIN OF INGRATITUDE. This psalm is about ingratitude. "They did not remember your many kindnesses" (verse 7). It is the root of all human sin: "They neither glorified him as God nor gave thanks to him" (Romans 1:21). That may not at first sound serious, but consider the crime of plagiarism. It is both theft and lie. It robs others of their due and creates the illusion that you are more able than you are. Sin is *cosmic* ingratitude. It gives you the delusion that you have the ability to conduct and hold your life together. Actually every day that your heart keeps pumping, your country is not invaded, and your brain keeps functioning is wholly an undeserved gift of God. We ought to live simple, normal, uneventful days full of amazed, thankful joy.

Prayer: Lord, I thank you for my routine mercies. I thank you for sustaining my life daily, for being endlessly patient with me, for shielding me from so many consequences of my foolish behavior, for the ways you have walked with me in trials, and for all my answered prayers. Amen.

October 1

READ Psalm 106:13–18. **13** But they soon forgot what he had done and did not wait for his plan to unfold. **14** In the desert they gave in to their craving; in the wilderness they put God to the test. **15** So he gave them what they asked for, but sent a wasting disease upon them. **16** In the camp they grew envious of Moses and of Aaron, who was consecrated to the LORD. **17** The earth opened up and swallowed Dathan; it buried the company of Abiram. **18** Fire blazed among their followers; a flame consumed the wicked.

BUT THEY SOON FORGOT. Every stanza of this poem makes the same point: Human beings fail at living as they should with God and their neighbors. No matter how many things God does for them, it doesn't change their hearts—their ingratitude (verse 13), their endless craving (verse 14), their sense of superiority to God (verse 14), or their envy and selfishness (verse 16). We need something to be done *in* us to save and transform us, because we can't do it ourselves. In the movie *Superman Returns*, Lois Lane says, "The world doesn't need a savior. And neither do I."[108] That expresses the deep language of the natural human heart, and it is utterly, fatally wrong.

Prayer: Lord, I praise you that you opened my heart to you, because I would never have done it myself. *"My heart owns none before thee, for thy rich grace I thirst; this knowing—if I love thee, thou must have loved me first."*[109] Amen.

October 2

READ Psalm 106:19–23. **19** At Horeb they made a calf and worshiped an idol cast from metal. **20** They exchanged their glorious God for an image of a bull, which eats grass. **21** They forgot the God who saved them, who had done great things in Egypt, **22** miracles in the land of Ham and awesome deeds by the Red Sea. **23** So he said he would destroy them—had not Moses, his chosen one, stood in the breach before him to keep his wrath from destroying them.

TO KEEP HIS WRATH. After the miracles of the exodus, "they forgot the God who saved them." (verse 21). We are no different (see verse 6). Our hearts think, "Back then you did that, but what have you done for me lately?" Don't just listen to your heart when it speaks like that; answer it like this. Moses turned away the divine wrath in prayer (verse 23). But on the cross Jesus *took* the divine wrath on himself (Hebrews 9:5; 1 John 2:2), so that if we believe in him, there is no wrath for us (John 3:36; Romans 8:1). When you are tempted to wonder if God still loves you, remember Jesus. Even if he never does another thing for any of us, *that's* what he's done lately.

Prayer: Lord, in Christ I have been forgiven, adopted into your family, made righteous in your sight, given the gift of the Spirit, and assured of my resurrection into glory unimaginable. Remind me that if you never did another thing for me, I should praise and serve you with my whole being for the rest of my life. Amen.

October 3

24 Then they despised the pleasant land; they did not believe his promise. **25** They grumbled in their tents and did not obey the LORD. **26** So he swore to them with uplifted hand that he would make them fall in the wilderness, **27** make their descendants fall among the nations and scatter them throughout the lands. **28** They yoked themselves to the Baal of Peor and ate sacrifices offered to lifeless gods; **29** they aroused the LORD's anger by their wicked deeds, and a plague broke out among them. **30** But Phinehas stood up and intervened, and the plague was checked. **31** This was credited to him as righteousness for endless generations to come.

HE SWORE TO THEM. When God promised punishment, even on oath (verses 26–27), it did not bring the people to obedience. There are many "scared straight" programs. Some expose at-risk juveniles to the realities of prison life; others show them the grim statistics and frightening consequences of drug addiction. Studies show that people who go through these programs are *more* likely to do the thing they are being warned against, not less.[110] Forbidding any behavior arouses in people a desire to do it and inspires a luxuriant growth of self-justifying internal reasoning why *they* are different. Paul said that when he most wanted to do the right thing, evil within him was aroused (Romans 7:14–24). We need a Savior.

Prayer: Lord, I grieve over the impurity and stubbornness of my heart. It is so both through the sin I inherited and through my life-long indulgence of it. How wretched I am! "Who will rescue me from this body that is subject to death? Thanks be to God, who delivers me through Jesus Christ our Lord!" (Romans 7:24–25). Amen.

October 4

READ Psalm 106:32–39. **32** By the waters of Meribah they angered the LORD, and trouble came to Moses because of them; **33** for they rebelled against the Spirit of God, and rash words came from Moses' lips. **34** They did not destroy the peoples as the LORD had commanded them, **35** but they mingled with the nations and adopted their customs. **36** They worshiped their idols, which became a snare to them. **37** They sacrificed their sons and their daughters to false gods. **38** They shed innocent blood, the blood of their sons and daughters, whom they sacrificed to the idols of Canaan, and the land was desecrated by their blood. **39** They defiled themselves by what they did; by their deeds they prostituted themselves.

THEY WORSHIPPED THEIR IDOLS. God's command to destroy the inhabitants of Canaan makes modern readers shudder, but this directive should be seen in the larger context of God's saving purposes for the world.[111] God had been patient with the violent, human-sacrificing Canaanites for centuries before he brought judgment on them through the Israelites (Genesis 15:16). Today God calls Christians not to assault but to seek the good of the unbelieving cities where we live (Jeremiah 29:7). Nevertheless, living in pluralistic societies means we must be all the more careful not to absorb the culture's idols or to abandon God's laws in order to conform to the world (verse 36). This combination of love yet deep difference will make us appear, in our neighbors' eyes, to be both weird and attractive at the same time (1 Peter 2:11–12).

Prayer: Lord Jesus, I confess that in my public life I am just not different enough from my neighbors to attract either hostility or interest in my faith. I am not visibly happier, kinder, humbler, or wiser than others. O Lord, help me to grow in grace so I can be a credit to you, to whom I owe everything. Amen.

October 5

READ Psalm 106:40–48. **40** Therefore the LORD was angry with his people and abhorred his inheritance. **41** He gave them into the hands of the nations, and their foes ruled over them. **42** Their enemies oppressed them and subjected them to their power. **43** Many times he delivered them, but they were bent on rebellion and they wasted away in their sin. **44** Yet he took note of their distress when he heard their cry; **45** for their sake he remembered his covenant and out of his great love he relented. **46** He caused all who held them captive to show them mercy. **47** Save us, LORD our God, and gather us from the nations, that we may give thanks to your holy name and glory in your praise. **48** Praise be to the LORD, the God of Israel, from everlasting to everlasting. Let all the people say, "Amen!" Praise the LORD.

BUT . . . HE HEARD THEIR CRY. Many times God turned to the people, but the people never turned to him. Nevertheless, he heard their cry (verses 43–44). Why does God not give up on us? It is because he remembers his covenant (verse 45). God made a covenant with Abraham, walking between the pieces of the dead animals, swearing to the point of death to save and bless Abraham's descendants (Genesis 15:8–21). We who believe in Christ are Abraham's children, receiving the blessing despite our sin because Jesus went to the point of death and took the curse we deserve (Galatians 3:10–14). Our unfaithfulness in light of his faithfulness makes ours more heinous. But his faithfulness in light of our unfaithfulness makes his more wonderful.

Prayer: Lord Jesus, I praise you for your indefatigable love! You were so committed to me that you were willing to lose your immortality, power, and glory for me and to be thrown into unimaginable depths for me. I cannot help but be lost in wonder, love, and praise. Amen.

October 6

READ Psalm 107:1–9. **1** Give thanks to the Lord, for he is good; his love endures forever. **2** Let the redeemed of the Lord tell their story— those he redeemed from the hand of the foe, **3** those he gathered from the lands, from east and west, from north and south. **4** Some wandered in desert wastelands, finding no way to a city where they could settle. **5** They were hungry and thirsty, and their lives ebbed away. **6** Then they cried out to the Lord in their trouble, and he delivered them from their distress. **7** He led them by a straight way to a city where they could settle. **8** Let them give thanks to the Lord for his unfailing love and his wonderful deeds for mankind, **9** for he satisfies the thirsty and fills the hungry with good things.

THEY HAD NO CITY. Here are people who are lost (verse 4), hungry (verse 5), exhausted (verse 5), and isolated because they did not live in a city (verses 5 and 7). At one level this shows that cities can be good places for human thriving. At the deepest level it means we need Jesus—to heal our spiritual lostness, remove our spiritual hunger, give rest for our spiritual exhaustion, and through his Body end our loneliness.[112] So believers work to make our cities good places for everyone to live (Jeremiah 29:7) and also call all to become citizens of the heavenly city (Revelation 21–22; Hebrews 12:22–24) through faith in God.

Prayer: Lord, save me from being so caught up in my own pursuits that I'm not a great neighbor to others in my city. But also save me from being seduced too much by the glitz and excitement of my earthly city. Let my heart rest in its citizenship of your heavenly one. Amen.

October 7

READ Psalm 107:10–16. **10** Some sat in darkness, in utter darkness, prisoners suffering in iron chains, **11** because they rebelled against God's commands and despised the plans of the Most High. **12** So he subjected them to bitter labor; they stumbled, and there was no one to help. **13** Then they cried to the LORD in their trouble, and he saved them from their distress. **14** He brought them out of darkness, the utter darkness, and broke away their chains. **15** Let them give thanks to the LORD for his unfailing love and his wonderful deeds for mankind, **16** for he breaks down gates of bronze and cuts through bars of iron.

THEY SIT IN CHAINS. Here are people who are guilty (verse 11). They rebelled against God and are now chained in a dungeon behind iron bars and gates (verse 16). This represents the darkness of a conscience and soul weighed down by shame and a sense of condemnation from which they cannot free themselves. In response to the people's cry God breaks their chains and bars (verses 14 and 16). But it was *he* who had chained them (verses 11–12). If they deserve his punishment, how can he do this? He can cut through his own bars because he bore his own judgment in Jesus (Isaiah 53:6; Galatians 3:13; Romans 3:25). Cry to the Lord—no matter how great the sin—and he will hear you.

Prayer: Lord, *"Long my imprisoned spirit lay fast bound in sin and nature's night; Thine eye diffused a quickening ray—I woke, the dungeon flamed with light; My chains fell off, my heart was free, I rose, went forth, and followed Thee."*[113] I praise your name for your radical forgiveness. Amen.

October 8

READ Psalm 107:17–22. **17** Some became fools through their rebellious ways and suffered affliction because of their iniquities. **18** They loathed all food and drew near the gates of death. **19** Then they cried to the LORD in their trouble, and he saved them from their distress. **20** He sent out his word and healed them; he rescued them from the grave. **21** Let them give thanks to the LORD for his unfailing love and his wonderful deeds for mankind. **22** Let them sacrifice thank offerings and tell of his works with songs of joy.

THE SELF-DAMAGED. Here are people who have ruined themselves. They are sick (verse 18) because they have become fools (verse 17). "Fools" in the Bible are not just regular sinners but those who become destructively self-absorbed and self-deceived. The picture is of those who have badly damaged their spiritual and physical health through foolish, self-indulgent lifestyles and addictions. "In such a context, verse 18 could well call to mind in modern times the drug-addict, but only as one example of man's perennial determination to get hurt."[114] When God responds, they are not merely forgiven but healed by his Word (verse 20), particularly by his unfailing love (verse 21). Believing the Gospel does not only bring pardon for sin but also renovates us wholly—mind, will, and emotions (Romans 6:15–23).

Prayer: Lord, I rejoice in forgiveness of sin, but I still limp along, half crippled by fears, self-pity, anger, self-consciousness, and discouragement. All could be healed so much further if I took the truths of the Gospel more to heart. Bring your Word in deep—let it dwell in me richly—that I can be more freed from the effects of sin. Amen.

October 9

23 Some went out on the sea in ships; they were merchants on the mighty waters. **24** They saw the works of the LORD, his wonderful deeds in the deep. **25** For he spoke and stirred up a tempest that lifted high the waves. **26** They mounted up to the heavens and went down to the depths; in their peril their courage melted away. **27** They reeled and staggered like drunkards; they were at their wits' end. **28** Then they cried out to the LORD in their trouble, and he brought them out of their distress. **29** He stilled the storm to a whisper; the waves of the sea were hushed. **30** They were glad when it grew calm, and he guided them to their desired haven. **31** Let them give thanks to the LORD for his unfailing love and his wonderful deeds for mankind. **32** Let them exalt him in the assembly of the people and praise him in the council of the elders.

THE STORM BATTERED. Here are people threatened by forces far beyond them. Sea travel can be a metaphor for life. There are clear days in which we feel that we are in control, that our seacraft can take us anywhere we want to go. But when great storms come up, we realize we are helpless before the enormity of the waves (verse 26). The illusion is shattered that life (or the sea) can be tamed through our management skills ("wits," verse 27). Life troubles will sink us, if we are on own. But God is our haven in storms (verse 30). And the New Testament reminds us that he helps us two ways—either by removing the storm (Mark 4:35–41) or by enabling us to walk through it, looking to him (Matthew 14:29–31).

Prayer: Lord, I confess my overconfidence about my ability to manage life through planning, knowing the right people, reading the right books. But then "out of the blue" comes a storm and I am lost. Teach me how to depend on you and lean on you moment by moment. Without you I can do nothing. Amen.

October 10

READ Psalm 107:33–43. **33** He turned rivers into a desert, flowing springs into thirsty ground, **34** and fruitful land into a salt waste, because of the wickedness of those who lived there. **35** He turned the desert into pools of water and the parched ground into flowing springs; **36** there he brought the hungry to live, and they founded a city where they could settle. **37** They sowed fields and planted vineyards that yielded a fruitful harvest; **38** he blessed them, and their numbers greatly increased, and he did not let their herds diminish. **39** Then their numbers decreased, and they were humbled by oppression, calamity and sorrow; **40** he who pours contempt on nobles made them wander in a trackless waste. **41** But he lifted the needy out of their affliction and increased their families like flocks. **42** The upright see and rejoice, but all the wicked shut their mouths. **43** Let the one who is wise heed these things and ponder the loving deeds of the LORD.

CONSIDER THE GREAT LOVE. Every stanza in this psalm was a case study in God's love (verse 43). Some brought their trouble on themselves (the guilty and the self-damaged) while some did not (the homeless and the storm tossed). Despite their radically different situations, there was one common factor. Every time the people "cried to the Lord" (verses 6, 13, 19, and 28) they were heard and given what they needed—community, forgiveness, healing, and haven. The lesson? The love of God is not earned; it's a gift of grace. You connect to it not by your merits or the quality of your life but through dependent prayer. Everyone who cried to God was heard. Behold how he loves us.

Prayer: Lord, there is only one password for getting into your infinite stores of grace and love. It is not "MyRighteousness" but "ChristsRighteousness." I praise you that, because of his work for me on the cross, I need only come with my need, and you will hear me. Amen.

October 11

READ Psalm 108:1–4. **1** My heart, O God, is steadfast; I will sing and make music with all my soul. **2** Awake, harp and lyre! I will awaken the dawn. **3** I will praise you, LORD, among the nations; I will sing of you among the peoples. **4** For great is your love, higher than the heavens; your faithfulness reaches to the skies.

COURAGE THROUGH SUFFERING. Psalm 108 combines the second halves of Psalm 57 and 60, both of which were desperate laments. But when they are combined here, the effect is dramatically different. This psalm is an expression of a "steadfast" heart, one with courage (verse 1). There is an aggressive joy here. Even if it is dark, the psalmist's song to God will *bring on* the dawn (verse 2). This is not a naive optimism but a confidence in God, literally pieced together out of former experiences of great vulnerability and need. This is why the Bible talks about strength coming out of weakness. The more times we are in narrow straits and we see God bring us through, the more peace and courage we will have as time goes on.

Prayer: Lord, I praise you for strengthening me not just in spite of my weakness but through it. As enormous pressure turns coal into diamonds, and fire turns ore into gold; let my experiences of suffering make me like your Son. Amen.

October 12

READ Psalm 108:5–13. **5** Be exalted, O God, above the heavens; let your glory be over all the earth. **6** Save us and help us with your right hand, that those you love may be delivered. **7** God has spoken from his sanctuary: "In triumph I will parcel out Shechem and measure off the Valley of Sukkoth. **8** Gilead is mine, Manasseh is mine; Ephraim is my helmet, Judah is my scepter. **9** Moab is my washbasin, on Edom I toss my sandal; over Philistia I shout in triumph." **10** Who will bring me to the fortified city? Who will lead me to Edom? **11** Is it not you, God, you who have rejected us and no longer go out with our armies? **12** Give us aid against the enemy, for human help is worthless. **13** With God we will gain the victory, and he will trample down our enemies.

COURAGE FOR HIS SAKE. "Steadfastness" (see verse 1) is courage—standing one's ground and doing right regardless of fears and consequences. Where does courage come from? Primarily it comes from wanting something more than your own safety. David wants all to see God's glory (verse 5). True courage is not "I can do it"—that is self-confidence. It is, rather, "This is more important than me." In the animal kingdom the mother undauntedly faces any size foe, not because she thinks she can win but for the sake of her young. David will face any foe for the sake of his Lord, whom he loves above all. He's not looking at himself. That is the secret of courage.

Prayer: Lord, give me such a sense of your living reality in my life that I live a more fearless life. Fear is just thinking of myself and my abilities instead of having my mind focused on you. Give me enough love for you to be brave. Amen.

October 13

READ Psalm 109:1–5. **1** My God, whom I praise, do not remain silent, **2** for people who are wicked and deceitful have opened their mouths against me; they have spoken against me with lying tongues. **3** With words of hatred they surround me; they attack me without cause. **4** In return for my friendship they accuse me, but I am a man of prayer. **5** They repay me evil for good, and hatred for my friendship.

BUT I AM A MAN OF PRAYER. David has given his attackers his friendship (verses 4 and 5), but in return they denounce him with words of hatred and lies (verses 2 and 3). How does David respond? Very simply he says, "But I am a man of prayer" (verse 4). It means he continues to pray for them even while they attack him (cf. Matthew 5:44). It also means that in times of terrible stress, he runs into the refuge of prayer. Is that how you respond to stress? And do you deal with attacks by praying fervently for your attackers (even as you may be seeking to right their wrongs or confront them)? It will make all the difference.

Prayer: Lord, my prayer is for my prayer. Help me change my heart toward those who trouble me. Through prayer drain away my ill will and desire to see them unhappy. I know those feelings harden and dehumanize me. Save me from them, please, Lord. Amen.

October 14

READ Psalm 109:6–15. **6** Appoint someone evil to oppose my enemy; let an accuser stand at his right hand. **7** When he is tried, let him be found guilty, and may his prayers condemn him. **8** May his days be few; may another take his place of leadership. **9** May his children be fatherless and his wife a widow. **10** May his children be wandering beggars; may they be driven from their ruined homes. **11** May a creditor seize all he has; may strangers plunder the fruits of his labor. **12** May no one extend kindness to him or take pity on his fatherless children. **13** May his descendants be cut off, their names blotted out from the next generation. **14** May the iniquity of his fathers be remembered before the LORD; may the sin of his mother never be blotted out. **15** May their sins always remain before the LORD, that he may blot out their name from the earth.

MAY THEIR SINS REMAIN. We cringe when we read David's white-hot cries for his enemies to pay for their sins. But we should be grateful that God hears cries against injustice (James 5:4). Also, we see how even here David leaves judgment to God (Romans 12:19). He doesn't say *he* will make his enemy's children beggars (verse 10). It is not wrong to be angry about wrongdoing if you leave it to the Lord to act. But merely venting our anger often leads to sinful bitterness, hate, and an unforgiving spirit.[115] On this side of the cross Christians should not curse but bless opponents (Romans 12:14) as did Jesus, who also was betrayed by a close friend.

Prayer: God of justice, I am thankful that you hear even our angry cries. Yet I need your strong help when I make them. Save me from letting my concern for justice devour my love and desire to see my opponents change and thrive. Let this be true in my politics as well as in my personal relationships. Amen.

October 15

READ Psalm 109:16–20. **16** For he never thought of doing a kindness, but hounded to death the poor and the needy and the brokenhearted. **17** He loved to pronounce a curse—may it come back on him. He found no pleasure in blessing—may it be far from him. **18** He wore cursing as his garment; it entered into his body like water, into his bones like oil. **19** May it be like a cloak wrapped about him, like a belt tied forever around him. **20** May this be the LORD's payment to my accusers, to those who speak evil of me.

SINS OF OMISSION. This description makes David's anger at his enemies more understandable. It also shows the justness of his prayer. David recognizes sin's recoil effect. God's judgment often works through natural consequences in which, over the long run, people receive back what they planned or chose for others (verses 17–19). This helps David and us leave vengeance in God's hands. The description also should convict and help us avoid the sin of self-congratulation. When we look at those doing sins of commission, like cursing and abusing people verbally (verse 17), we may feel pretty self-righteous if we don't do the same things. But the failure to think of doing a kindness (verse 16) is a sin of *omission,* one of which we are all guilty (James 4:17).

Prayer: Lord, I confess that so many of my sins are failures to serve and love people because I am too wrapped up in myself to think or notice their needs. O Lord, save me from sinful obliviousness. Amen.

October 16

BUT YOU, LORD. The phrase "But you, Sovereign Lord" here, as ever in the psalms, marks a great turning point. Hard prayers become softer, hopeless prayers more confident, sad prayers are filled with joy, and guilty prayers arrive in mercy. Our prayer may rightly begin with our own hurts, sins, enemies, surroundings, troubles. But it is only when you lay these things before God, see them in light of who he is, and say, "But you . . ."—that release, relief, growth, hope, and strength begin to come. The "But you . . ." of the psalms has its New Testament counterpart in Paul's great "*But* now. . . ." The entire human race is lost in sin (Romans 1:18–3:20), "but now apart from the law . . . righteousness is given through faith in Jesus Christ" (Romans 3:21–22).

Prayer: Lord, I thank you that your reality changes *everything.* I am weak—O, but you . . . I deserve nothing—O, but you . . . I don't see any way out of this—O, but you . . . My life seems to be derailed—O, but you . . . I don't know how to pray. Ah, but you will help me. Amen.

October 17

READ Psalm 109: 30–31. **30** With my mouth I will greatly extol the LORD; in the great throng of worshipers I will praise him. **31** For he stands at the right hand of the needy, to save their lives from those who would condemn them.

AT THE RIGHT HAND OF THE NEEDY. In ancient law courts your accuser would stand at your right hand, prosecuting his case against you. David declares that he is the victim of false indictments, and hopes that a prosecutor would be put at his enemy's right hand (see verse 6.) Now suddenly the scene changes, and God who stands "at the right hand of the needy" (verse 31) to defend them, not accuse them. In Jesus Christ God came to be our advocate (1 John 2:1–2). He stands for our defense when we are accused (cf. Acts 7:56.) And when Jesus the true advocate came, he forgave his betrayer and enemies (John 13:18–30). So should we.

Prayer: Lord, I confess my grudges. I justify them because I am not seeking repayment, but I avoid some people and I hope for them to fail. Help me forgive fully, all the way down, and begin to pray for their repentance and good. *"My sin, dear Savior, made thee bleed, yet thou didst pray for me!"*[116] Amen.

October 18

READ Psalm 110. **1** The LORD says to my lord: "Sit at my right hand until I make your enemies a footstool for your feet." **2** The LORD will extend your mighty scepter from Zion, saying, "Rule in the midst of your enemies!" **3** Your troops will be willing on your day of battle. Arrayed in holy splendor, your young men will come to you like dew from the morning's womb. **4** The LORD has sworn and will not change his mind: "You are a priest forever, in the order of Melchizedek." **5** The Lord is at your right hand; he will crush kings on the day of his wrath. **6** He will judge the nations, heaping up the dead and crushing the rulers of the whole earth. **7** He will drink from a brook along the way, and so he will lift his head high.

THE PRIEST-KING. David hears a word from God to his "lord" (verse 1). But since he was Israel's king, who could be his superior? Jesus says the verse refers to him (Mark 12:35–37). But this powerful king is also a sympathetic priest (verse 4; cf. Genesis 14:18–20; Hebrews 6:19–7:28) who represents the people to God. So Jesus is both human and divine, both a lion and a lamb (Revelation 5:5–6). While earthly kings conquer by filling the world with bodies (verse 6), Jesus conquers by converting and filling the earth with his body (Ephesians 1:22–23). So there is a battle to be fought, but with the weapons of love, service, and truth (2 Corinthians 10:4–5; Romans 12:9–21). Will you enlist (verse 3)?

Prayer: Lord, *"for not with swords loud clashing, nor roll of stirring drums; with deeds of love and mercy the heavenly kingdom comes."*[117] With your Spirit overcome my lack of generosity and my obsession with my own needs and security, so that I can truly be part of your work in the world. Amen.

October 19

READ Psalm 111. **1** Praise the LORD. I will extol the LORD with all my heart in the council of the upright and in the assembly. **2** Great are the works of the LORD; they are pondered by all who delight in them. **3** Glorious and majestic are his deeds, and his righteousness endures forever. **4** He has caused his wonders to be remembered; the LORD is gracious and compassionate. **5** He provides food for those who fear him; he remembers his covenant forever. **6** He has shown his people the power of his works, giving them the lands of other nations. **7** The works of his hands are faithful and just; all his precepts are trustworthy. **8** They are established for ever and ever, enacted in faithfulness and uprightness. **9** He provided redemption for his people; he ordained his covenant forever—holy and awesome is his name. **10** The fear of the LORD is the beginning of wisdom; all who follow his precepts have good understanding. To him belongs eternal praise.

THE ONE WE MUST RESEMBLE. Psalm 111 describes God and Psalm 112 how his people come to resemble their God. We were made in his "image" (Genesis 1:27). That means we were made to relate to him and reflect back to him his own character. So who is this God we should be like? God is a worker who makes things (verse 2). He is righteous (verse 3), compassionate (verses 4–5), and a God of truth (verses 7–8.) Finally, he is a God of integrity, who keeps his promises (verse 9). We will become like this not simply by obeying his rules (as important as that is) but through "the fear of the LORD" (verse 10), worshipping him with awe. We become like the things we love most.

Prayer: Lord, I may say my prayers and obey your commands, but it is true worship and adoration that will actually change me. Don't let me settle for the shallows of mere religious compliance. Fill me with the joyful fear that comes as we seek your face. Amen.

October 20

READ Psalm 112. **1** Praise the LORD. Blessed are those who fear the LORD, who find great delight in his commands. **2** Their children will be mighty in the land; the generation of the upright will be blessed. **3** Wealth and riches are in their houses, and their righteousness endures forever. **4** Even in darkness light dawns for the upright, for those who are gracious and compassionate and righteous. **5** Good will come to those who are generous and lend freely, who conduct their affairs with justice. **6** Surely the righteous will never be shaken; they will be remembered forever. **7** They will have no fear of bad news; their hearts are steadfast, trusting in the LORD. **8** Their hearts are secure, they will have no fear; in the end they will look in triumph on their foes. **9** They have freely scattered their gifts to the poor, their righteousness endures forever; their horn will be lifted high in honor. **10** The wicked will see and be vexed, they will gnash their teeth and waste away; the longings of the wicked will come to nothing.

THEIR LONGINGS COME TO NOTHING. Those who do not merely believe in God but fear him and so obey out of inner delight (see verse 1) have their characters transformed into his likeness (Ephesians 4:22–24). God is compassionate (111:4) and so they are generous (verses 4–5). God's word endures (111:8) and so those who fear him are steadfast even when news is bad (verse 7). God is righteous (111:3) and so are they (verse 3), but remember that "righteousness" in the Bible consists not only of traditional family values (verse 2) but also of helping the poor (verse 9). The psalm says without God your deepest longings won't be fulfilled (verse 10). That means that with God they will be (Psalm 16:11; John 6:35).

Prayer: Lord, I thank you that you give us the bread of life. All around me people are looking for meaning, satisfaction, freedom, connection. But these are all aspects of deep spiritual hunger, and only your grace and your face can satisfy that. Keep me from their cosmic wild goose chases. Let me taste and see that you are good. Amen.

October 21

READ Psalm 113. **1** Praise the LORD. Praise the LORD, you his servants, praise the name of the LORD. **2** Let the name of the LORD be praised, both now and forevermore. **3** From the rising of the sun to the place where it sets, the name of the LORD is to be praised. **4** The LORD is exalted over all the nations, his glory above the heavens. **5** Who is like the LORD our God, the One who sits enthroned on high, **6** who stoops down to look on the heavens and the earth? **7** He raises the poor from the dust and lifts the needy from the ash heap; **8** he seats them with princes, with the princes of his people. **9** He settles the childless woman in her home as a happy mother of children. Praise the LORD.

GREATNESS AND SMALLNESS. Praise God because there is nothing too great for him. He is over all time (verse 2), all places (verse 3), and all human power and authority (verse 4). But also praise him because there is no one too small for God (verses 7–9). He enthrones the poor (verse 7). The situation of the poor often is used to open them spiritually to the need for grace and the riches of salvation (Luke 6:20; Revelation 1:6). Materially God works for justice in history for the oppressed (Psalm 103:6, 140:12, 146:7). He loves working through the barren (think of Sarah, Hannah, and Elizabeth) and puts the lonely in community (verse 9). God's greatness is seen in his regard for the ungreat. In Jesus he proved to be great enough to become small himself.

Prayer: Lord Jesus, I praise you that one infinitely greater than the universe with all its galaxies would become a tiny infant who needed to be fed and carried and changed. And you did it for me. That humbles my heart and yet lifts it to the stars as well. Thank you, Lord. Amen.

October 22

READ Psalm 114. **1** When Israel came out of Egypt, Jacob from a people of foreign tongue, **2** Judah became God's sanctuary, Israel his dominion. **3** The sea looked and fled, the Jordan turned back; **4** the mountains leaped like rams, the hills like lambs. **5** Why was it, sea, that you fled? Why, Jordan, did you turn back? **6** Why, mountains, did you skip like rams, you hills, like lambs? **7** Tremble, earth, at the presence of the Lord, at the presence of the God of Jacob, **8** who turned the rock into a pool, the hard rock into springs of water.

SHAKING THE EARTH. As Israel left Egypt, things that seemed to be absolute barriers were removed by the power of God. The Red Sea parted and the mountains shook (Exodus 19:18; Hebrews 12:18–27). The psalmist taunts the earthly powers—saying the mountains "leaped like lambs" (verse 4). God's love for us shakes the world, because nothing can come between us and God's love (Romans 8:38). At both Jesus's death (Matthew 27:51) and his Resurrection (Matthew 28:2) the earth shook, indicating the coming of God's power to save. To get us to our true country to live with him, he will shake and destroy death itself (1 Corinthians 15:56–57). So let nothing move or intimidate you (1 Corinthians 15:58).

Prayer: Lord, how easily I get shaken. Criticism, a sense of failure, changes and losses—all these things rattle me. Help me to live in the "kingdom that cannot be shaken" (Hebrews 12:28). Teach me how to build my life every day on your Word and your love, which will endure when all other things pass away. Amen.

October 23

READ Psalm 115:1–8. **1** Not to us, LORD, not to us but to your name be the glory, because of your love and faithfulness. **2** Why do the nations say, "Where is their God?" **3** Our God is in heaven; he does whatever pleases him. **4** But their idols are silver and gold, made by human hands. **5** They have mouths, but cannot speak, eyes, but cannot see. **6** They have ears, but cannot hear, noses, but cannot smell. **7** They have hands, but cannot feel, feet, but cannot walk, nor can they utter a sound with their throats. **8** Those who make them will be like them, and so will all who trust in them.

THE POWER OF IDOLS. In the story *Something Wicked This Way Comes,* each person has a particular secret desire which they think will bring fulfillment—restored youth, sex with the beauty of their fantasies, athletic prowess, lots of money.[118] But when they sell everything to get their dream, they are enslaved by it rather than satisfied. That fits with the biblical teaching of idolatry. Anything more important to you than the real God is an alternate god. Idols have no power (verses 5–7) to give you the love, forgiveness, and guidance you need. But paradoxically they do have power to make you like them (verse 8) and to keep you both spiritually blind and unable to see as well as spiritually lame and unable to change.

Prayer: Lord, I confess that I make an idol out of people's approval. Let me be so satisfied with your love that I no longer respond to people out of fear of displeasing them but only in love, seeking what is best for them. Remove my idols of approval—which can never give me the approval I need. Amen.

October 24

READ Psalm 115:9–18. **9** All you Israelites, trust in the LORD—he is their help and shield. **10** House of Aaron, trust in the LORD—he is their help and shield. **11** You who fear him, trust in the LORD—he is their help and shield. **12** The LORD remembers us and will bless us: He will bless his people Israel, he will bless the house of Aaron, **13** he will bless those who fear the LORD—small and great alike. **14** May the LORD cause you to flourish, both you and your children. **15** May you be blessed by the LORD, the Maker of heaven and earth. **16** The highest heavens belong to the LORD, but the earth he has given to mankind. **17** It is not the dead who praise the LORD, those who go down to the place of silence; **18** it is we who extol the LORD, both now and forevermore. Praise the LORD.

BLESSING. The word "bless" or "blessed" is repeated five times. The word means richness, fullness, multidimensional thriving, and satisfaction. Idols cannot give it. When the psalmist speaks of blessing for "Israel" (verse 12), it reminds us of Jacob (named Israel) who had wrestled all his life to get his father Isaac's blessing (Genesis 28:1–41). One lonely night in the dark a mysterious figure began to wrestle with him. When Jacob realized this was a manifestation of the Lord himself, he said, "I won't let you go until you bless me." We don't know exactly what God said, but we learn, "Then he blessed him there" (Genesis 32:26–29). Nothing else in life will give you the deep blessing you crave most, but the Lord will do it.

Prayer: Father, your Son Jesus Christ gives me the meaning, value, and security I look for in other things. I ask that you help me to rejoice in him more fully than I do. *Break my schemes of earthly joy so I may find my all in Thee.*[119] Amen.

October 25

READ Psalm 116:1–11. **1** I love the LORD, for he heard my voice; he heard my cry for mercy. **2** Because he turned his ear to me, I will call on him as long as I live. **3** The cords of death entangled me, the anguish of the grave came over me; I was overcome by distress and sorrow. **4** Then I called on the name of the LORD: "LORD, save me!" **5** The LORD is gracious and righteous; our God is full of compassion. **6** The LORD protects the unwary; when I was brought low, he saved me. **7** Return to your rest, my soul, for the LORD has been good to you. **8** For you, LORD, have delivered me from death, my eyes from tears, my feet from stumbling, **9** that I may walk before the LORD in the land of the living. **10** I trusted in the LORD when I said, "I am greatly afflicted"; **11** in my alarm I said, "Everyone is a liar."

A THANKFUL LIFE. The psalmist almost died (verses 3 and 8). In his fear he called everyone a liar (verse 11), but he trusted God even when his emotions were out of control (verse 10). Now he has restructured his life on the basis of grateful love. The first mark of a thankful life is this: "I will call on him as long as I live" (verse 2). To call on God's name means two things in the Bible—to trust in him and nothing else for your salvation (Romans 10:12–13) and to orient your whole life to prayer and worship (Genesis 12:8). Grateful people should also *walk* before God (verse 9). This means to live conscious of him at all time. It is to be both "wholly exposed [and accountable] but wholly befriended [and loved]."[120] Love the Lord, for he listens.

Prayer: Lord, when I get into a tight place, my heart instinctively says, "I can fix this. I can handle this." I think about people to call—but it is all futile. I *can't* handle life, and the sooner I admit this deep in myself, the sooner I'll know the peace of always calling on you. Amen.

October 26

DELIVERED FROM DEATH. God saved the psalmist from death (verse 8) because his servants' deaths are costly ("precious") and painful to him (verse 15). The psalmist feels he has been virtually resurrected back into the land of the living (see verse 9). God does, of course, allow his people to die, but they are *so* precious to him that he will someday pay the ultimate price on the cross so that our physical death will be just an entrance into greater life (2 Corinthians 5:1–10). Therefore, we can drink "the cup of salvation" to him (verse 13), celebrating this salvation in worship. But that is only because he drank the cup of divine wrath on sin, for us (Luke 22:42).

Prayer: Lord, you died that I might not die forever, and you rose so I might live forever. For this may I *"sing your praise without delays."*[121] Help me live my days in joyful hope, helping my soul to remember that as sin *"consigned thee to dust, His life may make thee gold, and much more, just."*[122] Amen.

October 27

READ Psalm 117. **1** Praise the LORD, all you nations; extol him, all you peoples. **2** For great is his love toward us, and the faithfulness of the LORD endures forever. Praise the LORD.

SINGING TO THE NATIONS. All peoples should praise God (verse 1) for his "love toward *us*" (verse 2). The Gospel proclaims God has broken into history to save a people for himself and has done so supremely in Jesus. This challenges the narrowness of those who believe "all good people can go to heaven" whether they believe in Jesus or not. No—this salvation is open to all, even those who have not led good, moral, and pulled-together lives. It is not for those who think they are good enough but for those who know they can be saved only by God's *chesedh,* his grace (verse 2), and who believe in Jesus's saving work in history for *us.* If you pray or sing this psalm, it recoils on you. You must go out and sing God's praises to the nations too.

Prayer: Lord, I praise you that you care for *all* the races, nations, and peoples, that you want to encompass all of them with your saving love. I confess I am not nearly as generous, that some kinds of people I strongly dislike. Help me to see all as both sinful and yet the recipients of your loving offers. Amen.

October 28

READ Psalm 118:1–9. **1** Give thanks to the Lord, for he is good; his love endures forever. **2** Let Israel say: "His love endures forever." **3** Let the house of Aaron say: "His love endures forever." **4** Let those who fear the Lord say: "His love endures forever." **5** When hard pressed, I cried to the Lord; he brought me into a spacious place. **6** The Lord is with me; I will not be afraid. What can mere mortals do to me? **7** The Lord is with me; he is my helper. I look in triumph on my enemies. **8** It is better to take refuge in the Lord than to trust in humans. **9** It is better to take refuge in the Lord than to trust in princes.

DON'T TRUST IN MAN. What does it mean to "trust in humans" (verse 8)? It is to build your life on the approval of others. You may feel good about yourself only if someone is romantically in love with you, or if you are being praised and complimented on your looks, intellect, or talent. But this will make you too needy of both affirmation and sexual intimacy, too devastated by criticism, too starry-eyed about celebrity. What is it to "trust in princes" (verse 9)? It is to make an idol out of power, to want too much to have influential friends, to need too much to be in charge yourself. This will leave you increasingly lonely as time goes on, for the essence of love is humble service (Romans 15:3). Take refuge in God.

Prayer: Lord, when I forget the Gospel I become dependent on the smiles and evaluation of others. I hear all criticism as a condemnation of my very being. But you have said that "there is now no condemnation" for me (Romans 8:1). You delight and sing over me (Zephaniah 3:14–17); you see me as a beauty (Colossians 1:22). Let me always remember that! Amen.

October 29

READ Psalm 118:10–18. **10** All the nations surrounded me, but in the name of the LORD I cut them down. **11** They surrounded me on every side, but in the name of the LORD I cut them down. **12** They swarmed around me like bees, but they were consumed as quickly as burning thorns; in the name of the LORD I cut them down. **13** I was pushed back and about to fall, but the LORD helped me. **14** The LORD is my strength and my defense; he has become my salvation. **15** Shouts of joy and victory resound in the tents of the righteous: "The LORD's right hand has done mighty things! **16** The LORD's right hand is lifted high; the LORD's right hand has done mighty things!" **17** I will not die but live, and will proclaim what the LORD has done. **18** The LORD has chastened me severely, but he has not given me over to death.

CHASTENING. These verses describe an attack by enemies, which the psalmist, with God's help, drives back. But he discerns that behind the hostility of enemies, and despite God's help in escaping them (verse 17), God was nevertheless using it to chasten him (verse 18). The word "chasten" means "instruction with teeth." It means to shape someone through a severe regimen. Hebrews 12:4–12 uses the Greek word *gymnazdo* to convey that God "disciplines" those he loves. During a workout your muscles feel like they are getting weaker, but the pressure on them is making you stronger. This is why God, like a trainer, allows pressures and stresses into your life: to grow your faith, love, and hope. Can you discern his training in your life?

Prayer: Lord, I praise you for loving me enough to not just leave me as I am. I thank you for your training regimen in my life. Like all training it's exhausting—that's how it works. When I become impatient with it, help me remember Jesus, who was chastened voluntarily, not for his sins but for mine (Hebrews 12:1–3). Amen.

October 30

READ Psalm 118:19–29. **19** Open for me the gates of the righteous; I will enter and give thanks to the LORD. **20** This is the gate of the LORD through which the righteous may enter. **21** I will give you thanks, for you answered me; you have become my salvation. **22** The stone the builders rejected has become the cornerstone; **23** the LORD has done this, and it is marvelous in our eyes. **24** The LORD has done it this very day; let us rejoice today and be glad. **25** LORD, save us! LORD, grant us success! **26** Blessed is he who comes in the name of the LORD. From the house of the LORD we bless you. **27** The LORD is God, and he has made his light shine on us. With boughs in hand, join in the festal procession up to the horns of the altar. **28** You are my God, and I will give praise you; you are my God, and I will exalt you. **29** Give thanks to the LORD, for he is good; his love endures forever.

OPEN THE GATES. The nation's leaders rejected the psalmist as builders discard a useless stone. But God made him a cornerstone (verse 22). When he came to the temple's gates, where only the righteous might pass (verses 19–20), he was welcomed up to the horns of the altar (verse 27).[123] Later Jesus came to Jerusalem to the shouts of Psalm 118:26: "Blessed is he who comes." He too was rejected by the leaders and went to the altar, but as a sacrifice for sin (Isaiah 53:10; Hebrews 9:12), making us righteous so we can go in to God (Hebrews 10:22). When we pray, the "gates of the righteous" are opened. Through his sacrifice we have access to the Father by the Spirit (Ephesians 2:18).

Prayer: Lord, I praise you that your Son willingly paid a terrible price in order for me to gain access to you in prayer. If he was willing to come all the way from heaven to earth to do that, can I not rouse myself a bit earlier every morning to use this blood-bought gift? Lord, make me a person of prayer. Amen.

October 31

READ Psalm 119:1–8. **1** Blessed are they whose ways are blameless, who walk according to the law of the LORD. **2** Blessed are they who keep his statutes and seek him with all their heart— **3** they do no wrong but follow his ways. **4** You have laid down precepts that are to be fully obeyed. **5** Oh, that my ways were steadfast in obeying your decrees! **6** Then I would not be put to shame when I consider all your commands. **7** I will praise you with an upright heart as I learn your righteous laws. **8** I will obey your decrees; do not utterly forsake me.

THE WORD: WHAT IT IS. Psalm 1 said the key to knowing God is delight in God's Word. What is it? As his law, decrees, and commands his Word is absolutely authoritative and must be obeyed (verses 1 and 5–6). As his statutes it is permanently relevant for every time and place and must be trusted (verse 2). As his precepts it is consummate wisdom such that what he requires perfectly fits our needs and nature (verse 4). As his "ways" it is not a set of abstract rules but an expression of God's own character and nature (verse 3). So knowing the Bible is no end in itself. We know it in order to seek *him with all our heart*—to know fellowship with God (verse 2).

Prayer: Lord, for years I thought that you could be active in my life through the Spirit and that the Bible was just a book of rules and inspirational stories. Thank you for showing me that the Bible *is* the way that, through the Spirit, you are active in my life. Let me know you through your Word. Amen.

November 1

READ Psalm 119:9–16. **9** How can a young person stay on the path of purity? By living according to your word. **10** I seek you with all my heart; do not let me stray from your commands. **11** I have hidden your word in my heart that I might not sin against you. **12** Praise be to you, LORD; teach me your decrees. **13** With my lips I recount all the laws that come from your mouth. **14** I rejoice in following your statutes as one rejoices in great riches. **15** I meditate on your precepts and consider your ways. **16** I delight in your decrees; I will not neglect your word.

THE WORD: WHAT WE SHOULD DO. How should we use the Word? We should see amazing riches in the Word (verse 14) and meditate on it long and hard (verses 15–16). We must hide the word of God in our hearts through closely reading and memorizing it. We ought to work the truths of Scripture into our affections until they shape our loves, hopes, and imagination. Jesus was the preeminent example of this. In his darkest moments, when he is being forsaken (Matthew 26:31), betrayed (Matthew 26:53–56), and killed (Matthew 27:46)—he quotes Scripture. His heart was so shaped by Scripture that it came to mind whenever he was in need or difficulty. The Word of God should also "dwell in us richly" (Colossians 3:16). Does it?

Prayer: Lord, there is nothing valuable in life that does not require enormous work—why should knowing you through your Word be any different? I confess I neglect your word. Even when I read it I neglect to digest and apply it. Help me! Amen.

November 2

READ Psalm 119:17–24. **17** Be good to your servant while I live, that I may obey your word. **18** Open my eyes that I may see wonderful things in your law. **19** I am a stranger on earth; do not hide your commands from me. **20** My soul is consumed with longing for your laws at all times. **21** You rebuke the arrogant, who are accursed, those who stray from your commands. **22** Remove from me their scorn and contempt, for I keep your statutes. **23** Though rulers sit together and slander me, your servant will meditate on your decrees. **24** Your statutes are my delight; they are my counselors.

THE WORD IS OUR COUNSELOR. One way to face isolation (verse 19), scorn, contempt, and slander (verses 22–23) is by seeking out counselors. The Bible itself can become a wonderful counselor (verse 24) but only if you are able to see "wonders" in it (verse 18). Paul speaks of a spiritual veil or covering over our minds (2 Corinthians 3:14–18). We may see various facts in the Bible, but without the Spirit's help we can't see the gloriousness and wonder of the Bible's teaching, and of Christ himself. The Spirit can remove the veil (2 Corinthians 3:18). Ask God to open your eyes to the beauties and glories of Scripture (verse 18). Then it can become the physician of your soul.

Prayer: Lord Jesus, you have been called Wonderful Counselor, and indeed you are! But it is within the pages of your Word that I have found your priceless advice and comfort. Open my eyes to understand the Scriptures so I can receive more and more of your counsel. Amen.

November 3

READ Psalm 119:25–32. **25** I am laid low in the dust; preserve my life according to your word. **26** I gave an account of my ways and you answered me; teach me your decrees. **27** Cause me to understand the way of your precepts, that I may meditate on your wonderful deeds. **28** My soul is weary with sorrow; strengthen me according to your word. **29** Keep me from deceitful ways; be gracious to me and teach me your law. **30** I have chosen the way of faithfulness; I have set my heart on your laws. **31** I hold fast to your statutes, LORD; do not let me be put to shame. **32** I run in the path of your commands, for you have broadened my understanding.

THE WORD IS OUR EXAMINER. The psalmist surveys his life (verse 26) using the Word to examine himself. Verse 29, "Keep me from deceitful ways," shows that the Word of God keeps you from being deceived about who you are, as well as from being a deceiver of others. Contemporary people tend to examine the Bible, looking for things they can't accept, but Christians should reverse that, allowing the Bible to examine *us*, looking for things God can't accept. Verse 30 says the psalmist has set his heart on being faithful to God's laws. We can't truly understand the Scripture unless we make a basic commitment, saying "whatever I find in your Word, I will do." This seems restrictive but will lead to freedom (see verse 45).

Prayer: Lord, I indeed need to search the Scriptures. But once I learn what a Scripture means, I must let it search *my* heart to its depths. Give me enough humility and love to do that. Amen.

November 4

READ Psalm 119:33–40. **33** Teach me, LORD, the way of your decrees, that I may follow it to the end. **34** Give me understanding, so that I may keep your law and obey it with all my heart. **35** Direct me in the path of your commands, for there I find delight. **36** Turn my heart toward your statutes and not toward selfish gain. **37** Turn my eyes away from worthless things; preserve my life according to your word. **38** Fulfill your promise to your servant, so that you may be feared. **39** Take away the disgrace I dread, for your laws are good. **40** How I long for your precepts! In your righteousness preserve my life.

THE WORD AND THE SELVES. The psalmist wants to keep God's law (verse 34) but finds the heart is easily turned to more self-interested ends (verse 36) and to idols ("worthless things," verse 37). Ephesians 4:22–24 tells us that believers have an "old self" and a "new self." Christians know that the old self struggles constantly with a sense of disgrace it dreads (verse 39), a feeling we aren't good enough. That is a true intuition! But your moral efforts won't address it. Only in Christ is the disgrace removed and a whole new identity given (Romans 8:1; Hebrews 10:22). Every day is a battle—will you operate out of your old self or your new self?

Prayer: Lord, I confess my old self, my old way of earning my acceptance and security, is still very present. It is why I still feel this sickening, vague dread of being exposed, found out as an impostor, a failure. Lord, burn deep into my conscience and heart this truth: The blood of Jesus Christ cleanses us from all sin. Amen.

November 5

READ Psalm 119:41–48.
41 May your unfailing love come to me, LORD, your salvation, according to your promise; **42** then I can answer anyone who taunts me, for I trust in your word. **43** Never take your word of truth from my mouth, for I have put my hope in your laws. **44** I will always obey your law, for ever and ever. **45** I will walk about in freedom, for I have sought out your precepts. **46** I will speak of your statutes before kings and will not be put to shame, **47** for I delight in your commands because I love them. **48** I reach out for your commands, which I love, that I may meditate on your decrees.

THE WORD AND FREEDOM. The more the psalmist seeks to obey God, the more he "walk[s] about in freedom" (verse 45). If God is not ruling us, something else is: sin and habit (verse 133), need for love and approval (verse 42), anxiety, or desire for money and success (verse 36). But when God is in charge, these things lose their inordinate power over us. Not even kings are feared (verse 46). Also, with God comes the freedom of "the mind-stretching encounter with a greater wisdom and vision than one's own. Verse 45 literally means 'at large.' . . . Moffatt's paraphrase of the verse is . . . 'thou dost open up my life.'"[124] Being near creative people frees you to think new thoughts. How much more an encounter with the living God and his Word?

Prayer: Lord, you do indeed "open up my life." I used to think climbing the ladder of this world was all there was, but now I realize there are untold spiritual realities and eternity and glory to look forward to. I praise you for the astonishing vision of life you give me through your Word. Amen.

November 6

READ Psalm 119:49–56. **49** Remember your word to your servant, for you have given me hope. **50** My comfort in my suffering is this: Your promise preserves my life. **51** The arrogant mock me unmercifully, but I do not turn from your law. **52** I remember, LORD, your ancient laws, and I find comfort in them. **53** Indignation grips me because of the wicked, who have forsaken your law. **54** Your decrees are the theme of my song wherever I lodge. **55** In the night, LORD, I remember your name, that I may keep your law. **56** This has been my practice: I obey your precepts.

THE WORD AND THE CULTURE. It is difficult to believe in a culture in which people mock you for believing in God's truth (verse 51). Why should anyone be concerned for antiquated ("ancient") laws that are clearly outdated (verse 52)? Despite this cultural scorn, the psalmist holds on to the Word resolutely (verses 51–52.) The result is a life "preserve[d]" (verse 50). Elsewhere God's Word is said to preserve life, and while in some cases that might mean literal survival, here it means more. The Bible creates endurance. Its promises lift the heart and its panoramic insights strengthen the will. It truly is spiritual manna that keeps us on our feet and able to go on.

Prayer: Lord Jesus, they mocked you pitilessly. "Prophesy to us, Messiah. Who hit you?" (Matthew 26:68). If you endured derision and scorn for me so patiently, surely I can take it for you. Let me remember how you were laughed at for me. Help me to be brave when I open my mouth about my beliefs. Amen.

November 7

READ Psalm 119:57–64. **57** You are my portion, LORD; I have promised to obey your words. **58** I have sought your face with all my heart; be gracious to me according to your promise. **59** I have considered my ways and have turned my steps to your statutes. **60** I will hasten and not delay to obey your commands. **61** Though the wicked bind me with ropes, I will not forget your law. **62** At midnight I rise to give you thanks for your righteous laws. **63** I am a friend to all who fear you, to all who follow your precepts. **64** The earth is filled with your love, LORD; teach me your decrees.

GOD'S LOVE FILLS THE EARTH. The whole "*earth* is filled with [God's] love" (verse 64). God created the world and cares for it in love. Jesus says we can trust God because he cares even for the birds of the air (Matthew 6:26) and loves everything he has made (Psalm 145:9). It is because he loves all people he created that he wants them to receive also his redeeming love. "I take no pleasure in the death of anyone. . . . Repent and live!" (Ezekiel 18:32). It is important to neither think God loves only believers nor to think he loves everyone in the world in exactly the same way. How should we respond to such a loving God? We should align all parts of our lives with God's Word (verses 59–60).

Prayer: Lord, I praise you that you have always loved me, but I praise you that you opened my heart to receive your saving love as well. *"Your sovereign mercy called me and taught my opening mind; the world had else enthralled me, to heavenly glories blind."*[125] Thank you for your grace. Amen.

November 8

READ Psalm 119:65–72. **65** Do good to your servant according to your word, LORD. **66** Teach me knowledge and good judgment, for I trust your commands. **67** Before I was afflicted I went astray, but now I obey your word. **68** You are good, and what you do is good; teach me your decrees. **69** Though the arrogant have smeared me with lies, I keep your precepts with all my heart. **70** Their hearts are callous and unfeeling, but I delight in your law. **71** It was good for me to be afflicted so that I might learn your decrees. **72** The law from your mouth is more precious to me than thousands of pieces of silver and gold.

THE SCHOOL OF SUFFERING. Suffering is a school where students learn things about themselves, about God, and about life that they would never have learned without it (verses 66–67). Looking back on the priceless lessons he learned, the sufferer is able to say to the one who appointed it all, "You are good, and what you do is good" (verse 68, cf. verses 65 and 71). If we go through this school immersing ourselves in God's Word, we develop real sensitivity of heart (verse 70) and our eyes are opened to see unthought-of treasures in the Bible itself (verse 72). How remarkable that, with the Word of God, a sufferer can come through it all deeper, wiser, richer, more loving, and even happier.

Prayer: Lord, you call yourself teacher and Lord, but I am such a slow pupil! I grit my teeth through my troubles as I wait for them to pass. Instead, every time something bad happens, help me to ask, "Is there anything I should be learning here?" Show me the way. Amen.

November 9

READ Psalm 119:73-80. 73 Your hands made me and formed me; give me understanding to learn your commands. **74** May those who fear you rejoice when they see me, for I have put my hope in your word. **75** I know, LORD, that your laws are righteous, and that in faithfulness you have afflicted me. **76** May your unfailing love be my comfort, according to your promise to your servant. **77** Let your compassion come to me that I may live, for your law is my delight. **78** May the arrogant be put to shame for wronging me without cause; but I will meditate on your precepts. **79** May those who fear you turn to me, those who understand your statutes. **80** May I wholeheartedly follow your decrees, that I may not be put to shame.

THE WITNESS OF SUFFERING. The psalmist reflects on how his suffering affects other believers—"those who fear you" (verses 74 and 79). He believes his suffering has been appointed by God "in faithfulness," that is, in love and wisdom (verse 75; cf. Genesis 50:20 and Romans 8:28). When others see him trusting God like that, they will get joy through his courageous hope (verse 74). During his trouble the psalmist meditates on the Word deeply enough for comfort (verse 76), delight (verse 77), and wholeheartedness (verse 80), "an inward being in which every capacity is perfectly integrated around the word."[126] When other believers see the power of the Word in his life, it draws them together and deepens loving fellowship. Suffering, rightly met, creates rich community and friendship.

Prayer: Lord, when I am licking my wounds I don't think of anyone else and I want to be alone. But help me at such times to be open to others' help, and show me ways to encourage them in my times of difficulty. Lord, you thought only of me during your suffering, so let me think of my community during mine. Amen.

November 10

READ Psalm 119:81–88. **81** My soul faints with longing for your salvation, but I have put my hope in your word. **82** My eyes fail, looking for your promise; I say, "When will you comfort me?" **83** Though I am like a wineskin in the smoke, I do not forget your decrees. **84** How long must your servant wait? When will you punish my persecutors? **85** The arrogant dig pits to trap me, contrary to your law. **86** All your commands are trustworthy; help me, for I am being persecuted without cause. **87** They almost wiped me from the earth, but I have not forsaken your precepts. **88** In your unfailing love preserve my life, that I may obey the statutes of your mouth.

LIFE PRESERVERS. The psalmist has reached the end of his rope. He's at the end of his ability to endure (verses 81–82). His suffering is not deserved (verse 86) and yet there is no relief. In such extreme moments what is there to do? Do what you have been doing—staying in the Word and praying honestly and fervently, as we see here. When suffering comes, prayer and Bible reading are the first activities to go. In reality they are your only life preservers. "The chief means for attaining wisdom . . . are the holy Scriptures, and prayer. The one is the fountain of living water, the other the bucket with which we are to draw."[127]

Prayer: Lord, when I have reached the end of my rope, of my wisdom and strength, that doesn't mean I've run out of *your* rope. It is always there beside me in my access to you through prayer and your Word. Don't let me neglect my life preservers! Amen.

November 11

READ Psalm 119:89–96. **89** Your word, LORD, is eternal; it stands firm in the heavens. **90** Your faithfulness continues through all generations; you established the earth, and it endures. **91** Your laws endure to this day, for all things serve you. **92** If your law had not been my delight, I would have perished in my affliction. **93** I will never forget your precepts, for by them you have preserved my life. **94** Save me, for I am yours; I have sought out your precepts. **95** The wicked are waiting to destroy me, but I will ponder your statutes. **96** To all perfection I see a limit, but your commands are boundless.

THE ETERNAL WORD. The psalmist speaks of the eternal Word of the Lord that is "in the heavens" (verse 89), sustaining and directing the world (verse 91; cf. Hebrews 1:3). But the psalmist then seamlessly identifies that eternal Word with the written Word of Scripture (verses 91–92). The same mind running the universe expresses itself in the Bible. So there is no limit to the perfect trustworthiness and truth of the Scripture (verse 96). It is therefore the only solid foundation on which to build a life. Human cultures, philosophies, and trends of "progress" rise up but within a generation or two become obsolete and forgotten. But "through all generations" (verse 90) "your word, LORD, is eternal" (verse 89).

Prayer: Lord, things my grandparents believed in their youth with the rest of society are now laughable or offensive. There are ascendant ideas in our culture that charge the Bible with being "regressive" but which themselves will be thrown into the dustbin of history. Help me remember that your Word is both perfect and eternal. Amen.

November 12

READ Psalm 119:97–104. **97** Oh, how I love your law! I meditate on it all day long. **98** Your commands are always with me and make me wiser than my enemies. **99** I have more insight than all my teachers, for I meditate on your statutes. **100** I have more understanding than the elders, for I obey your precepts. **101** I have kept my feet from every evil path so that I might obey your word. **102** I have not departed from your laws, for you yourself have taught me. **103** How sweet are your words to my taste, sweeter than honey to my mouth! **104** I gain understanding from your precepts; therefore I hate every wrong path.

THE WORD OF WISDOM. Wisdom is knowing the right path to take in every situation (verse 101). Nothing provides it like the Word of God. Neither scholarship and research (verse 99) nor sophistication and accomplishment (verse 100) can tell you as much about the human heart, human nature, and the ways of the world. Both Jesus (Luke 10:21) and Paul (1 Corinthians 1:18–25) point out that the Gospel tends to be rejected by the knowledgeable and high ranking, but embraced by the needy and the humbled. Wisdom, then, comes not to people who merely learn the facts of the Bible. It appears to those who humbly receive it in love (verse 97), obedience (verse 101), and delight (verse 103).

Prayer: Lord, your Word is full of *"infinite sweetness! Let my heart [savor] every letter."*[128] It has a medicine for every wound. Teach me how not just to learn but to savor and relish the teachings of your Word. Amen.

November 13

READ Psalm 119:105–112. **105** Your word is a lamp for my feet and a light on my path. **106** I have taken an oath and confirmed it, that I will follow your righteous laws. **107** I have suffered much; preserve my life, LORD, according to your word. **108** Accept, LORD, the willing praise of my mouth, and teach me your laws. **109** Though I constantly take my life in my hands, I will not forget your law. **110** The wicked have set a snare for me, but I have not strayed from your precepts. **111** Your statutes are my heritage forever; they are the joy of my heart. **112** My heart is set on keeping your decrees to the very end.

THE WORD MY LAMP. You need a lamp for walking if the place is too dark for your unaided eyes. So life itself is too dark for our unaided wisdom. We will go astray without the illumination of God's Word (verse 105). The Word will be a lamp to you only if you follow it nonbegrudgingly even when you don't like what it shows you. "My heart is set on keeping your decrees to the very end" (verse 112). "Joy without obedience is frivolity; obedience without joy is moralism."[129] Remember Jesus in the darkness of his temptation (Luke 4:1–13). Every time Satan tried to envelop Christ in darkness, Christ used Scripture after Scripture to dispel it.

Prayer: Lord, let me be so immersed in your Word that, as they did for Jesus, your words spring to my mind, interpreting my moment, guiding my choices, and strengthening my heart. Amen.

November 14

READ Psalm 119:113–120. **113** I hate double-minded people, but I love your law. **114** You are my refuge and my shield; I have put my hope in your word. **115** Away from me, you evildoers, that I may keep the commands of my God! **116** Sustain me, my God, according to your promise, and I will live; do not let my hopes be dashed. **117** Uphold me, and I will be delivered; I will always have regard for your decrees. **118** You reject all who stray from your decrees, for their delusions come to nothing. **119** All the wicked of the earth you discard like dross; therefore I love your statutes. **120** My flesh trembles in fear of you; I stand in awe of your laws.

KNOWING GOD. Verse 120 ties the fear of God closely to awe of the Word. There is an awe before the Word itself (verse 120) as we see its grandeur, coherence, and wisdom. This leads directly to the fear of God, the deep, trembling joy and wonder that increase as we relate to him not as we imagine him to be but as he truly is. How can we be sure we are encountering the real God and not the God we want him to be? Only through the Word. The Bible is "the primary means by which God presents himself to us, in such a way that we can know him and remain in a faithful relationship with him."[130]

Prayer: Lord, take me into the infinities and immensities of your Word. Give me a strong sense of its divine origin. Let it take my breath away as do the dawn and sunset. Let it break my heart with its beauty as do the mountains and sea. For then I'm only a moment from seeing your face. Amen.

November 15

READ Psalm 119:121–128. **121** I have done what is righteous and just; do not leave me to my oppressors. **122** Ensure your servant's well-being; do not let the arrogant oppress me. **123** My eyes fail, looking for your salvation, looking for your righteous promise. **124** Deal with your servant according to your love and teach me your decrees. **125** I am your servant; give me discernment that I may understand your statutes. **126** It is time for you to act, LORD; your law is being broken. **127** Because I love your commands more than gold, more than pure gold, **128** and because I consider all your precepts right, I hate every wrong path.

IT IS TIME FOR YOU TO ACT. In the psalmist's culture God's laws are being despised (verse 126) and believers are being oppressed (verses 121–122). No one is listening to the Word of God (verse 123). You too may find that when you speak about your faith you are vigorously ignored or even shouted down. What does the psalmist do? He asks God to "act" (verse 126), which means, "I am out of ideas and energy! I put it all in your hands." There comes a time when all there is to do is to pray, to tend to your own heart and life, and to wait for God to open a door (Revelation 3:8).

Prayer: Lord, I confess that I try to be the Holy Spirit. When people I love don't listen to the truth, I sometimes beat on the outside of hearts that can be unlocked only from inside. Only your Spirit can go in there. I can't. Lord, I will wait for you to act. Amen.

November 16

READ Psalm 119:129–136. **129** Your statutes are wonderful; therefore I obey them. **130** The unfolding of your words gives light; it gives understanding to the simple. **131** I open my mouth and pant, longing for your commands. **132** Turn to me and have mercy on me, as you always do to those who love your name. **133** Direct my footsteps according to your word; let no sin rule over me. **134** Redeem me from human oppression, that I may obey your precepts. **135** Make your face shine upon your servant and teach me your decrees. **136** Streams of tears flow from my eyes, for your law is not obeyed.

THE UNFOLDING WORD. When the psalmist calls God's Word "wonderful," he is using a word that means "supernatural" (verse 129). It is not a merely human book. This is why the Bible "unfolds" its depths for those patient enough to plumb them. While the Scripture is clear enough in its basic message for a child to understand, it will not yield its astonishing riches except to trusting (verse 133), obedient (verse 136), diligent (verse 131) study and sustained reflection. If this price is paid, however, the return is infinitely greater than the cost.

Prayer: Lord, I take time for only the most superficial Bible study. But everyone makes time for the things they feel most important. I confess that my heart has little desire to know the Word. Let Psalm 119 break my heart's indifference. Amen.

November 17

READ Psalm 119:137–144. **137** You are righteous, LORD, and your laws are right. **138** The statutes you have laid down are righteous; they are fully trustworthy. **139** My zeal wears me out, for my enemies ignore your words. **140** Your promises have been thoroughly tested, and your servant loves them. **141** Though I am lowly and despised, I do not forget your precepts. **142** Your righteousness is everlasting and your law is true. **143** Trouble and distress have come upon me, but your commands give me delight. **144** Your statutes are always righteous; give me understanding that I may live.

THE RIGHTEOUS WORD. When the Bible says that God is righteous (verses 137 and 142), it means he is completely just and fair; he never exploits or abuses. God's Word perfectly reflects this same righteousness (verses 138 and 144). This is hard for modern people, who live in the most authority-averse culture in world history. Much in the Word seems on the surface unfair and even exploitive to us. However, this is the testimony of millions of people—and of the Word itself: If you trust God's Word, "thoroughly testing" it in the crucible of your life over the years (verse 140), you will find it not only true (verse 142) but also delightful (verse 143). You will come to love it (verse 140).

Prayer: Lord, there were once many things in your Word that seemed too harsh and severe to me, but as time has gone on, they have become fewer. Your Word has proven true. Open doors for me to tell others, in this most suspicious of all cultures, that the Word of the Lord can be trusted. Amen.

November 18

READ Psalm 119:145-152. **145** I call with all my heart; answer me, LORD, and I will obey your decrees. **146** I call out to you; save me and I will keep your statutes. **147** I rise before dawn and cry for help; I have put my hope in your word. **148** My eyes stay open through the watches of the night, that I may meditate on your promises. **149** Hear my voice in accordance with your love; preserve my life, LORD, according to your laws. **150** Those who devise wicked schemes are near, but they are far from your law. **151** Yet you are near, LORD, and all your commands are true. **152** Long ago I learned from your statutes that you established them to last forever.

USING THE WORD. These verses give a glimpse of a day in the life of a man of the Word. He gets up before dawn to pray and hope in God's Word (verse 147); late at night he meditates on its promises (verse 148). Verse 164 says that he praises God seven times a day for his word. Many monastic orders follow this literally and have seven set daily times for prayer and reading. But since the number seven signifies completeness or totality, we learn that we should make the prayerful study of the Word one of the top priorities for our time, something that is never squeezed out by other things.

Prayer: Lord, when I am done with this prayer I am going to make a plan and take action to read your Word more and more often. Help me, so that my plan will be neither too unrealistic to work nor too unambitious to make a difference. Amen.

November 19

READ Psalm 119:153–160. **153** Look on my suffering and deliver me, for I have not forgotten your law. **154** Defend my cause and redeem me; preserve my life according to your promise. **155** Salvation is far from the wicked, for they do not seek out your decrees. **156** Your compassion, LORD, is great; preserve my life according to your laws. **157** Many are the foes who persecute me, but I have not turned from your statutes. **158** I look on the faithless with loathing, for they do not obey your word. **159** See how I love your precepts; preserve my life, LORD, in accordance with your love. **160** All your words are true; all your righteous laws are eternal.

THE DOCTRINE OF THE WORD. The psalmist says that "all your words are true" (verse 160; see also 151). Everything the Bible asserts is true. It must be followed, regardless of our emotional likes, cultural custom, or popular opinion. Also, God's word is "eternal" (verse 160; see also verse 152). Nothing the Bible says can go out of date. We do not need to modernize, correct, or supplement it. Certainly the Word is more than simply a book of true statements. It is the way to know God and his strengthening love (verse 159). But this encounter is based on these doctrinal commitments to the full inspiration and authority of the Bible. If we can't trust what it says of God, we can't know the God it shows us.

Prayer: Lord, my grandparents lived in a time in which your Word was respected but ignored. I live in a time in which it is attacked and dismembered. Make me able to defend the truth of your Word to my own mind and then, when opportune, to others. Amen.

November 20

READ Psalm 119:161–168. **161** Rulers persecute me without cause, but my heart trembles at your word. **162** I rejoice in your promise like one who finds great spoil. **163** I hate and detest falsehood but I love your law. **164** Seven times a day I praise you for your righteous laws. **165** Great peace have those who love your law, and nothing can make them stumble. **166** I wait for your salvation, LORD, and I follow your commands. **167** I obey your statutes, for I love them greatly. **168** I obey your precepts and your statutes, for all my ways are known to you.

THE TREASURED WORD. The psalmist "trembles at [God's] word" (verse 161). He is fiercely devoted to the Scripture because he rightly identifies the Word so closely with its author. If God is the source of life, then his Word will give life; if God is wholly truthful, then the Word cannot err. And if God is glorious, the Bible is a treasure. "I rejoice in your promise like one who finds great spoil" (verse 162). "Spoil" is what soldiers received after a hard-fought battle. To learn and digest the Word of God requires a fight. We must fight our busy schedules, our distracted minds, our stubborn hearts, and the world's opinion and disdain. But if we win, the result is pure gold.

Prayer: Lord, indeed your Word *"is like a deep, deep mine, and jewels rich and rare are hidden in its mighty depths for every searcher there."*[131] Give me the energy for study of your Word that comes from a deep sense of the value of what I will find there. Amen.

November 21

READ Psalm 119:169–176. **169** May my cry come before you, LORD; give me understanding according to your word. **170** May my supplication come before you; deliver me according to your promise. **171** May my lips overflow with praise, for you teach me your decrees. **172** May my tongue sing of your word, for all your commands are righteous. **173** May your hand be ready to help me, for I have chosen your precepts. **174** I long for your salvation, LORD, and your law gives me delight. **175** Let me live that I may praise you, and may your laws sustain me. **176** I have strayed like a lost sheep. Seek your servant, for I have not forgotten your commands.

THE POWERFUL WORD. Psalm 119 has given us many directions about what to do with the Scripture. We are to read, learn, and understand it—to meditate on, memorize, and follow it. We are to take time to do this morning and night without fail. But all this is in vain unless God seeks you as you read his Word (verse 176). The Word of God is alive and active, penetrating and healing like a surgeon's knife (Hebrews 4:12–13). If you aren't sure about the Bible's trustworthiness—or if you have friends who are aren't sure—just give yourselves to reading it. Even if you don't believe a knife is sharp, if it is, it can still cut you.

Prayer: Lord, here is the wonderful mirror *"that mends the looker's eyes: this is the well that washes what it shows. Who can endear its praise too much?"*[132] What healing, shaping power it has! Let me eagerly give myself to the Word. Amen.

November 22

READ Psalm 120. **1** I call on the LORD in my distress, and he answers me. **2** Save me, LORD, from lying lips and from deceitful tongues. **3** What will he do to you, and what more besides, you deceitful tongue? **4** He will punish you with a warrior's sharp arrows, with burning coals of the broom bush. **5** Woe to me that I dwell in Meshek, that I live among the tents of Kedar! **6** Too long have I lived among those who hate peace. **7** I am for peace; but when I speak, they are for war.

EXILE. This is the first of fifteen "Songs of Ascent" sung by those ascending Mount Zion for the annual feasts.[133] The psalmist seeks peace, but those around him want only conflict with him and his faith (verse 7). This is "the resentment of one way of life against its opposite . . . which no amount of goodwill, short of capitulation or conversion, can resolve."[134] In this situation the Bible forbids either compromise (2 Corinthians 6:14ff) or retaliation (Romans 12:14–21). The psalmist leaves vengeance to God (verse 3–4), but even when believers peacefully serve their neighbors, they may attract hostility (1 Peter 2:12). So we follow our Lord, who was also a man of peace in a culture of war (1 Peter 2:21–25).

Prayer: Lord, it breaks my heart, and often my patience, when despite my overtures of peace a person remains implacably adversarial. And I live in a culture where many think constant, angry indignation is a moral virtue. Lord, I ask your help to continue loving and offering respect to those who are against me and what I believe. Amen.

November 23

HELP. In a search for help the psalmist looks to the mountains (verse 1), which could be either a place to hide or a lair for enemies. But the mountains are nothing (as either threat or help) compared with the help of the Lord, the one who made the mountains (verse 2). What is God's help? It is spiritual refreshment ("shade," verse 5) through his presence. It is God's enabling us to avoid foot slipping or sin (verse 3; cf. Psalm 73:2). An ounce of sin can harm us more than a ton of suffering. Sin can harden our hearts so we lose everything, but suffering, if handled rightly, can make us wiser, happier, and deeper.

Prayer: Lord, my life is filled with pressures that are like the sun beating down and draining me of all strength. But I have known times when your smile, sensed in prayer, was like cool shade or like a refreshing breeze to my heart. Give me the grace to know you more as my shade and my help. Amen.

November 24

READ Psalm 122. 1 I rejoiced with those who said to me, "Let us go to the house of the LORD." **2** Our feet are standing in your gates, Jerusalem. **3** Jerusalem is built like a city that is closely compacted together. **4** That is where the tribes go up—the tribes of the LORD—to praise the name of the LORD according to the statute given to Israel. **5** There stand the thrones for judgment, the thrones of the house of David. **6** Pray for the peace of Jerusalem: "May those who love you be secure. **7** May there be peace within your walls and security within your citadels." **8** For the sake of my family and friends, I will say, "Peace be within you." **9** For the sake of the house of the LORD our God, I will seek your prosperity.

CHURCH. Those attending the annual festivals approached Jerusalem with joy (verse 1). They loved the city and prayed for its flourishing (verses 6–7). What Jerusalem was to the ancient Jews the church is to believers in Christ. When we come to faith in Christ, we become citizens in the heavenly Jerusalem (Hebrews 12:22–24; Philippians 3:20). The manifestation of that heavenly (and future) city is the counterculture of the Christian church, a society where the world can see human life lived according to God's will. Through the Gospel, different races and nations are "closely compacted together" (verse 3; cf. Ephesians 2:11–22). People who would never get along outside the church love one another inside it. We must joyfully seek out the church; the Bible knows nothing of solitary religion.

Prayer: Lord, I praise you for what the church *could* be—an alternative human society that shows the world your glory. But I confess I am part of what the church *is,* a flawed community far from reflecting your character. Give me the understanding and the love I need to become part of the solution, not the problem. Amen.

November 25

READ Psalm 123. **1** I lift up my eyes to you, to you who sit enthroned in heaven. **2** As the eyes of slaves look to the hand of their master, as the eyes of a female slave look to the hand of her mistress, so our eyes look to the LORD our God, till he shows us his mercy. **3** Have mercy on us, LORD, have mercy on us, for we have endured no end of contempt. **4** We have endured no end of ridicule from the arrogant, of contempt from the proud.

FOCUS. Believers feel the pain of the world's contempt (verses 3–4). How do we keep from either adopting its views or becoming resentful and withdrawn? We must lift our eyes to God (verse 1). This is more than simply to "take a look." It denotes a steady, reflective, adoring gaze (verses 1 and 2) filled with longing and desire (Matthew 6:23; cf. Joshua 7:21). The psalmist focuses both his attention and the yearnings of his heart on God in prayer (verse 2). He became like a domestic servant, trained to respond to every indication of his master's will (verse 2). In short, the psalmist overcomes all distractions and makes knowing God experientially and serving God obediently the main business of his life. Pray this psalm daily until God shows you his mercy.

Prayer: Lord, I live in an "attention deficit disorder" society. One thing after another comes into my sight and is gone. Oh, teach me how to focus on you. Let me always keep you in mind during the day. And help me gaze long and lovingly on you in prayer. Amen.

November 26

READ Psalm 124. **1** If the LORD had not been on our side—let Israel say— **2** if the LORD had not been on our side when people attacked us, **3** they would have swallowed us alive when their anger flared against us; **4** the flood would have engulfed us, the torrent would have swept over us, **5** the raging waters would have swept us away. **6** Praise be to the LORD, who has not let us be torn by their teeth. **7** We have escaped like a bird from the fowler's snare; the snare has been broken, and we have escaped. **8** Our help is in the name of the LORD, the Maker of heaven and earth.

COVENANT. Four times (verses 1, 2, 6, and 8) God is called the LORD, the God who enters into a covenant with us by grace. This unfamiliar word means his love is "locked on to us" in unending commitment. Thus he is always *for* us (verses 1–2). But the psalmist could not see what we see. God is ever on our side, because in Christ our sins can't bring us into condemnation (Romans 8:1, 34–35). So not "trouble or hardship or persecution or famine or nakedness or danger or sword . . . will be able to separate us from the love of God that is in Christ Jesus our Lord" (Romans 8:35, 39). Since the maker of heaven and earth is (through Christ) our help, we will not fear (verse 8). What could be against us (Romans 8:31)?

Prayer: Lord, you are a covenant-keeping God. Your Son vowed to save us, and not even hell itself, coming down on him with its full force, could stop him from keeping his promise. Now make me like him. *"Take my will, and make it Thine; it shall be no longer mine. Take myself, and I will be, ever, only, all for Thee."*[135] Amen.

November 27

ENDURANCE. In ancient times there was no more militarily secure position for a city than to be behind encircling mountains. Trusting in God is like being in a mountain fastness (verse 2). How? Trusting God provides a superior vantage point. It helps us see our own sin and see that wickedness only pays in the short term. Trusting God is also the way to eventually get breathtaking sights of God himself. When Isaiah saw the Holy One, high and lifted up, it permanently changed his view of everything (Isaiah 6:1–8). Most of all, trusting God means connecting yourself to the one person who will endure forever. And that means you will endure as well (verse 1). In a world in which seemingly everything changes and nothing lasts, fix your mind on that.

Prayer: Lord, I find the relentless transitions and changes of life exhausting. But you do not change, and you are my dwelling place. Help me calm my heart through this truth. *"For his mercies, they endure; Ever faithful, ever sure."*[136] Amen.

November 28

READ Psalm 126. 1 When the LORD restored the fortunes of Zion, we were like those who dreamed. 2 Our mouths were filled with laughter, our tongues with songs of joy. Then it was said among the nations, "The LORD has done great things for them." 3 The LORD has done great things for us, and we are filled with joy. 4 Restore our fortunes, LORD, like streams in the Negev. 5 Those who sow with tears will reap with songs of joy. 6 Those who go out weeping, carrying seed to sow, will return with songs of joy, carrying sheaves with them.

RESTORATION. Israel had eras of great spiritual fruitfulness and vitality (verses 1–3) marked by joy (verse 2). But communities of faith often have "Negev" times of great spiritual dryness. (The Negev was an arid, desertlike land.) Sometimes a flood of God's Spirit comes down powerfully and suddenly, like the streams from distant mountain rainstorms, and the community is restored dramatically (verse 4). But there is also a slower path to renewal. Those who "sow with tears" (verses 5 and 6) are those who have painstakingly prayed and wept over their own sins and also over people without faith. As in actual farming, sowing does not show immediate fruit. But faithful prayer and service will eventually bear fruit. The desert will become a garden (Isaiah 35:1–2).

Prayer: Lord, I am praying for my church, my country, and several people I love—that they will be spiritually empowered and renewed. Help me to rest in your timing, knowing that my tears in prayer are like seeds that will come to fruition in the lives of those I care for. Amen.

November 29

READ Psalm 127. **1** Unless the LORD builds the house, its builders labor in vain. Unless the LORD watches over the city, the guards stand watch in vain. **2** In vain you rise early and stay up late, toiling for food to eat—for he grants sleep to those he loves. **3** Children are a heritage from the LORD, offspring a reward from him. **4** Like arrows in the hands of a warrior are children born in one's youth. **5** Blessed is the man whose quiver is full of them. They will not be put to shame when they contend with their opponents in court.

REST. Prosperity and security are not ultimately your accomplishments but God's gifts (verse 1). So overwork, worry, and strain are foolish and wrong (verse 2). So too thriving, happy children are God's doing (verses 3–5). "Helicopter" parenting and overinvolvement in our children's lives, cannot ensure their health and happiness. Unless the Lord enters their lives, all our watching is in vain. Giving our children to God is the only way we get to keep them. If you know that the one who loves you unfailingly is in complete charge of history, you will be able to sleep well (verse 2). And if you *are* overworked and overstressed, you are forgetting who God is. Jesus said it most bluntly: "Apart from me you can do nothing" (John 15:5).

Prayer: Lord, admitting my accomplishments are your gift is a bittersweet thing to do. It stings at first because it humbles. But then it is so very sweet and brings such peace. It is not up to me, and it never was. Let me work hard, with this liberating insight removing the pressure I sinfully put on myself. Amen.

November 30

READ Psalm 128. **1** Blessed are all who fear the LORD, who walk in obedience to him. **2** You will eat the fruit of your labor; blessings and prosperity will be yours. **3** Your wife will be like a fruitful vine within your house; your children will be like olive shoots around your table. **4** Yes, this will be the blessing for the man who fears the LORD. **5** May the LORD bless you from Zion; may you see the prosperity of Jerusalem all the days of your life. **6** May you live to see your children's children—peace be on Israel.

FAMILY. A loving spouse and growing children are a great blessing (verses 3–4). But sin in the heart and evil in the world have disrupted the life of the human family. Many wish to have families who don't, and many who have families wish they had very different ones. There are also people who have suffered terrible abuse within their families. Jesus said that his family did not consist of his biological relatives: "Whoever does God's will is my brother and sister and mother" (Mark 3:35). The church must not only support and repair families but also find a way to become the family of God where everyone, married and single, childless or not, can flourish in love.

Prayer: Lord, too many of us today relate to others at church as fellow customers rather than as brothers and sisters. We go to get religious services, not to live out our common lives together like family. Change my thinking; help me to help my church become a family. Amen.

December 1

READ Psalm 129. **1** "'They have greatly oppressed me from my youth,'" let Israel say; **2** "they have greatly oppressed me from my youth, but they have not gained the victory over me. **3** Plowmen have plowed my back and made their furrows long. **4** But the LORD is righteous; he has cut me free from the cords of the wicked." **5** May all who hate Zion be turned back in shame. **6** May they be like grass on the roof, which withers before it can grow; **7** a reaper cannot fill his hands with it, nor one who gathers fill his arms. **8** May those who pass by not say to them, "The blessing of the LORD be on you; we bless you in the name of the LORD."

OPPRESSION. The psalmist talks about slaves with backs scarred by whips (verse 3) who are liberated by God (verse 4). God "works righteousness and justice for all the oppressed" (Psalm 103:6) and hates world rulers who are tyrants (Luke 22:25–27), so their power is always temporary (verse 5). We should therefore be working for social justice in the world. But Christians can read this at another level. There was one who voluntarily gave his back to the smiters (Isaiah 50:6), by whose wounds and stripes we are healed (Isaiah 53:5). When we meet people who oppose the gospel ("hate Zion," verse 5), we should follow Jesus by defeating evil through forgiveness and love (Romans 12:14–21; 1 Peter 2:22–24) and calling them to repent (Ezekiel 18:30–32).

Prayer: Lord, they came with "swords and clubs" (Matthew 26:47) and flogged you. *"With clubs and staves they sought you, like a thief, you who are the Way, the true relief; Most true to those, who are your greatest grief."*[137] Thank you for being true to me in that hour and healing me with your stripes. Amen.

December 2

READ Psalm 130. **1** Out of the depths I cry to you, LORD; **2** Lord, hear my voice. Let your ears be attentive to my cry for mercy. **3** If you, LORD, kept a record of sins, Lord, who could stand? **4** But with you there is forgiveness, so that we can, with reverence, serve you. **5** I wait for the LORD, my whole being waits, and in his word I put my hope. **6** I wait for the Lord more than watchmen wait for the morning, more than watchmen wait for the morning. **7** Israel, put your hope in the LORD, for with the LORD is unfailing love and with him is full redemption. **8** He himself will redeem Israel from all their sins.

FORGIVENESS. What do we owe a God who gives us all we have and keeps us alive every second? We ought to love him and serve him without rival. But *no* one does this, so no one can "stand" on Judgment Day based on their record (verse 3; cf. Romans 3:10). Waiting for God's mercy may seem hopeless, like a sleepless person longing for morning, which never seems to come (verse 6). But here's the Gospel: "He *himself* will redeem Israel from all their sins" (verse 8). Jesus is God himself, dying to save his people from their sins. God's forgiveness and mercy generates a joyful fear and wonder that empowers our lives (verse 4). Morning has broken!

Prayer: Lord, I thank you for the joy of forgiveness. I remember the surprise of it. My guilt was like low-level chronic pain. When it was removed, I realized it had drained my life of joy and confidence. Let me remember my forgiveness so that I have a light heart that is quick to enjoy life and other people. Amen.

December 3

CONTENTMENT. There can be an inordinate desire for greatness and accomplishment (verse 1). "Should you then seek great things for yourself? Do not seek them" (Jeremiah 45:5). This self-seeking creates great restlessness and discontent—but the psalmist has left all that behind. A nursing child, held by its mother, is highly aware of the milk she can offer and will squirm and cry if denied. A child who has been "weaned" (verse 2), however, and no longer nurses, is content just to *be* with its mother, enjoying her closeness and love without wanting anything else. We so often approach God only for what he can give, rather than simply to rest in his presence. Do *that* now, through the Word and prayer, in Jesus's name.

Prayer. Lord, you tell me to bring you my needs. But help me also to rest in your presence, joyfully content to just be with you. Sometimes give me that level of nearness and love. I need it so much. Amen.

December 4

READ Psalm 132:1–10. **1** LORD, remember David and all his self-denial. **2** He swore an oath to the LORD, he made a vow to the Mighty One of Jacob: **3** "I will not enter my house or go to my bed, **4** I will allow no sleep to my eyes or slumber to my eyelids, **5** till I find a place for the LORD, a dwelling for the Mighty One of Jacob." **6** We heard it in Ephrathah, we came upon it in the fields of Jaar: **7** "Let us go to his dwelling place; let us worship at his footstool, saying, **8** 'Arise, LORD, and come to your resting place, you and the ark of your might. **9** May your priests be clothed with righteousness; may your faithful people sing for joy.'" **10** For the sake of your servant David, do not reject your anointed one.

NEARNESS. David promised to bring the Ark of the Covenant (God's "footstool," verse 7; cf. 1 Chronicles 28:2) to Jerusalem and to build God a dwelling (verse 7; cf. 2 Samuel 7:1–17). This was not just a political move. In verse 5 David remembers the Lord as the God "of Jacob," who wrestled with the patriarch but gave him the deep blessing he had looked for all his life (Genesis 32:29). David wants God near, at whatever cost, in order to know God's blessing in his heart. And the text tells us it cost David much "suffering" to establish God's house in Jerusalem (verse 1). We too should pay any price to get near God, remembering the one who took a vow like David's and bore the infinite cost to come near to us (Hebrews 10:5–10).

Prayer: Lord, in ancient times people had to journey to Jerusalem to know your presence in the temple. I praise you that today, through Jesus, we can draw near to you anytime and anyplace. I confess that I neglect this gift, bought at infinite price. Help me draw near to you, Lord, and then please draw near to me. Amen.

December 5

READ Psalm 132:11–18. **11** The LORD swore an oath to David, a sure oath that he will not revoke: "One of your own descendants I will place on your throne— **12** if your sons keep my covenant and the statutes I teach them, then their sons will sit on your throne for ever and ever." **13** For the LORD has chosen Zion, he has desired it for his dwelling, saying, **14** "This is my resting place for ever and ever; here I will sit enthroned, for I have desired it. **15** I will bless her with abundant provisions; her poor will I satisfy with food. **16** I will clothe her priests with salvation, and her faithful people will ever sing for joy. **17** "Here I will make a horn grow for David and set up a lamp for my anointed one. **18** I will clothe his enemies with shame, but the crown on his head will be adorned with a radiant crown."

ASSURANCE. The emphasis of this psalm is on God's oath, which he cannot fail to keep. God promised that a descendant of David would bring God's presence into the world in a way David could hardly ever imagine (verse 11; cf. 2 Samuel 7:11–16). Jesus, the greater David, has indeed come, and he has brought the presence of God into our lives—making *us* the dwelling place (1 Peter 2:4–10). We are his dwelling place not because we have worked and earned it but because we were chosen by grace (verse 13). You will get no comfort from your salvation if you are not sure you have it. God's promise assures us that he will never leave us.

Prayer: Lord, *"the soul who on Jesus does lean for repose, you will not—you will not—desert to its foes. That soul though all hell should endeavor to shake, you'll never, no never, no never forsake."*[138] I ask that your Spirit speak this truth to my heart (Romans 8:16). Amen.

December 6

READ Psalm 133. **1** How good and pleasant it is when God's people live together in unity! **2** It is like precious oil poured on the head, running down on the beard, running down on Aaron's beard, down upon the collar of his robes. **3** It is as if the dew of Hermon were falling on Mount Zion. For there the LORD bestows his blessing, even life forevermore.

UNITY. The unity of God's people brings opposites together, symbolized by tall Hermon in the rural north and the little hill of Zion in the urban south (verse 3). For Hermon's dew to fall on Zion would be a miracle—and so is the supernatural bond that brings people far divergent in culture, race, and class together in the Lord. The unity and love he gives us is like precious oil in ancient times (verse 2), making people fragrant and attractive to us who otherwise we would dismiss or reject. So "be patient, bearing with one another in love. Make every effort to keep the unity of the Spirit through the bond of peace" (Ephesians 4:2–3).

Prayer: Lord, the world will know us by our love for one another across the racial and cultural barriers that divide the rest of the human race. Yet the church is often too much like the world in this. Teach me how to help the church be the diverse, unified Body it was meant to be. And let me do this in a non-self-righteous way. Amen.

December 7

READ Psalm 134. **1** Praise the LORD, all you servants of the LORD who minister by night in the house of the LORD. **2** Lift up your hands in the sanctuary and praise the LORD. **3** May the LORD bless you from Zion, he who is the Maker of heaven and earth.

WORSHIP. The pilgrims finally arrive in Jerusalem and come into the temple. They see the priests and Levitical singers singing at night (verse 1; cf. 1 Chronicles 23:30). Perhaps those who worked the "night shift" got little public attention or acknowledgment. Yet by being able to pray and praise him in his presence, they had "the one thing needful" (Luke 10:42, King James Version). Though they were laboring in relative obscurity, God blessed them, as he does all who are faithful to their calling. So the greatest thing is to live in his presence, always singing thankfully in our hearts to him (Ephesians 5:19–20) but remembering we can only do so "from Zion," the place of blood sacrifice for sins. Today that means remembering Jesus's blood poured out (Hebrews 10:1–22).

Prayer: Lord, I want to consciously worship you all day. Then every good thing I'd see as a gift from your heart, and every bad thing as a test from your hand. Please give me a moment-by-moment God-centeredness. Amen.

December 8

READ Psalm 135:1–12. **1** Praise the LORD. Praise the name of the LORD; praise him, you servants of the LORD, **2** you who minister in the house of the LORD, in the courts of the house of our God. **3** Praise the LORD, for the LORD is good; sing praise to his name, for that is pleasant. **4** For the LORD has chosen Jacob to be his own, Israel to be his treasured possession. **5** I know that the LORD is great, that our Lord is greater than all gods. **6** The LORD does whatever pleases him, in the heavens and on the earth, in the seas and all their depths. **7** He makes clouds rise from the ends of the earth; he sends lightning with the rain and brings out the wind from his storehouses. **8** He struck down the firstborn of Egypt, the firstborn of people and animals. **9** He sent his signs and wonders into your midst, Egypt, against Pharaoh and all his servants. **10** He struck down many nations and killed mighty kings— **11** Sihon king of the Amorites, Og king of Bashan, and all the kings of Canaan— **12** and he gave their land as an inheritance, an inheritance to his people Israel.

THE GOD TO PRAISE. Why should we praise God? We should praise him because *he* is good (verse 3). But we should also praise him because *it* is good; it brings us true pleasure (verse 3) because it fits our most fundamental longings and created nature. And we should praise him because, astonishingly, in his grace he finds *us* good. He regards us as his treasure (verse 4), a profoundly comforting claim. Finally, we should praise him because he works all things together for good (verse 6; cf. Romans 8:28). You are surrounded by his love!

Prayer: Lord, I praise you that whatever you will is good— because you are good. And I praise you that this is no affront to my freedom but rather its grounding. I can't, ultimately, mess up my life, because you are in charge, and because you love me. Amen.

December 9

READ Psalm 135:13–21. **13** Your name, Lord, endures forever, your renown, LORD, through all generations. **14** For the LORD will vindicate his people and have compassion on his servants. **15** The idols of the nations are silver and gold, made by human hands. **16** They have mouths, but cannot speak, eyes, but cannot see. **17** They have ears, but cannot hear, nor is there breath in their mouths. **18** Those who make them will be like them, and so will all who trust in them. **19** All you Israelites, praise the LORD; house of Aaron, praise the LORD; **20** house of Levi, praise the LORD; you who fear him, praise the LORD. **21** Praise be to the LORD from Zion, to him who dwells in Jerusalem. Praise the LORD.

THE GODS NOT TO PRAISE. These verses on idolatry reproduce the teaching of Psalm 115 (see the October 23 devotional). Idols are usually good things turned into ultimate things because we look to them to give us the significance and security that can come only from God. How can we "put away" our idols? Whenever you see your heart in the grip of some kind of temptation, anxiety, or fit of anger, ask: How are my feelings being caused by an inordinate hope for something to give me what only Jesus can? How does Christ give me so much more fully and graciously and suitably the very things I am looking for elsewhere?

Prayer: Lord, I will never be able to love you as I ought until I discard competing loves. Purify my heart to rejoice in you above all things. Oh, how much better and wiser will I love all the other people and things in my life if I love you the best of all! Amen.

December 10

READ Psalm 136:1–9. **1** Give thanks to the LORD, for he is good. *His love endures forever.* **2** Give thanks to the God of gods. *His love endures forever.* **3** Give thanks to the Lord of lords: *His love endures forever.* **4** to him who alone does great wonders, *His love endures forever.* **5** who by his understanding made the heavens, *His love endures forever.* **6** who spread out the earth upon the waters, *His love endures forever.* **7** who made the great lights— *His love endures forever.* **8** the sun to govern the day, *His love endures forever.* **9** the moon and stars to govern the night; *His love endures forever.*

PRAISED THEOLOGY. Every verse in this psalm points to truths elsewhere in the Bible. However, sound theology is not an end in itself but must be turned into praise. Even obedience alone is not enough. Ethical compliance without fervent worship means you've given God your will but not your heart. Notice too that this praise is not solitary. This psalm gives us a glimpse of how many of the psalms were sung responsively in the worshipping congregation. So you must not rest content with biblical knowledge and sound doctrine but you must turn it all into worship that encompasses your whole heart and life. And you must not stop at individual, private spirituality but must know God in the assembly and obey him as part of a whole community.

Prayer: Lord, in your presence is fullness of joy and pleasures forevermore (Psalm 16:11), yet I work harder at my career and even hobbies than at learning to pray. These things are like playing in a mud puddle when you have set a table for me filled with your love, peace, and joy. Lord, teach me to pray and show me a church where I can learn it. Amen.

December 11

READ Psalm 136:10–16. **10** to him who struck down the first-born of Egypt *His love endures forever.* **11** and brought Israel out from among them *His love endures forever.* **12** with a mighty hand and out-stretched arm; *His love endures forever.* **13** to him who divided the Red Sea asunder *His love endures forever.* **14** and brought Israel through the midst of it, *His love endures forever.* **15** but swept Pharaoh and his army into the Red Sea; *His love endures forever.* **16** to him who led his people through the wilderness; *His love endures forever.*

AND WONDERS OF HIS LOVE. "His love endures forever" is repeated. But why "love"? Don't his righteousness and power endure too? None of the attributes of God can be understood without the others. Still, Paul hints that while God's greatness can be logically deduced from the created world (Romans 1:20), God's *love* is a complete surprise and wonder. Looking at the human heart and history, you would never conclude that God loves us. But he does! Paul asks for help to grasp not God's righteousness but "how wide and long and high and deep is the love of Christ." (Ephesians 3:18). God's love is his most amazing trait, and likewise love should be his followers' most evident mark (John 13:35). Is it yours?

Prayer: Lord, the mark of a Christian is love, and so I should be known as a loving person not just by friends but also by acquaintances. I confess that this is not true. With your Spirit eat away at the reasons for this—my overbusyness, my pride, and, yes, my fear of being too vulnerable. Amen.

December 12

READ Psalm 136:17–26. **17** who struck down great kings, *His love endures forever.* **18** and killed mighty kings— *His love endures forever.* **19** Sihon king of the Amorites *His love endures forever.* **20** and Og king of Bashan— *His love endures forever.* **21** and gave their land as an inheritance, *His love endures forever.* **22** an inheritance to his servant Israel. *His love endures forever.* **23** He remembered us in our low estate *His love endures forever.* **24** and freed us from our enemies. *His love endures forever.* **25** He gives food to every creature. *His love endures forever.* **26** Give thanks to the God of heaven. *His love endures forever.*

OUR LOW ESTATE. God's love was so great he came into our low estate (verse 23) in Jesus Christ. Meditate on this love in a poet's imagining of Jesus speaking from the cross:

O all ye who pass by, behold and see; Man stole the fruit, but
  I must climb the tree;
The tree of life to all, but only me: Was ever grief like mine?

"Now heal thy self, Physician; now come down." Alas! I did
  so, when I left my crown
And father's smile for you, to feel his frown: Was ever grief
  like mine?

In healing not my self, there doth consist all that salvation,
  which ye now resist;
Your safety in my sickness doth subsist: Was ever grief like
  mine?[139]

Prayer: Lord, your love endures but I wax hot and cold, usually cold. O Holy Spirit, do to me what this psalm is trying to do to me. Relentlessly instill the truth of your love down into my heart until it kindles my love—the love I owe and want to feel. Amen.

December 13

READ Psalm 137. **1** By the rivers of Babylon we sat and wept when we remembered Zion. **2** There on the poplars we hung our harps, **3** for there our captors asked us for songs, our tormentors demanded songs of joy; they said, "Sing us one of the songs of Zion!" **4** How can we sing the songs of the LORD while in a foreign land? **5** If I forget you, Jerusalem, may my right hand forget its skill. **6** May my tongue cling to the roof of my mouth if I do not remember you, if I do not consider Jerusalem my highest joy. **7** Remember, LORD, what the Edomites did on the day Jerusalem fell. "Tear it down," they cried, "tear it down to its foundations!" **8** Daughter Babylon, doomed to destruction, happy is the one who repays you for what you have done to us. **9** Happy is the one who seizes your infants and dashes them against the rocks.

THE SONGS OF ZION. In Babylon the exiles sought the city's peace (Jeremiah 29:4–7), but when captors asked them to sing psalms as entertainment they refused (verses 2–4). They would not relativize the claims of their faith. The songs of Zion are not cultural artifacts but *the* story of God's saving plan. Their cry, asking that the oppressors (verse 7) get what they gave others (verses 8–9), startles us. But we should not close our ears to the pain of the oppressed of the world. Notice, again, that even these singers leave judgment to God (verse 7). Christians also know that *God's* Son Jesus became an infant who was also eventually crushed by oppressors (verses 8–9). He received the punishment injustice deserves. So Christians can forgive and pray for reconciliation.

Prayer: Lord, I urgently ask help for your church today. We believe in absolute truth in a relativistic world. We are invited to "be religious" but only on the culture's terms, only if we grant that our faith isn't *the* truth as revealed by God. How do we serve our neighbors and lovingly insist on the Gospel? Help us, O Lord. Amen.

December 14

READ Psalm 138. **1** I will praise you, LORD, with all my heart; before the "gods" I will sing your praise. **2** I will bow down toward your holy temple and will praise your name for your unfailing love and your faithfulness, for you have so exalted your name solemn decree that it surpasses your fame. **3** When I called, you answered me; you greatly emboldened me. **4** May all the kings of the earth praise you, LORD, when they hear what you have decreed. **5** May they sing of the ways of the LORD, for the glory of the LORD is great. **6** Though the LORD is exalted, he looks kindly on the lowly; though lofty, he sees them from afar. **7** Though I walk in the midst of trouble, you preserve my life. You stretch out your hand against the anger of my foes; with your right hand you save me. **8** The LORD will vindicate me; your love, LORD, endures forever—do not abandon the works of your hands.

HE LOOKS UPON THE LOWLY. David turns away from the "gods"—high and powerful beings and people (verse 1). He perceives that though high and exalted himself, God is always close to the lowly (verse 6)—in two senses. He loves the poor and the widowed (cf. Psalm 113:7–8). And he comes into the hearts and lives only of those humble enough to know they need a savior (Isaiah 57:15; 1 Peter 5:6; Matthew 5:3). It is people without resources who know best the lavishness of God's love. Self-sufficient people don't go to God with the same desperation and so never discover his love and his power on their behalf.

Prayer: Lord, I live in a culture that calls for self-assertion. Yet if you withdrew your upholding strength I would cease to exist in the blink of an eye. I confess that I forget that and think I am holding myself and the world together. I ask that you would heal me of my damnable self-sufficiency.

December 15

READ Psalm 139:1–12. **1** You have searched me, LORD, and you know me. **2** You know when I sit and when I rise; you perceive my thoughts from afar. **3** You discern my going out and my lying down; you are familiar with all my ways. **4** Before a word is on my tongue you, LORD, know it completely . **5** You hem me in behind and before, and you lay your hand upon me. **6** Such knowledge is too wonderful for me, too lofty for me to attain. **7** Where can I go from your Spirit? Where can I flee from your presence? **8** If I go up to the heavens, you are there; if I make my bed in the depths, you are there. **9** If I rise on the wings of the dawn, if I settle on the far side of the sea, **10** even there your hand will guide me, your right hand will hold me fast. **11** If I say, "Surely the darkness will hide me and the light become night around me," **12** even the darkness will not be dark to you; the night will shine like the day, for darkness is as light to you.

YOU DISCERN. God knows everything (verses 1–6) and fully exists everywhere at once—he is *omnipresent* (verses 7–12). This should be a comfort (verse 10) but it feels more like a threat ("you hem me in," verse 5) because we feel the need to hide from God (Genesis 3:7). In Christ, however, we are clothed with Jesus's righteousness (Philippians 3:9). When we know that, we can bear to let God expose us and to overcome our distorted self-views, which are so confused and biased. When someone we know is absolutely committed to us points out our flaws, though it is hard, we can listen. The upholding love enables us to accept the unpleasant truth, and then the prospects for growth become unlimited. So it is with God.

Prayer: Lord, I confess that when things go wrong in my life, I seldom stop to consider whether you are lovingly trying to show me something that needs to change. Friends tell friends the truth, even when it hurts. So help me to be open to your friendship and critique. Amen.

December 16

READING Psalm 139:13–24. 13 For you created my inmost being; you knit me together in my mother's womb. 14 I praise you because I am fearfully and wonderfully made; your works are wonderful, I know that full well. 15 My frame was not hidden from you when I was made in the secret place, when I was woven together in the depths of the earth. 16 Your eyes saw my unformed body; all the days ordained for me were written in your book before one of them came to be. 17 How precious to me are your thoughts, God! How vast is the sum of them! 18 Were I to count them, they would outnumber the grains of sand—when I awake, I am still with you. 19 If only you, God, would slay the wicked! Away from me, you who are bloodthirsty! 20 They speak of you with evil intent; your adversaries misuse your name. 21 Do I not hate those who hate you, LORD, and abhor those who are in rebellion against you? 22 I have nothing but hatred for them; I count them my enemies. 23 Search me, God, and know my heart; test me and know my anxious thoughts. 24 See if there is any offensive way in me, and lead me in the way everlasting.

WHEN I AWAKE. God also is *omnipotent* (verses 13–18). This should be a vast comfort to us. No matter what the future holds, God is in control with a power greater than death. The psalmist says God will never let go of our hand no matter how dark it gets (see verses 11–12), so that "when I awake I am still with you" (verse 18). As Psalm 17:15 says, God is *so* committed in love to always be with us that he won't even let death separate us (Romans 8:38–39). We will be with him forever.

Prayer: Lord, I confess there was a time in which the idea that my days were "ordained" in "your book" felt limiting to me. But as time goes by, and I can see how limited *our* wisdom is, my only hope becomes reliance on yours. I praise you that I am fearfully and wonderfully made! Amen.

December 17

READ Psalm 140. **1** Rescue me, LORD, from evildoers; protect me from the violent, **2** who devise evil plans in their hearts and stir up war every day. **3** They make their tongues as sharp as a serpent's; the poison of vipers is on their lips. **4** Keep me safe, LORD, from the hands of the wicked; protect me from the violent, who devise ways to trip my feet. **5** The arrogant have hidden a snare for me; they have spread out the cords of their net and have set traps for me along my path. **6** I say to the LORD, "You are my God." Hear, LORD, my cry for mercy. **7** Sovereign LORD, my strong deliverer, you shield my head in the day of battle. **8** Do not grant the wicked their desires, LORD; do not let their plans succeed. **9** Those who surround me proudly rear their heads; may the mischief of their lips engulf them. **10** May burning coals fall on them; may they be thrown into the fire, into miry pits, never to rise. **11** May slanderers not be established in the land; may disaster hunt down the violent. **12** I know that the LORD secures justice for the poor and upholds the cause of the needy. **13** Surely the righteous will praise your name and the upright will live in your presence.

CHANGE THE WORLD. David prays for protection (verses 1–5). While he takes practical measures to guard himself, he acknowledges that only God can keep him safe (verses 6–8). He asks God to be himself and establish justice in society (verses 11–12), bringing down those who exploit and oppress. By the end of this prayer, David's confidence has grown (verse 13). David prays to change the world. He prays that the plans of the exploitative and violent will not succeed and that the poor and downtrodden will be lifted up—and we should pray for the same thing. Affecting world events through prayer is not wishful thinking; we influence the course of current events through appealing to our Father in heaven to intervene.

Prayer: Lord, help me to remember that you have promised that we "do not have because [we] do not ask" (James 4:2). Forgive me for sinning against many of my friends by failing to pray for them. Use my prayers to do good things in the world. Amen.

December 18

READ Psalm 141. **1** I call to you, LORD; come quickly to me; hear me when I call to you. **2** May my prayer be set before you like incense; may the lifting up of my hands be like the evening sacrifice. **3** Set a guard over my mouth, LORD; keep watch over the door of my lips. **4** Do not let my heart be drawn to what is evil so that I take part in wicked deeds along with those who are evildoers; do not let me eat their delicacies. **5** Let a righteous man strike me—that is a kindness; let him rebuke me—that is oil on my head. My head will not refuse it, for my prayer will still be against the deeds of evildoers. **6** Their rulers will be thrown down from the cliffs, and the wicked will learn that my words were well spoken. **7** They will say, "As one plows and breaks up the earth, so our bones have been scattered at the mouth of the grave." **8** But my eyes are fixed on you, Sovereign LORD; in you I take refuge—do not give me over to death. **9** Keep me safe from the traps set by evildoers, from the snares they have laid for me. **10** Let the wicked fall into their own nets, while I pass by in safety.

SPEAKING AND LISTENING. David again calls for help, but this time it is for protection from his heart's susceptibility to evil (verse 4). He asks that good people hold him accountable, "rebuke" him (verse 5). This would be a "kindness" (verse 5). Inviting and listening to criticism is an irreplaceable component of wisdom (Proverbs 27:5, 6, 27; 28:23; 29:5). He also asks that God "set a guard over [his] mouth" (verse 3). Careless words not only harm others but also fortify the worst parts of our own nature (James 3:1–12). Our words should be honest, few, wise, apt, and kind. "Speaking the truth in love" (Ephesians 4:15) knits this all together—right speaking and friends who are willing to confront us.

Prayer: Lord, I ask for two things. Make me a friend who can speak the truth in love. And give me friends who are willing to do this for me—to exhort me lovingly but candidly, lest I be hardened by the deceitfulness of my own heart (Hebrews 3:13). Amen.

December 19

1 I cry aloud to the LORD; I lift up my voice to the LORD for mercy. **2** I pour out before him my complaint; before him I tell my trouble. **3** When my spirit grows faint within me, it is you who watch over my way. In the path where I walk people have hidden a snare for me. **4** Look and see, there is no one at my right hand; no one is concerned for me. I have no refuge; no one cares for my life. **5** I cry to you, LORD; I say, "You are my refuge, my portion in the land of the living." **6** Listen to my cry, for I am in desperate need; rescue me from those who pursue me, for they are too strong for me. **7** Set me free from my prison, that I may praise your name. Then the righteous will gather about me because of your goodness to me.

EMOTIONS AND PRAYER. This psalm and Psalm 57 come from the same experience—when David was hiding in a cave from King Saul. The two psalms together show us how wildly our emotions can fluctuate within the same circumstances and the same framework of belief in God. In Psalm 57 David sees the cave as a place of God's protection, but now it looks like a death trap to him (verses 3–4). He is not ashamed to use the word "cry" three times. He is begging God to hear him, to care for him, to see his desperate need, and to rescue him. Decorous prayer has its place, but desperate prayer, from the heart, is something that God honors. Yet hope is kindled (verse 7).

Prayer: Father, your Son was no Stoic. He was a man of sorrows, acquainted with grief. He was constantly weeping, sighing, and exulting in spirit. I confess that I either deny my emotions, trying to put on a good front, or let them simply carry me away. Show me how to bring them honestly yet submissively to you. Amen.

December 20

READ Psalm 143. 1 LORD, hear my prayer, listen to my cry for mercy; in your faithfulness and righteousness come to my relief. 2 Do not bring your servant into judgment, for no one living is righteous before you. 3 The enemy pursues me, he crushes me to the ground; he makes me dwell in darkness like those long dead. 4 So my spirit grows faint within me; my heart within me is dismayed. 5 I remember the days of long ago; I meditate on all your works and consider what your hands have done. 6 I spread out my hands to you; I thirst for you like a parched land. 7 Answer me quickly, LORD; my spirit fails. Do not hide your face from me or I will be like those who go down to the pit. 8 Let the morning bring me word of your unfailing love, for I have put my trust in you. Show me the way I should go, for to you I entrust my life. 9 Rescue me from my enemies, LORD, for I hide myself in you. 10 Teach me to do your will, for you are my God; may your good Spirit lead me on level ground. 11 For your name's sake, LORD, preserve my life; in your righteousness, bring me out of trouble. 12 In your unfailing love, silence my enemies; destroy all my foes, for I am your servant.

NO ONE IS RIGHTEOUS. In psalms David often claims "blamelessness." The impression is that he thought he was sinless. Not so. David professed innocence of the particular accusations against him. But he knew that if God were to try him for his whole life he would not pass. Here he confesses that no human beings are righteous before God, not even the best ones (verse 2; Romans 3:10–18). He is not only saying that everyone sins but also that everyone is lost. But wait! How can David ask God *not* to bring him into judgment (verse 2), when a judge who justifies the wrongdoer is an abomination (Proverbs 17:15)? Only the cross would reveal the answer (1 John 1:9–2:2).

Prayer: Father, I praise you for the beauty of salvation—that justice was served and yet sinners redeemed, that you can be both just and justifier of those who believe (Romans 3:26). Simply help me to adore you for this. Amen.

December 21

READ Psalm 144:1–8. 1 Praise be to the LORD my Rock, who trains
my hands for war, my fingers for battle. **2** He is my loving God and my
fortress, my stronghold and my deliverer, my shield, in whom I take refuge, who subdues peoples under me. **3** LORD, what are human beings that
you care for them, mere mortals that you think of them? **4** They are like a
breath; their days are like a fleeting shadow. **5** Part your heavens, LORD,
and come down; touch the mountains, so that they smoke. **6** Send forth
lightning and scatter the enemy; shoot your arrows and rout them.
7 Reach down your hand from on high; deliver me and rescue me from
the mighty waters, from the hands of foreigners **8** whose mouths are full
of lies, whose right hands are deceitful.

WHY DOES HE CARE? "Human beings . . . are like a breath;
their days are like a fleeting shadow" (verses 3–4). Life is nasty,
brutish, and short. So why would God even notice us, let alone
love us? (verse 3). That question can be asked in skepticism or
awe. The skeptic asks why any force capable of generating this
vast universe would have regard for tiny, short-lived beings on a
speck of dust called Earth? But for those who know "my loving
God" (verse 2) that's just the point. There *is* no good reason for
God to care about us. But amazingly he does. He doesn't love
us because we benefit him in some way. How could we? He
loves us simply because he loves us (Deuteronomy 7:7). That's
why we praise him.

Prayer: Lord, I praise you that someone of your immeasurable
greatness would not just set his love on me but would also shrink
down infinitely to enter the universe he had made in order to be
crushed like an insect—and all for me. *"Amazing love, how can it
be that Thou, my God, shouldst die for me?"*[140] Amen.

December 22

READ Psalm 144:9–15. **9** I will sing a new song to you, my God; on the ten-stringed lyre I will make music to you, **10** to the One who gives victory to kings, who delivers his servant David. **11** From the deadly sword deliver me; rescue me from the hands of foreigners whose mouths are full of lies, whose right hands are deceitful. **12** Then our sons in their youth will be like well-nurtured plants, and our daughters will be like pillars carved to adorn a palace. **13** Our barns will be filled with every kind of provision. Our sheep will increase by thousands, by tens of thousands in our fields; **14** our oxen will draw heavy loads. There will be no breaching of walls, no going into captivity, no cry of distress in our streets. **15** Blessed is the people of whom this is true; blessed are the people whose God is the LORD.

THANKSGIVING. This hymn marks David's deliverance from King Saul and perhaps his enthronement. It also shows how to respond when God gives a major answer to prayer: with thanksgiving. A thankful spirit combines humility (because you see God's answer was a sheer gift) with confidence (because you know a loving God always hears prayer). We see this unique humble boldness now pervading David's mind and heart. David's first response to God's answer was to ask amazed how God could even notice us (see verses 3–4). But his joy does not turn to complacency; he prays fervently for a prosperous (verses 12–13) and just (verse 14) society. But his plea does not turn into anxiety. There is great exuberance throughout the psalm. Such is the rich, textured character of a life marked by grateful joy.

Prayer: Lord, I thank you that there are an infinite number of things to thank you for, if I reflect for even a moment! Now help me to take that time and to give you thanks for your many gifts I take for granted. Then let thankfulness begin to transform all my attitudes, toward you, myself, others, and life. Amen.

December 23

praise your name for ever and ever. **2** Every day I will praise you and extol your name for ever and ever. **3** Great is the LORD and most worthy of praise; his greatness no one can fathom. **4** One generation will commend your works to another; they will tell of your mighty acts. **5** They speak of the glorious splendor of your majesty, and I will meditate on your wonderful works. **6** They tell of the power of your awesome works, and I will proclaim your great deeds. **7** They celebrate your abundant goodness and joyfully sing of your righteousness. **8** The LORD is gracious and compassionate, slow to anger and rich in love. **9** The LORD is good to all; he has compassion on all he has made.

THE GLORY OF HIS LOVE. When Moses asked God, "Show me your glory" (Exodus 33:18), God proclaimed, "The Lord is gracious and compassionate, slow to anger and rich in love" (verse 8; see also Exodus 34:5–6). Yes, God is absolute in power, yet there is no greater manifestation of his glory than his compassion for all. Jonah quoted verse 8 to God in anger because he had showed compassion to a race Jonah despised (Jonah 4:2). God rebuked him, telling Jonah he cared not only about the wicked Ninevites but even about their animals (Jonah 4:11), showing the truth of verse 9. Celebrate his abundant goodness! (verse 6).

Prayer: Lord, I confess I am much like Jonah. I want you to be loving only to certain people. I give lip service to "loving everyone," but I don't really do it. Teach me to be compassionate to all you have made. Help me start by being patient with that person in my life I struggle so much to love. Amen.

December 24

READ Psalm 145:10–21. **10** All your works praise you, LORD; your faithful people extol you. **11** They tell of the glory of your kingdom and speak of your might, **12** so that all people may know of your mighty acts and the glorious splendor of your kingdom. **13** Your kingdom is an everlasting kingdom, and your dominion endures through all generations. The LORD is trustworthy in all he promises and faithful in all he does. **14** The LORD upholds all who fall and lifts up all who are bowed down. **15** The eyes of all look to you, and you give them their food at the proper time. **16** You open your hand and satisfy the desires of every living thing. **17** The LORD is righteous in all his ways and faithful in all he does. **18** The LORD is near to all who call on him, to all who call on him in truth. **19** He fulfills the desires of those who fear him; he hears their cry and saves them. **20** The LORD watches over all who love him, but all the wicked he will destroy. **21** My mouth will speak in praise of the LORD. Let every creature praise his holy name for ever and ever.

BRILLIANT LOVE. The love of God is richer than we think. There is God's universal love for *all* he has made (see verse 8). God also has a redeeming love for all those he saves. He is near in a different, heightened way to all those who "call on him in truth" and "fear him" (verses 18–19). Without this saving faith we will be lost eternally (verse 20). Finally, there is God's yearning love for all who are broken and fallen. "The Lord upholds *all* who fall and lifts up *all* who are bowed down" (verse 14). It is a mistake to say he loves everyone uniformly or that there is anyone on earth he does not love. God's love is as beautifully and brilliantly multifaceted as a diamond.

Prayer: Lord, since it is you who feed us and you who meet our needs, ordinary human labor such as farming, cooking, and knitting have great dignity. They are means by which you love your creation. Help me to sense that dignity so I can do the simplest of tasks to your glory. Amen.

December 25

PRAISE FOR JUSTICE. The final five psalms are all praise and joy. This teaches us that "the Psalms are a miniature of our story as a whole, which will end in unbroken blessing and delight."[141] It also teaches us that all true prayer "pursued far enough, becomes praise."[142] It may take a long time or a lifetime, but all prayer that engages God and the world as they truly are will eventually end in praise. This particular psalm praises God because he guarantees justice. He cares for the poor, hungry, prisoner, physically impaired, soul weary, immigrant, and single parent (verses 7–9). He cared so much he became a helpless baby born to poor parents. Praise the Lord!

Prayer: Lord, I thank you that you cared so much for us that you became a vulnerable mortal and died to satisfy the demands of justice against sin. I praise you for your unspeakable gift this Christmas Day. Amen.

December 26

READ Psalm 147:1–11. **1** Praise the LORD. How good it is to sing praises to our God, how pleasant and fitting to praise him! **2** The LORD builds up Jerusalem; he gathers the exiles of Israel. **3** He heals the brokenhearted and binds up their wounds. **4** He determines the number of the stars and calls them each by name. **5** Great is our Lord and mighty in power; his understanding has no limit. **6** The LORD sustains the humble but casts the wicked to the ground. **7** Sing to the LORD with grateful praise; make music to our God on the harp. **8** He covers the sky with clouds; he supplies the earth with rain and makes grass grow on the hills. **9** He provides food for the cattle and for the young ravens when they call. **10** His pleasure is not in the strength of the horse, nor his delight in the legs of the warrior; **11** the LORD delights in those who fear him, who put their hope in his unfailing love.

HE CALLS THE STARS. The number of stars is still uncountable by human science, yet God knows them by name (verse 4; cf. Isaiah 40:26). Job speaks of the creation, when "the morning stars sang together and all the angels shouted for joy" (Job 38:7). Psalm 19 tells us that, unless you repress it, you can still hear the stars singing about their maker. "In Reason's Ear they all rejoice, and utter forth a glorious voice; For ever singing, as they shine, "The Hand that made us is Divine."[143] Yet this unimaginably immense God is given *pleasure,* real joy and delight, when human beings put their life's hope in his gracious love (verse 11). Great is our Lord!

Prayer: Lord, it is astonishing that I can bring *you* delight. And this delight does not wax and wane depending on my performance but is unvarying because I am in Jesus Christ (Ephesians 1:3–4). Let me start every day from the platform that "the only eyes in the universe that count are delighted in me." Amen.

December 27

READ Psalm 117:12–20. 19 Extol the LORD, Jerusalem, praise your
God, Zion. **13** He strengthens the bars of your gates and blesses your people within you. **14** He grants peace to your borders and satisfies you with the finest of wheat. **15** He sends his command to the earth; his word runs swiftly. **16** He spreads the snow like wool and scatters the frost like ashes. **17** He hurls down his hail like pebbles. Who can withstand his icy blast? **18** He sends his word and melts them; he stirs up his breezes, and the waters flow. **19** He has revealed his word to Jacob, his laws and decrees to Israel. **20** He has done this for no other nation; they do not know his laws. Praise the LORD.

PRAISE AND OBEDIENCE. A little boy left his toys out and went in to practice the piano, using hymns for his lesson. When his mother called him to pick up his toys, he said, "I can't come; I'm singing praise to Jesus." His mother responded: "There's no use singing God's praises when you're being disobedient."[144] God delights not merely in words of acclaim but in people who obey his laws (verses 19–20; verse 11). If you get an emotional experience out of a worship service but aren't willing to obey, you are using him without giving yourself to him. Christians are saved by faith, not by obeying the law, but the law shows us how to please, love, and resemble the one who saved us by grace.

Prayer: Lord, ethical behavior without joy-filled worship *or* exuberant praise without whole-life obedience—both of these are counterfeit Christianities. I have veered in both directions in my life. Keep me on the straight path. I offer you my whole life, mind, will, and emotions. Amen.

December 28

READ Psalm 148:1–6. **1** Praise the LORD. Praise the LORD from the heavens, praise him in the heights above. **2** Praise him, all his angels, praise him, all his heavenly hosts. **3** Praise him, sun and moon, praise him, all you shining stars. **4** Praise him, you highest heavens and you waters above the skies. **5** Let them praise the name of the LORD, for at his command they were created, **6** and he established them for ever and ever—he issued a decree that will never pass away.

THE PRAISE OF CREATION. Praise comes to God from all he has made. It begins in the highest heaven (verses 1–4). It comes from the sun and moon and stars (verse 3), from the clouds and rain (verse 4). The second half of the psalm will include sea creatures, mountains, trees, animals, and flying birds (verses 7–10). The psalmist commands all of them to praise the Lord, as he does the inhabitants of the earth (verses 11–13). But the reader of the Bible knows that the nonhuman creation is already fully praising God. All of nature sings God's glory; we alone are out of tune. The question is this: How can we be brought back into the great music?

Prayer: Lord, when I try to praise you, I can sense that I'm out of tune, that I am an extremely unskillful musician. But "tune my heart to sing thy grace"[145] by the truth of your Word and by the moving of the Spirit in my heart. Amen.

December 29

READ Psalm 148:7–14. / Praise the LORD from the earth, you great sea creatures and all ocean depths, 8 lightning and hail, snow and clouds, stormy winds that do his bidding, 9 you mountains and all hills, fruit trees and all cedars, 10 wild animals and all cattle, small creatures and flying birds, 11 kings of the earth and all nations, you princes and all rulers on earth, 12 young men and women, old men and children. 13 Let them praise the name of the LORD, for his name alone is exalted; his splendor is above the earth and the heavens. 14 And he has raised up for his people a horn, the praise of all his saints, of Israel, the people close to his heart. Praise the LORD.

PRAISE THAT UNITES. We see extremes brought together in praise (verses 10–12): wild animals and kings, old and young. "Young men and maids, old men and babes."[146] How can humans be brought into the music? "He has raised up for his people a horn" (verse 14), a strong deliverer. The Gospels tell us this is Jesus (Luke 1:69), who brings us to God (verse 14). When your soul through grace begins to praise God, you come into harmony with the rest of the universe, which is also singing. Your redeemed voice contributes its own unique chord and adds to the overwhelming beauty. Praise unites us also with one another. Here is "the only potential bond between the extremes of mankind: joyful preoccupation with God."[147] Praise the Lord!

Prayer: Lord, glorify yourself before the world and put forth your power to unite the extremes of humankind in the church of Jesus Christ. Unite the races, the classes, the genders, the tribes—all in praise. You have begun this good work; now bring it to completion in Jesus Christ. Amen.

December 30

READ Psalm 149. **1** Praise the LORD. Sing to the LORD a new song, his praise in the assembly of his faithful people. **2** Let Israel rejoice in their Maker; let the people of Zion be glad in their King. **3** Let them praise his name with dancing and make music to him with timbrel and harp. **4** For the LORD takes delight in his people; he crowns the humble with victory. **5** Let his faithful people rejoice in this honor and sing for joy on their beds. **6** May the praise of God be in their mouths and a double-edged sword in their hands, **7** to inflict vengeance on the nations and punishment on the peoples, **8** to bind their kings with fetters, their nobles with shackles of iron, **9** to carry out the sentence written against them—this is the glory of all his faithful people. Praise the LORD.

THE PRAISE OF THE REDEEMED. His people praise him because he has made them his people (verses 2–3) and because he honors and delights in them (verses 4 and 5)—though they don't deserve it (verse 4). Knowing this, we are sent out into the world to further God's cause. For Israelites this meant waging literal warfare against the nations that rejected God (verses 6–9). But a Christian's sword is the Gospel of the Word of God, which penetrates heart defenses to the Gospel (Hebrews 4:12). We conquer through Christ's blood and our testimony to what he has done in our lives (Revelation 12:11). Gospel joy, knowing how honored and loved we are in Christ (verse 5), makes us ready for this mission.

Prayer: Lord, *"Take my feet and let them be swift and beautiful for thee. Take my voice and let me sing, always, only, for my King. Take my lips and let them be filled with messages from thee."*[148] Amen.

December 31

READ Psalm 150. **1** Praise the LORD. Praise God in his sanctuary; praise him in his mighty heavens. **2** Praise him for his acts of power; praise him for his surpassing greatness. **3** Praise him with the sounding of the trumpet, praise him with the harp and lyre, **4** praise him with timbrel and dancing, praise him with the strings and pipe, **5** praise him with the clash of cymbals, praise him with resounding cymbals. **6** Let everything that has breath praise the LORD. Praise the LORD.

AN ETERNITY OF PRAISE. The psalms are, in the end, a miniature of life. Every possible experience, if prayed to the God who is really there, is destined to end in praise. Confession leads to the joy of forgiveness. Laments lead to a deeper resting in him for our happiness. If we could praise God perfectly, we would love him completely and then our joy would be full. The new heavens and new earth are perfect because everyone and everything is glorifying God fully and therefore enjoying him forever. So Psalm 150 gives us a glimpse of that unimaginable future. So praise him everywhere (verse 1) for everything (verse 2) in every way (verses 3–5). "Let everything that has breath praise the Lord" (verse 6).

Prayer: Lord, you have given so much to me. Give me one thing more—a heart for praising you. *"Not thankful, when it pleaseth me; as if thy blessings had spare days: But such a heart, whose pulse may be Thy praise."*[149] Amen.

ACKNOWLEDGMENTS

When asked to do a devotional book, Tim and I immediately thought of the psalms; after all, he had decades of material, so it would be a piece of cake, right? Never say that!

Between a difficult year of health issues for me, ministry commitments for Tim, and the death of our dear friend David, whom this book is meant to honor, Tim started off behind schedule. The first manuscript was, unfortunately, awful—so crammed full of information and ideas on every page that it was as dense as haiku, as I regretfully told my husband.

Well, that manuscript was scrapped and another one appeared, but our editor, Brian Tart, wisely and rightly rejected it because the format was too complex and not accessible enough.

By then we were frantic (I pitched in to help), but we finally simplified everything to the version you have in your hands. It has been the most difficult book to write, in some ways, and yet the sweetest—and in the end the most personal and intimate of all Tim's books.

When it was done we looked at each other and said, "What are we going to do now that we're not spending fifteen hours every day in the psalms?" The answer is, I guess, go back and spend each day with a psalm or part of a psalm, just as everyone else should be doing.

For those of you who upheld us in so many ways during the writing (and writing and writing) of this book, thank you so much. Ray and Gill Lane, for hosting us at The Fisherbeck, their bed-and-breakfast hotel in the Lake District of England; Lynn Land and Jane and Brian McGreevy in Charleston; Janice Worth in Florida; and Louise Midwood.

Tim in particular wants to acknowledge his deep debt to the late Derek Kidner, whose commentary on the psalms has been his main resource for understanding the Psalter over the last four decades. This commentary is unsurpassed for its wisdom and spiritual eloquence. Kidner's sensitivity to the nuances of poetry is wonderful, and he has been an enormous help to us less skillful readers. Tim also wants to recommend the psalms commentaries of both Alec Motyer (in *The New Bible Commentary: 21st-Century Edition*) and Tremper Longman (in the Tyndale Series). Tremper's volume gives the most help on how to read the psalms from the perspective of the New Testament and of the Gospel of Christ. Motyer's commentary is the shortest and pithiest, and is brimming with nuggets of insight. The pastoral hearts and Christ-centered perspectives of these three authors make them essential reading for anyone who wants the most out of the psalms.

Thanks are also due to our children and grandchildren, who kept us involved in real life: love to David, Jen, and Charlotte; Michael, Sara, Lucy, and Kate; and Jonathan, Ann-Marie, and to-be-named Baby Boy Keller.

Thanks also to our agent, David McCormick, who has the gift of encouragement and, for this volume, negotiated the difficulties of permission to use the NIV translation in a plethora of countries. You are the best, David.

We also thank God who, in his wisdom, plunged the two of us into the psalms for these months in order to deepen our love for him, for each other, and to give us a glimpse of our future True Country.

"Together we will take the road that leads into the West,
And far away will find a land where both our hearts
may rest."[150]

NOTES

1. Gordon Wenham, *The Psalter Reclaimed: Praying and Praising with the Psalms* (Crossway, 2013), p. 16.
2. J. Calvin, *Commentary on the Psalms* (electronic ed.) (Albany, OR: Ages Software, 1998), comment on Psalm 20:1–2.
3. Quoted in Wenham, *Psalter Reclaimed*, p. 15.
4. Alec Motyer, *A Christian's Pocket Guide to Loving the Old Testament* (Ross-shire, Scotland: Christian Focus, 2015), p. 97.
5. Ibid., p. 34.
6. Ibid., p. 26. Wenham shows how "speech-act" theory explains why the reciting and praying of the psalms is a transformative experience.
7. Eugene H. Peterson, *Answering God: The Psalms as Tools for Prayer* (Harper San Francisco, 1989), pp. 5–6.
8. Derek Kidner, *Psalms 1–72: An Introduction and Commentary* (Leicester, England: InterVarsity Press, 1973), p. 53.
9. John Newton, "Approach, My Soul, the Mercy Seat," *Olney Hymns* (London: W. Oliver, 1779), number 12, available at http://www.hymntime.com/tch/htm/a/p/p/approach.htm.
10. Ibid.
11. Ibid.
12. Kidner, *Psalms 1–72*, p. 113.
13. C. S. Lewis, "The Weight of Glory" (sermon, Church of St. Mary the Virgin, Oxford, June 8, 1942), available at http://www.verber.com/mark/xian/weight-of-glory.pdf.
14. Kidner, *Psalms 1–72*, p. 121.
15. Newton, "Approach, My Soul, the Mercy Seat."
16. Adapted from Thomas Cranmer, "Second Collect for Good Friday," in *The Collects of Thomas Cranmer*, eds. C. Frederick Barbee and Paul F. M. Zahl (Grand Rapids, MI: William B. Eerdmans, 2006), p. 48.
17. Kidner, *Psalms 1–72*, p. 111.
18. Ibid., p. 133.
19. Lewis, "Weight of Glory."
20. Kidner, *Psalms 1–72*, p. 140.
21. From Thomas Cranmer, "The Collect for the Second Sunday in Advent," in Barbee and Zahl, *Collects of Thomas Cranmer*, p. 4.
22. Kidner, *Psalms 1–72*, p. 128.
23. Adapted from Thomas Cranmer, "Collect for the Fourth Sunday After Easter," in Barbee and Zahl, *Collects of Thomas Cranmer*, p. 58.
24. Tom LeCompte, "The Disorient Express," *Air and Space*, September 2008, http://www.airspacemag.com/military-aviation/the-disorient-express-474780/.
25. C. S. Lewis, *Reflections on the Psalms* (San Diego, CA: Harcourt Brace, 1964), p. 94.
26. Last sentence adapted from John Newton, "How Sweet the Name of Jesus Sounds" in *Olney Hymns*: "Weak is the effort of my heart, and cold my warmest thought; But when I see Thee as Thou art, I'll praise Thee as I ought."

27. George Herbert, "Love (III)," *George Herbert and the Seventeenth-Century Religious Poets* (W. W. Norton, 1978), available at http://www.poetryfoundation.org/learning/poem/173632.

28. Kidner, *Psalms 1–72*, pp. 155–56.

29. Ibid., p. 158. See also Sinclair B. Ferguson, *The Whole Christ: Legalism, Antinomianism, and Gospel Assurance: Why the Marrow Controversy Still Matters* (Wheaton, IL: Crossway Books, 2016).

30. Lewis, "Weight of Glory."

31. The comparison of Paul's paradoxes in 2 Corinthians with this part of Psalm 37 comes from Kidner, *Psalms 1–72*, pp. 169–70.

32. Newton, "How Sweet the Name of Jesus Sounds."

33. George Herbert, "Discipline," in *The Temple* (1633).

34. Newton, "Approach, My Soul, the Mercy Seat."

35. Kidner, *Psalms 1–72*, p. 157.

36. From John Newton, "We Were Once as You Are," in *The Works of John Newton*, vol. 3 (1824) (repr. Banner of Truth, 1985), p. 572.

37. Kidner, *Psalms 1–72*, p. 179.

38. Isaac Watts, "O God Our Help in Ages Past," hymn.

39. C. S. Lewis, *Perelandra* (New York: Macmillan, 1965), pp. 121–22.

40. J.R.R. Tolkien, *The Return of the King* (New York: Del Ray Books, 1986), p. 209.

41. Kidner, *Psalms 1–72*, p. 201.

42. Ibid., p. 207.

43. Alec Motyer, "The Psalms," in *The New Bible Commentary: 21st Century Edition*, ed. D. A. Carson et al. (Downers Grove, IL: Intervarsity Press, 1994), p. 523.

44. Tremper Longman, *Psalms: An Introduction and Commentary* (Downers Grove, IL: IVP Academic, 2014), p. 242.

45. James Proctor, "It Is Finished," hymn.

46. For more on what it means to behold Christ by faith in such a way that fully engages the affections of the heart, see John Owen, "Meditations and Discourses on the Glory of Christ," in *Works of John Owen*, vol. 1, ed. W. Goold (Edinburgh: Banner of Truth, 1965), pp. 274–461.

47. Kidner, *Psalms 1–72*, p. 227.

48. Kidner, *Psalms 1–72*, p. 252.

49. John Newton, "Begone Unbelief," in *Olney Hymns*.

50. Ibid.

51. This is the title of a book on confession of sin by Søren Kierkegaard.

52. C. S. Lewis, "A Word About Praising," in *Reflections on the Psalms* (New York: Harcourt, Brace, and World, 1958), p. 95.

53. J.R.R. Tolkien, *The Two Towers* (New York: Del Ray Books, 1986), p. 327.

54. Kidner, *Psalms 1–72*, p. 238.

55. See George Herbert, "Time," in *George Herbert: The Complete English Poems*, ed. John Tobin, (London: Penguin Books, 1991), p. 114. Herbert addresses time and death:

    And in his blessing thou art blessed;
    For where thou only wert before
    An executioner at best;
    Thou art a gard'ner now, and more,
    An usher to convey our souls
    Beyond the utmost stars and poles.

56. Kidner, *Psalms 1–72*, p. 263.
57. John Newton, "Letter VII to the Reverend Mr. R_____," in *The Works of the Reverend John Newton* (New York: Robert Carter, 1847), p. 337.
58. Kidner, *Psalms 1–72*, p. 28.
59. C. S. Lewis, ed., *George MacDonald: An Anthology* (New York: HarperCollins Paperback, 2001), p. 44.
60. George Herbert, "Praise (2)," in Tobin, *George Herbert*, p. 137.
61. Elisabeth Elliot, in David Howard, "The Intrepid Missionary Elisabeth Elliot," *Wall Street Journal*, June 25, 2015.
62. Adapted from Thomas Cranmer, "Collect for the Twelfth Sunday After Trinity," in Barbee and Zahl, *Collects of Thomas Cranmer*, p. 92.
63. Motyer, "Psalms," in Carson, *New Bible Commentary*, p. 530.
64. John Newton, *Letters of John Newton* (London: Banner of Truth Trust, 1960), p. 179.
65. Adapted from Thomas Cranmer, "Collect for the Fifth Sunday After Trinity," Barbee and Zahl, *Collects of Thomas Cranmer*, p. 78.
66. Helen H. Lemmel, "Turn Your Eyes Upon Jesus," hymn.
67. Augustine, *Confessions*, trans. R. S. Pine-Coffin (London: Penguin Classics, 1961), book 2, chapters 4–8.
68. Ibid., book 4, p. 61.
69. Adapted from George Herbert, "Joseph's Coat," in Tobin, *George Herbert*, p. 137.
70. Elisabeth Elliot, "Epilogue II," in *Through the Gates of Splendor*, 40th ann. ed., (Tyndale, 1996), p. 267.
71. See Longman, *Psalms*, p. 242: "With the coming of Jesus, there was no longer a need for a special holy place, because Jesus himself was the very presence of God (John 1:14), and after he ascended to heaven, he sent the Holy Spirit who dwells in our midst."
72. Adapted from *The Poems of Robert Herrick: A Selection from Hesperides and Noble Numbers* (BiblioLife, 2012), p. 379.
73. I have shown verse 10 as it appears in the alternate translation contained in the footnotes to the *New International Version*.
74. Thomas Cranmer, "Collect for the First Sunday After Trinity," in Barbee and Zahl, *Collects of Thomas Cranmer*, p. 70.
75. William Cowper, "Walking with God," in *Olney Hymns*. See also http://cyberhymnal.org/htm/o/f/oforaclo.htm
76. Adapted from Cowper, "Walking with God."
77. Charlotte Elliott, "O Jesus Make Thyself to Me," hymn.
78. Derek Kidner, *Psalms 73–150: An Introduction and Commentary* (Downers Grove, IL: InterVarsity Press, 1975), pp. 324–25.
79. Kidner, *Psalms 73–150*, p. 327.
80. Longman, *Psalms*, p. 52.
81. Westminster Shorter Catechism: "Q. 1. What is the chief end of man? A. Man's chief end is to glorify God, and to enjoy him forever."
82. Kidner, *Psalms 73–150*, p. 313.
83. George Herbert, "Discipline," in *The English Poems of George Herbert*, ed. Helen Wilcox (Cambridge: Cambridge University Press, 2007), p. 621.
84. John Newton, "Glorious Things of Thee Are Spoken," hymn based on Psalm 87, *Olney Hymns*.
85. Charlotte Elliott, "O Jesus Make Thyself to Me," hymn.
86. John Newton, "The Resurrection and the Life," in *Olney Hymns*.

87. John Newton, "Let Us Love and Sing and Wonder," in *Olney Hymns.*

88. George Herbert, "Virtue," in Tobin, *George Herbert,* p. 81.

89. George Herbert, "Avarice," Tobin, *George Herbert,* p. 70.

90. Kidner, *Psalms 73–150,* p. 374.

91. Charles Wesley, "Jesus, Lover of my Soul," hymn.

92. Kidner, *Psalms 73–150,* p. 380.

93. Kidner, *Psalms 73–150,* p. 349.

94. Newton, "How Sweet the Name of Jesus Sounds," published under the title "The Name of Jesus," *Olney Hymns.*

95. John Newton, "Dagon Before the Ark."

96. Newton, "How Sweet the Name of Jesus Sounds." See note 99.

97. George Herbert, "Antiphon (1)," in Tobin, *George Herbert,* p. 47.

98. Kidner, *Psalms 73–150,* p. 359.

99. Motyer, "Psalms," in Carson, *New Bible Commentary,* p. 551.

100. Samuel Rutherford, *The Letters of the Rev. Samuel Rutherford* (New York: Robert Carter and Brothers, 1863) pp. 40 and 166.

101. Motyer, "Psalms," in Carson, *New Bible Commentary,* p. 552.

102. Jonathan Edwards [1722], The "Miscellanies": (Entry Nos. a–z, aa–zz, 1–500) (WJE Online Vol. 13), entry a) "Of Holiness." Edwards describes a common spiritual experience, that when we are singing God's praises the most, we sense that the mountains and ocean and trees are "singing" as well (Psalm 19:1–5).

103. Robert Grant, "O Worship the King," hymn.

104. Joseph Addison, "The Spacious Firmament," hymn.

105. This is a quote from a lecture that we (Tim and Kathy Keller) heard Elisabeth Elliot deliver at Gordon-Conwell Seminary in 1974.

106. Isaac Watts, "When I Survey the Wondrous Cross," hymn.

107. Ibid.

108. *Superman Returns* (2006), Warner Bros. Pictures, directed by Bryan Singer.

109. Josiah Conder, "'Tis Not That I Did Choose Thee," hymn.

110. David Lapp, "Do Scary Statistics Change People's Behavior?" *Family Studies,* June 16, 2015, http://family-studies.org/do-scary-statistics-change-peoples-behavior/.

111. This is a question that cannot be fully answered in this short space. To begin an exploration of this issue, see Tremper Longman and Daniel G. Reid, "When God Declares War," *Christianity Today,* October 28, 1996, and Tremper Longman, "The God of War," *Christianity Today,* May 1, 2003.

112. Kidner, *Psalms 73–150,* pp. 418–19.

113. Charles Wesley, "And Can It Be?," hymn.

114. Ibid., p. 420.

115. "What we retreat from is not the fact that [David] prayed, but the realism in which he couched his prayers. When any measure of hostility disturbs our comfortable lives we rouse ourselves to say 'Lord, help me to love my enemies as Jesus taught, and, please, will you deal with them for me.' The psalmist was more realistic: how will God 'deal with them' except in ways that he has revealed in his word? False accusers must receive what they purposed to achieve (Dt. 19:16–19, cf. 2 with 6); those who disobey have no tenure on earth (Dt. 4:1, cf. 8); sinners bring disaster on their descendants (Ex. 34:7, cf. 9–12). If we retreat into unreality with a general petition where the psalmist ventured to express scriptural realism, we should at least be aware of what we are doing. But our retreat is understandable and accords with Paul's caution (Eph. 4:26) that allowable anger is near neighbor to sin. J. L. McKenzie (*American Ecclesiastical Review, III,* 1944, pp. 81–96) asks

whether 'the imprecatory psalms are not a model, not because of their lower degree of perfection but because they are too lofty for . . . us to imitate without danger.'" Motyer "Psalms," in *New Bible Commentary*, ed. Carson et al., p. 551.

116. John Newton, "Father, Forgive Them," *Olney Hymns*.
117. Ernest W. Shurtleff, "Lead On O King Eternal," hymn.
118. See the book by Ray Bradbury, *Something Wicked This Way Comes* (New York: Avon Reprint, 2006), as well as the 1983 movie of the same name starring Jonathan Pryce. The list on this page is more reflective of the characters in the movie, which are not all identical to those in the book. Note Bradbury's quote from W. B. Yeats on the frontispiece of the book, "Man is in love, and loves what vanishes," and compare it with the teaching of Psalm 115 about idols.
119. Adapted from John Newton, "I Asked the Lord," *Olney Hymns*.
120. Kidner, *Psalms 73–150*, p. 409.
121. George Herbert, "Easter," in Tobin, *George Herbert*, p. 37.
122. Ibid.
123. Here I am following the interpretation of Motyer, "Psalms," in Carson, *New Bible Commentary*, p. 565.
124. Kidner, *Psalms 73–150*, p. 421.
125. Conder, "'Tis Not That I Did Choose Thee," hymn.
126. Motyer, "Psalms," in Carson, *New Bible Commentary*, p. 569.
127. J. Newton and Richard Cecil, *The Works of John Newton*, vol. 1 (London: Hamilton, Adams, 1824), p. 141.
128. George Herbert, "The Holy Scriptures (1)," in Tobin, *George Herbert*, p. 52.
129. Motyer, "Psalms," in Carson, *New Bible Commentary*, p. 570.
130. Timothy Ward, *Words of Life: Scripture as the Living and Active Word of God* (Downers Grove, IL: IVP Academic, 2009), p. 177.
131. Edwin Hodder, "Thy Word Is Like a Garden, Lord," hymn.
132. Herbert, " Holy Scriptures (1)," in Tobin, *George Herbert*, p. 52.
133. Tremper Longman, *How to Read the Psalms* (Downers Grove, IL: InterVarsity Press, 1988), pp. 44–45; see also Kidner, *Psalms 1–72*, p. 43.
134. Kidner, *Psalms 73–150*, p. 430.
135. Frances R. Havergal, "Take My Life."
136. John Milton, "Let Us with a Gladsome Mind," hymn.
137. George Herbert, "The Sacrifice," in Tobin, *George Herbert*, p. 24.
138. Adapted from anonymous, "How Firm a Foundation," hymn.
139. George Herbert, "The Sacrifice," in Tobin, *George Herbert*, pp. 29–30. Notice the "Tree" is the cross. The cross is a Tree of Life for us because it was a tree of death for him.
140. Charles Wesley, "And Can It Be?," hymn.
141. Kidner, *Psalms 73–150*, p. 483.
142. Peterson, *Answering God*, p. 128.
143. Joseph Addison, "The Spacious Firmament," hymn.
144. This is an anecdote from a lecture that we (Tim and Kathy Keller) heard Elisabeth Elliot deliver at Gordon-Conwell Seminary in 1974.
145. Robert Robinson, "Come Thou Fount of Every Blessing," hymn.
146. William Billings, "O Praise the Lord of Heaven" (based on Psalm 148), hymn.
147. Kidner, *Psalms 73–150*, p. 488.
148. Frances R. Havergal, "Take My Life and Let It Be," hymn.
149. George Herbert, "Gratefulness," in Tobin, *George Herbert*, p. 114.
150. J.R.R. Tolkien, *The Two Towers* (New York: Del Ray Books, 1986), p. 81.